ANGELS
AND
ALIENS

UFOs AND THE
MYTHIC IMAGINATION

KEITH THOMPSON

A William Patrick Book

▲▼ **Addison-Wesley Publishing Company, Inc.**
Reading, Massachusetts   Menlo Park, California   New York
Don Mills, Ontario   Wokingham, England   Amsterdam   Bonn
Sydney   Singapore   Tokyo   Madrid   San Juan
Paris   Seoul   Milan   Mexico City   Taipei

The Divine Comedy by Dante Aligheri; Inferno. Translated by Allen Mandelbaum. Copyright © 1940, renewed 1968. Reprinted by permission of Random House, Inc.

Thompson, Keith, 1954–
    Angels and aliens : UFOs and the mythic imagination / Keith Thompson.
        p.   cm.
    Includes bibliographical references and index.
    ISBN 0-201-55084-9
    1. Unidentified flying objects.   I. Title
TL789.T46   1991
001.9′42--dc20   91-21306
                                                                      CIP

Jacket design by Richard Rossiter
Text design by Joyce C. Weston
Set in 11-point Garamond by CopyRight, Inc.

1 2 3 4 5 6 7 8 9-MA-9594939291
First printing, October 1991

For Tyler

'Tis no disparagement to be a stranger, or so irksome to be an exile. The rain is a stranger to the earth, rivers to the Sea, Jupiter in Egypt, the Sun to us all. The Soul is an alien to the Body, a Nightingale to the air, a Swallow in an house, and Ganymede in Heaven, an Elephant at Rome, a Phoenix in India; and such things commonly please us best which are most strange, and come farthest off.

— Robert Burton
The Anatomy of Melancholy

CONTENTS

PROLOGUE

I HAVE never seen a UFO. I have never noticed anything in the sky that didn't seem to belong there, nor can I claim to have been invited — or hauled against my will — inside a landed saucer.

During my formative years I read no books promising to present the "startling, never-before-revealed facts" about UFOs. I wasn't even acquainted with the world of science fiction prior to taking a university course called "the literature of the fantastic." (Although I have probably seen every episode of the 1960s television program "Green Acres," I can't recall watching more than two or three episodes of "Star Trek" from beginning to end.) And over the years nothing about the respective claims of UFO disciples and UFO debunkers has convinced me of the need to reach definitive conclusions about the ultimate nature and origins of this puzzling phenomenon.

Instead, I have watched with fascination as a persistent body of remarkable stories (or in UFO jargon, "sighting reports") has given rise to provocative mythic horizons and imaginal realms. In the pages that follow, I explore the ways in which these symbolic worlds are real, vital, and filled with significance *whether or not* any particular UFO was the planet Venus or a Venusian starship.

In *Creation Myth*, Scottish religion scholar R. J. Stewart defines a myth as "a story embodying and declaring a pattern of relationship between humanity, other forms of life, and the environment." Joseph Campbell, in turn, writes that "the first and most essential service of a mythology is this one of opening mind and heart to the utter wonder of all being." Both definitions are relevant to this study, as are questions concerning parallels between modern UFO events and accounts in world mythology of human interactions with extraordinary beings.

To the extent that the figures of myth are characteristically depicted as quarreling, cheating, vulnerable, seeking revenge, tearing apart and being torn apart, we find evidence of "mythic patterns" among competing UFO researchers as they contend to fashion for the UFO phenomenon a consistent *mythos*, or plot; and as their very efforts to do so forms a mythos of its own: an epic drama of individuals seeking to make meaning of epic events and experiences in which (to borrow an apt phrase from the psychologist James Hillman) "the supposed surety of fact and illusion of fiction exchange their clothes."

Time after time, this exchange reaches the same impasse: testimony from The People on one side, dismissive responses from The Authorities on the other. In the fertile void of this deadlock, extraordinary possibilities — about the nature of mind and matter, spirit and soul, heaven and earth, the destiny of the cosmos, *their* plans for *us* — enter the debate, transforming the traditional celestial UFO into a metaphysical one.

"We have here a golden opportunity of seeing how a legend is formed," wrote the great philosopher-psychologist Carl Jung about flying saucers. I heartily agree. For over forty years, the curiously compelling acronym "UFO" — *as an idea at work in the world soul* — has shaped human belief and imagination in complicated ways. A robust contemporary prodigy has emerged in our midst, enticing us with the vivid ambivalence of its images, systematically resisting definitive explanation, fostering rancorous debate, comprising a provocative enigma of global proportions.

This is a chronicle of the wanderings of that prodigy.

ONE

———— ✕ ————

IN THE early summer of 1947, this Associated Press dispatch came across the wire in newsrooms throughout the United States:

PENDLETON, Ore., June 25 (AP) — Nine bright saucer-like objects flying at "incredible speed" at 10,000 feet altitude were reported here today by Kenneth Arnold, Boise, Idaho, pilot who said he could not hazard a guess as to what they were.

Arnold, a United States Forest Service employee engaged in searching for a missing plane, said he sighted the mysterious objects yesterday at 3 P.M. They were flying between Mount Rainier and Mount Adams, in Washington state, he said, and appeared to wave in and out of formation. Arnold said he clocked and estimated their speed at 1,200 miles an hour.

Inquiries at Yakima last night brought only blank stares, he said, but he added he talked today with an unidentified man from Utah, south of here, who said he had seen similar objects over the mountains near Ukiah yesterday.

"It seems impossible," Arnold said, "but there it is."

Arnold first told of his sighting to several people he met at the Yakima, Washington, airport. During Arnold's flight later the same day to Pendleton, Oregon, a member of his Yakima audience telephoned details of Arnold's account to the Pendleton airport, where several skeptical reporters gathered to meet him on his arrival. At their request, Arnold repeated his remarkable tale. Because he was a well-regarded citizen — rescue pilot, businessman, deputy sheriff — "skepticism changed to wonder and the journalists reported the incident as a serious news item," writes historian David Jacobs in *The UFO Controversy in America*.

A local reporter named Bill Bequette is credited with capturing Arnold's passing statement that the nine disk-shaped objects made an undulating motion like "a saucer skipping over water." Within a matter of hours, Arnold's story — trumpeted by the evocative phrase "flying saucer," a creation of anonymous headline writers — became front-page news throughout the nation. The next day an Associated Press story carried this follow-up lead:

> Army and CAA spokesmen expressed skepticism over a report of nine mysterious objects — big as airplanes — whizzing over Western Washington at 1,200 miles an hour.

Within days, Kenneth and Doris Arnold's Boise, Idaho, home was besieged by reporters seeking additional details about the nine mysterious craft. "I can't begin to estimate the number of people, letters, telegrams, and phone calls I tried to answer," Arnold recalled. "After three days of this hubbub I came to the conclusion that I was the only sane one in the bunch." On June 27, United Press wired this report to its affiliates:

> PENDLETON, Ore., June 27 (UP) — Kenneth Arnold said Friday (June 27) he would like to get on one of his 1,200 mile-an-hour "Flying Saucers" and escape from the furor caused by his story of mysterious aircraft flashing over Southern Washington.

People throughout the United States, many of them quite credible, responded to Arnold's story with their own reports about unconventional objects seen in the sky. Because many of these sightings occurred *before* Arnold's, early press coverage was evenhanded, sometimes even sympathetic; but not for long. Reporters became more dubious as the stories grew increasingly bizarre and some turned out to be hoaxes. In the absence of corroborating physical evidence of flying saucers, newspapers turned to satire.

The *New York Times* editorialized that Arnold had seen nothing more than "atoms escaping from an overwrought bomb," later suggesting that

the silver objects were probably coins scattered by "high-riding government officials" to reduce the country's economic pressures. In a
similar spirit, *Life* magazine quoted a Harvard anthropologist's theory
that saucers were "misplaced halos searching for all the people who
were killed over the Fourth of July." Being the most famous saucer-
sighter, Arnold presented an easy target, alongside his already legendary
account.

"If I saw a ten-story building flying through the air I would never
say a word about it," Arnold announced on reading various accounts
dismissing his competence as an observer. "Half the people I see look
at me as a combination of Einstein, Flash Gordon, and Screwball."
For its part, the air force could find evidence of only the third category. In a private memorandum, an air force investigator reported to
his superiors that the anointed Father of the Flying Saucer had become
"practically a moron in the eyes of the majority of the population of
the United States."

IN STRICTLY factual terms, the widely held view that the UFO
phenomenon began with Arnold's sighting is mistaken. Beginning the
year before and continuing until 1948, witnesses in Sweden and Finland
reported seeing strange, cigar-shaped objects flying close to the Soviet
border, leading United States Army intelligence agents to fear that these
"ghost rockets," as they came to be known, might be Soviet secret
weapons developed in collaboration with German scientists. Fully 20
percent of these sightings found no explanation. During World War
II, pilots reported unusual balls of light and disklike objects following
them — in some cases, "dancing" on the wingtips of their aircraft —
as they flew bombing runs. The origin of these phenomena likewise
remains a mystery.

Half a century earlier, between November 1896 and May 1897,
thousands of people in nineteen mostly western and midwestern states
reported seeing dirigible-type cylindrical airships sailing through the
skies. Because this was five years before the Wright brothers' famous
experiments with heavier-than-air flight at Kitty Hawk, these reports
caused a sensation not unlike the early response to flying saucers. Today's
UFO researchers remain characteristically divided concerning this late-
nineteenth-century phenomenon, some attributing the sightings to contagious rumors and deliberate hoaxes, others arguing that at least some

of these aerial events emerged from the same mysterious dimensions beyond time and space as did their eventual descendants, flying saucers.

But in terms of what Carl Jung was to describe as "a modern myth of things seen in the skies," there can be no doubt that Kenneth Arnold's legendary sighting did indeed mark the beginning of the UFO phenomenon. A widely published Gallup poll of August 19, 1947, less than two months after Arnold's legendary sighting, revealed that nine out of ten Americans knew about the flying saucers, whereas considerably fewer had heard of the Marshall Plan for the postwar reconstruction of Europe.

The Age of the Saucers had arrived, and in no small way.

THE ensuing summer and fall of 1947 featured a rash of public activity that fostered a fertile milieu in which the phrase "flying saucer" would quickly lodge in the public imagination, where it began to crackle like a low-grade neon sign. Consider this surreal succession of responses that appeared in the context of Arnold's sighting:

- A preliminary study of UFOs has "not produced enough fact to warrant further investigation," according to an official air force statement of July 4. The same public statement notes that the air force would *continue to study* several sightings of interest in Texas and the Pacific Northwest.
- "Nine shiny objects flying at a high rate of speed, such as described by a Boise, Idaho, pilot, were reported by W.I. Davenport, a carpenter, to have been sighted here yesterday" (Associated Press, June 26, Kansas City).
- Reports of flying saucers subsequent to Kenneth Arnold's sighting were caused by a "mild case of meteorological jitters" combined with "mass hypnosis," according to Gordon A. Atwater, astronomer at the Hayden Planetarium (*New York Times*, July 6).
- FLYING SAUCERS SEEN IN MOST STATES NOW (*San Francisco Chronicle* headline, July 7).
- RAAF CAPTURES FLYING SAUCER IN ROSWELL REGION. NO DETAILS OF FLYING DISKS ARE REVEALED (Roswell, New Mexico, *Daily Record* headline, July 8). "The many rumors regarding the flying disc became a reality yesterday when the intelligence office of the 509th Bomb Group of the Eighth Air Force, Roswell Army Air

Field, was fortunate enough to gain possession of a disc through the co-operation of one of the local ranchers and the Sheriff's office of Chaves County" (*San Francisco Chronicle*, July 9; picked up by the Associated Press, the *New York Times* wire service, and the prestigious *London Times*).

- A private pilot named Vernon Baird reports knocking a "pearl gray, clam-shaped" craft resembling a "yo-yo" out of the sky over Montana. The story is carried by newspapers throughout the nation. In a one-paragraph report the following day, Baird admits he fabricated the story while shooting the breeze with other pilots around the hangar. He promises not to do it again.
- Flying saucers belong in the same category as the Loch Ness monster, insists Dr. Newton Smith of the United States Bureau of Standards (*New York Times*, December 27, 1947).
- A savvy press agent advertises a radio program featuring the "Flying Saucer Blues."

MATTERS were hardly more promising in private quarters such as the Technical Intelligence Divisions of the Air Materiel Command (AMC), headquartered at Wright Field in Dayton, Ohio. This branch of the air force had begun collecting and filing newspaper accounts on an informal basis prior to receiving a classified order to investigate all reports it received. Headed from 1951 to 1953 by Captain Edward J. Ruppelt, the AMC was split down the middle between those who felt UFOs would be revealed as terrestrial in origin (atmospheric phenomena, Soviet secret weapons, or perhaps a classified air force plane rumored to be called the "Flying Flapjack") and others who thought the objects eventually would be proved extraterrestrial (spaceships or "space animals").

One of the most significant episodes of these early years occurred entirely behind the scenes. As with secret government activity in general, the impact (subtle and not so) of this classified transaction would eventually return to the public domain, where it would echo at various levels.

On September 23, 1947, Lieutenant General Nathan F. Twining, commander of the AMC, responded to a Pentagon request for a UFO update by writing a memo saying that "the reported phenomenon is something real and not visionary or fictitious." Citing reported operating characteristics (including extreme rates of climb, maneuverability, and evasiveness) as indicating possible manual control, Twining recommended that a detailed classified formal study of the disks begin at once.

Twining's memo led to the establishment of an air force classified project to determine whether flying saucers posed a threat to the national security. "The attitude toward this task varied from a state of near panic, early in the life of the project, to that of complete contempt for anyone who even mentioned the words 'flying saucer,'" recalled Captain Ruppelt in his classic account of the period, *The Report on Unidentified Flying Objects*. Located at Wright Field, Project Sign, known publicly as Project Saucer, began work on January 22, 1948, two weeks after military and civilian witnesses sighted a UFO that looked like "an ice cream cone topped with red" over Godman Air Force Base in Kentucky. Four National Guard F-51 planes were scrambled to take a closer look.

The flight leader, Captain Thomas Mantell, radioed the Godman Tower that "it appears to be a metallic object . . . tremendous in size . . . directly ahead and slightly above . . . I'm trying to close in for a better look." That was his last radio contact with the tower.

Later that day, Captain Mantell's decapitated body was found in the wreckage of his plane, near Fort Knox. Subsequent investigation indicated that Mantell had most likely blacked out from lack of oxygen and suffocated before the crash. But what had Mantell seen, and chased?

The air force's preliminary verdict — *Mantell had died while chasing the planet Venus, which he had mistaken for a flying saucer* — met with hoots of derision from the press and much of the American public. The hoots became howls of indignant satisfaction when subsequent investigation showed no meaningful correlation between Venus and the object. Three years later, the navy revealed that a top-secret, high-altitude, photographic reconnaissance Skyhook balloon, capable of expanding to a diameter of 100 feet, had been in the area. It was determined that this was what Mantell had pursued.

But by then it was too late for the air force to rebound from its fateful assertion that Mantell met his death en route to Venus. In the interim, filling a void left by the military's unconvincing response, a vivid legend had taken hold: *a man had died in a dramatic encounter with a UFO and the air force had conspired to conceal the truth*. Whether this legend was strictly or even loosely true is beside the point, in terms of the legend's primary effect on the collective imagination. The legend held.

The provocative notion that the government had definitive answers that it systematically kept from the public was now in place. For decades to come, this theme would capture the energies and passions of a small but vocal cadre of self-styled civilian researchers, whose cries of "cover-up!" served as a lightning rod for a percentage of followers inclined toward conspiracy theories (for some, the more elaborate and less verifiable the theory, the better).

Six months later, things got worse for the air force when Clarence Chiles and John Whitted, pilot and copilot of an Eastern Airlines DC-3, flying at 5,000 feet between Montgomery and Mobile, Alabama, reported seeing a torpedo-shaped, wingless craft over 100 feet long, "powered by some jet or other type of power-shooting flame from the rear some 50 feet," according to Captain Chiles. The massive object, with two horizontal rows of large square windows, reminded Whitted of "one of those Fantastic Flash Gordon rocket ships in the funny papers" as it streaked past their aircraft at nearly 700 miles per hour at 2:45 A.M.

The Pentagon responded by claiming the pilot and copilot (and one passenger who awoke in time to catch a brief glimpse) had seen a weather balloon, but this explanation was abruptly withdrawn. Air force consultant J. Allen Hynek remarked that "no astronomical explanation" was possible "if we accept the report at face value." UFO archskeptic Donald Menzel, a distinguished Harvard astronomer, dismissed the sighting as an unusually bright meteor embellished by flight-weary imaginations, but the pilot and copilot vehemently disagreed. The air force eventually adopted Menzel's theory, listing the event as a fireball.

Notwithstanding their increasingly strained assurances that all was well in the sky, Project Sign's staff were plainly worried about the public relations fallout from the Mantell and Chiles-Whitted cases. Deciding a bold move was in order, the Sign staff wrote a confidential "Estimate of the Situation" memorandum documenting the history of UFO sightings and concluding, for the first time, that UFOs were extraterrestrial in origin. Chief of Staff General Hoyt S. Vanenberg, the memo's intended recipient, rejected this hypothesis for lack of evidence and returned the document to Sign headquarters with an order to burn all copies.

Consequently, those Sign staff members who held to the extraterrestrial hypothesis lost influence to those who believed UFO sightings could and would be explained in mundane terms. In February 1949, Sign issued a report concluding that there was insufficient evidence to prove the objective reality of UFOs (which encouraged skeptics), while admitting that the study was unable to find a "reasonable and convincing explanation" for 20 percent of the sightings (which encouraged proponents).

On December 16, 1948, the military study received a new code name, Project Grudge — a name that, if unintentionally, mirrored the air force's barely concealed contempt for its subject. Grudge was charged to find an explanation for every sighting received, by way of assuring the public that the air force was indeed on top of the situation. "Instead of seeking the origin of a possibly unique phenomenon, as Sign had done, Grudge usually denied the objective reality of that phenomenon," notes historian David Jacobs.

Project Grudge's first attempt to shape public opinion by cooperating wholeheartedly with the author of a two-part *Saturday Evening Post* series was a notable failure. Although the articles explicitly sought to debunk UFOs and to mock the people who reported them, author Sidney Shallet conceded that explanations for a few sightings had not been found. A few days after the second installment hit the newsstands, UFO sightings reached an all-time high. In response, the air force issued a lengthy news release repeating its increasingly familiar mantra: *All UFOs can be explained as hoaxes, hallucinations, and misidentifications.*

Instead of reassuring the public, this whole sequence only raised new doubts. For the first time, civilians began studying the UFO phenomenon for themselves, marking a new chapter in the unfolding UFO epic. Civilian interest shot upward when, six months after its inception, Project Grudge revealed that 23 percent of the sightings it studied remained unidentified. The Grudge staff decided to try a new tack, arguing that the very reporting of UFOs constituted a danger to the national security. By this logic it was but one short step further to Grudge's recognition that the continuing existence of a UFO investigatory body could only *encourage* such reports. Project Grudge folded on December 27, 1949.

THE focus of the simmering UFO debate shifted to publishing when the January 1950 issue of *True* magazine featured a sensational article by retired Marine Corps Major Donald E. Keyhoe. Short on facts and high on speculation, this widely read and controversial article interpreted the new official silence on UFOs as clear evidence that the air force was hiding something big. To Keyhoe this could be only one thing, stated in the author's characteristically unambiguous terms: "For the past 175 years, the planet Earth has been under systematic close-range examination by living, intelligent observers from another planet." This assertion and others like it were based primarily on reconstructed conversations with anonymous individuals supposedly "in the know," conversations resembling dialogue from the less distinguished detective novels of the period.

> "Charley, there's a rumor that airline pilots have been ordered not to talk," I told Planck. "You know anything about it?"
> "You mean ordered by the Air Force or the companies?"
> "The Air Force and the C.A.A."
> "If the C.A.A.'s in on it, it's a top level deal," said Charley.

Keyhoe later expanded his article into an influential and no less sensational book, *The Flying Saucers Are Real*, which sold 500,000 copies.

At roughly the same time, a popular author named Frank Skully wrote a melodramatic book called *Behind the Flying Saucers*. This account chronicled the alleged air force capture of three landed saucers and several four-foot-tall dead aliens. Although the story turned out to be bogus, its impact — like that of Keyhoe's article and book — was enormous. Skully will be remembered in the annals of saucerology for introducing themes that, over the decades, would become staples in an ever-widening UFO mythology: crashed saucers, alien corpses, and elaborate cover-ups of the truth awaiting unveiling by intrepid investigators.

In short order, there followed several national magazine articles on the subject: *Time* asserting that all UFOs were actually Skyhook balloons, *U.S. News and World Report* announcing that all saucers were actually navy secret weapons, *Cosmopolitan* scathingly depicting people who reported UFOs as "true believers," "screwballs," "gagsters," and members of the "lunatic fringe."

These early book and magazine treatments — like the emotionally unsatisfying air force verdicts on the Mantell and Chiles-Whitted cases, and the official admission that a persistent percentage of sightings eluded definitive identification — offered little to clarify the remarkable "happenings" variously called flying saucers and UFOs. Neither did they do much to discourage public fascination with the charges and countercharges leveled between proponents and skeptics (some of whom took delight in attempting to "debunk" UFOs as a whole).

To the contrary, the emerging controversy simply further enhanced the mythic status of an apparently new class of events that seemed to travel an interface between mind and matter: a "twilight zone." A strangely consistent plot was beginning to take shape.

TWO

—————— ⨉ ——————

SPEAKING mythically, the early happenings of the UFO phenomenon were founding events, precursors of what was to come, reflective of psychic boundaries more fundamental than the simple temporal beginnings indicated by calendars.

Mythic events, writes the great Hungarian scholar Karl Kerenyi, "form the ground or foundation of the world, since everything rests on them." They comprise archetypal first principles "to which everything individual and particular goes back and out of which it is made, while they remain ageless, inexhaustible, invincible in timeless primordiality, in a past that proves imperishable because of its eternally repeated rebirths."

Kenneth Arnold's famous experience of June 24, 1947, constituted just such an Eternal Beginning. As the Associated Press story of Arnold's sighting of "nine bright saucer-like objects flying at 'incredible speed' at 10,000 feet" percolated through the collective psyche, primordial times drew close. Taken out of the idiom of twentieth-century journalism and considered as a modern creation myth, here is how Arnold's sighting might sound:

> In the beginning were nine bright objects, and Kenneth Arnold looked upon them, and he saw that their speed was enormous, and he was amazed, for he knew not what they were nor how to name them. Soon

he spoke forth what he saw, and through the inexhaustible darkness there echoed two words, *flying saucer*. In this moment the world was born.

"The world" was that of the UFO phenomenon, a universe organized around compelling sightings of strange *unknown* objects with their own mythic name: Unidentified Flying Objects, UFOs. This acronym was conceived by air force investigators, who, finding the phrase "flying saucer" too rich for its imaginal palate, settled on the term "UFO" because its colorless objectivity suited the pervasive rationalism and scientism of the postwar era. Even so, from the outset many observers had problems with the logic of this acronym, not the least being that it simply asserted what needed to be shown, namely that actual *objects* were being seen. And "unidentified"? Perhaps witnesses did not recognize what they saw in specific cases, but this is different from the idea that the events witnessed were *unidentifiable*.

These were important factual considerations, yet also somewhat beside the point. For, from a mythic standpoint, there was an unspoken *ceremonial necessity* that these events receive the formal designation "unidentifed," no matter what they were or where they were from in an ultimate sense. Soon enough, like the acronyms "CIA" and "laser" [l(ight) a(mplication by) s(timulated) e(mission of) r(adiation)], "UFO" attained popular associations far exceeding the bare denotation of three initials: alien visitations . . . hoaxes. . . angels . . . cover-up . . . mis-identifications . . . planetary poltergeists . . . hallucinations . . . visionary rumors.

These themes — and countless more as the epic developed steam — were the subject of fierce debate among players with mythic roles of their own: "debunker," "skeptic," "proponent" (and "contactee," as we will learn in future chapters). Indeed, a world had been born — apparently new, yet with echoes of ancient spirits visible at diffuse edges, as we shall see.

In simple historical terms, Arnold's sighting stands as a temporal reference point for the beginning of what was widely seen as a new phenomenon. Mythically, however, Arnold's sighting signifies something far more: ufology's *ongoing* beginning, its *primordial* present, its *continuously unfinished* thematic ground. Indeed, the more time that passes between the present moment and the UFO phenomenon's formal birth on June 24, 1947, the more charisma this date accrues.

In 1967, for instance, UFO research conferences were held on the theme "Twenty Years of UFOs." By 1987, the theme had become "Forty Years of UFOs." It is almost impossible to attend any of several annual midsummer UFO research conferences and not hear someone — or many — conjure the Primordial Beginning, often along these lines: "Now, if Kenneth Arnold *himself* were here today, he would demand that UFO research take stock of itself and look to new directions. . . ."

Through a tacit transformation that began long before his death in 1984, Kenneth Arnold was to become ufology's archetypal ancestor, its primal progenitor, its First Man. But this is not to say ufologists worship Arnold as a hero, martyr, or saint; the matter is far more complex. It is true that, over forty years later, Kenneth Arnold's case is regularly depicted by UFO proponents as the start of a new and altogether important chapter in the evolving saga of scientific discovery. Yet the details of his sighting are also regularly revisited by debunkers. They point to inconsistencies in Arnold's account to argue that his basic observations were mistaken and, consequently, that the UFO phenomenon must be seen as little more than an extended variation — a jazz riff — on Arnold's aboriginal delusion.

Martin Kottmeyer does not consider himself a debunker, nor even a ufologist. Yet he is a fierce critic of what he sees as the abysmal naivete of most UFO researchers and their theories, and he makes this clear in the articles he writes when he is not working on his small family farm in rural Illinois. In an article in the British magazine *Magonia*, Kottmeyer described returning to Arnold's original sighting report and discovering that, contrary to popular opinion, Arnold had not described nine objects in the shape of saucers. Instead he said the objects *moved like* a saucer skipping across water.

It was by jumbling the metaphoric intent of the description, Kottmeyer proposed, that reporters labeled the objects *flying saucers*. Arnold later complained that this phrase arose from "a great deal of misunderstanding," but the public had only the news story to go on, not having seen Arnold's sketches of objects. "People started looking for flying saucers and that is exactly what they found," said Kottmeyer. "They reported flat, circular objects that look like flying saucers sound like they should look like."

The implications of this journalistic error are "staggering in the extreme," Kottmeyer writes. Besides indicating a cultural origin of the entire flying saucer phenomenon — he says — this affair inserts a first-order paradox into efforts to interpret UFOs in extraterrestrial terms. "Why would extraterrestrials redesign their craft to conform to Bequette's error?" he said, referring to the local reporter who wrote those first misleading accounts.

Appearing over forty years after the phrase "flying saucer" was first spoken, Kottmeyer's article dutifully took its place in a debate that increasingly resembles disagreements among religious scholars about what Jesus *really* said to his disciples about the Kingdom. Others returning to the case in the future — perhaps to challenge Kottmeyer's perspective — will likewise be stepping back onto the Primal Ground hallowed by Arnold's fateful visual coincidence. All the more evidence that Arnold's sighting remains — for both sides of the debate — the *necessary* point of commencement for the entire UFO mythos.

From this perspective, the Arnold inception — like Origin in all creation mythologies — is the same as *authenticity* for those "inside" the UFO universe. This is because myth, according to scholar Kerenyi, "always sets up some precedent as an ideal and as a guarantee of the continuance of the ideal." With the emergence of the gods of Greek history, a new world emerged, a world lived by the Greeks under the rule of Zeus. Likewise, a new world emerged with Kenneth Arnold's report of objects skipping across the sky — a world under the "rule" of a "god" named UFO. The mythologist Bronislaw Malinowski elaborates:

> The myth . . . in its original living form . . . is not a mere tale told but a reality lived. It is not in the nature of an invention such as we have read in our novels today, but living reality, believed to have occurred in primordial times and to be influencing ever afterwards the world and the destinies of men. . . . [Myth asserts] an original, greater, and more important reality through which the present life, fate, and work of mankind are governed, and the knowledge of which provides men on the one hand with motives for ritual and moral acts, on the other with directions for their performance.

Kerenyi's fascinating idea, that myth in its "original, living form" provides "motives for ritual," helps us understand how, in the wake of Arnold's report, other themes took lasting ground in the emerging UFO mythos, where they, too, would offer ufologists "directions for their performance."

• • •

*T*HERE *must be a pattern capable of connecting the dots, capable of revealing what is concealed, capable of solving the UFO phenomenon right away.* This is the essence of the single assumption shared by key players in the early years of the unfolding UFO drama. Despite their disagreeing on most everything else, there was an unquestioned commitment to *explaining* UFOs. The agreed-on key was to *reveal* what was *hidden*.

Deception — intentional and otherwise — was the problem. The air force was deceiving the public by keeping the facts about UFOs from the public, said leading civilian UFO researchers. These researchers were deceiving the public by repeating this absurd claim over and over, the air force responded. According to debunkers, there were only two kinds of UFO witnesses: those who were deceived by their senses, and those who sought to deceive the public through hoaxed claims. No: the greatest deception of all, said UFO witnesses and their advocates, was to be found in the commitment of debunkers to explaining every sighting in conventional terms, no matter what the evidence showed.

Beneath surfaces — beyond disguise, distortion, dissembling, and disinformation — meaningful patterns awaited; this was the well-articulated mantra of most players in the drama's early years. *Exposed*, the phenomenon would *reveal its truths*. The challenge, simply enough, lay in directing attention to the phenomenon's observable variables and founding a theory on these variables.

But matters were not quite so simple. This "first observe, then theorize" formula overlooked a crucial point made by Einstein in 1926: "It is the theory which decides what we can observe." It neglected as well an important observation made by the German physicist Werner Heisenberg, namely that nature never reveals itself to us as it is, but rather always through the questions we put to it. From this perspective, it is not enough merely to challenge the assertion that the UFO phenomenon is "full of sound and fury, signifying nothing." The more important — and more difficult — question has to do with *which pattern, or patterns, to look for.*

Mathematician G. Spencer Brown has noted, "If two observers habitually look for different kinds of pattern they are bound to disagree upon the series which they call random." This touches the core of the conundrum that had bedeviled the UFO debate from the very outset: the capacity of these strange aerial events to outdistance each attempt to corner them definitively.

• • •

LOOKING at the evidence in terms of extraterrestrial visitation, the authors of the 1948 "Estimate of the Situation" memorandum found the pattern they were looking for. General Hoyt Vanenberg could — and did — dismiss this conclusion for lack of evidence. The memo's authors and recipient were looking for different patterns in the same data, and found them (or did not find them, in Vanenberg's case, which amounts to a different sort of pattern).

Likewise, Donald Keyhoe's research led him to find a pattern of massive government conspiracy. Others — including Keyhoe's pro-UFO colleagues — looked at the same evidence and reached different conclusions.

Viewing through his "lens" as a trained observer of astronomical and meteorological phenomena, Donald Menzel found evidence of such phenomena in the UFO cases he studied, contrary to others who, not searching for those sorts of patterns, examined the same cases.

The French scientist Aime Michel, in turn, found evidence that the magnitude of the intelligence behind UFO sightings was leagues beyond the limited cognitive capacities of human beings. If the reported contacts are real, and if contact occurs on their level rather than ours, Michel suggested, "then no matter what we do, it will forever remain imperceptible to us, just as most of our relationships with animals are altogether undiscoverable by them." In fact, because we are able to perceive phenomena that appear at our own psychic level or below it, we humans stand as much of a chance to comprehend UFOs as the mouse that nibbles on the corner of a leather-bound copy of *Macbeth* stands to comprehend the motives of Shakespeare. Michel was not alone in this view.

The *New York Times* adopted a more prosaic stance. UFO sightings continued to constitute little more than the latest "silly season," which, like past seasons featuring the Loch Ness monster, would, they hoped, soon be over. The evidence for this assertion — as for all the others — was "clear."

How could a phenomenon lend itself to so many seemingly contradictory interpretations at the same time? This question signals that it is time to draw back into the mythic imagination and make the acquaintance of one of this epic's leading players, even though he seldom appears as "himself." His arrival during the previous chapter wasn't even noticed, even though his role in the opening scenes was a major one — as it will be in many episodes to come.

I'm speaking of the Greek god Proteus, the son of Okeanos and Tethys. His dwelling place was the depths of the sea, whose changeability he mimicked in his remarkable capacity to change himself into myriad shapes and forms — a lion, panther, swine, serpent, or, if desperate, the contour of water or fire — in order to avoid those who would press him to demonstrate his prophetic powers. As the psychologist James Hillman put it, Proteus's "ceaselessly changing image that could take on any shape or nature represented the multiple and ambiguous form of the soul."

Ufologists seeking to verify the protean UFO's extraordinary nature — its "prophetic powers" — have found themselves rewarded, often to their dismay, with similar aesthetic riches: Arnold's splendid image of nine celestial objects undulating, like saucers skipping over water . . . Captain Mantell's fateful pursuit of an object described by witnesses as an ice-cream cone topped with red . . . a torpedo-shaped wingless craft trailing a massive flame as it caromed by an Eastern airline flight over Alabama . . . balls of light dancing on the wings of aircraft during World War II . . . "ghost rockets" over Sweden and Finland. UFOs have also been reported in the shape of stars, cigars, spheres, fireballs, dumbbells, footballs, hats, diamonds, plates pressed rim to rim, and washtubs.

But there are limits to this god's expressiveness. A passage from Homer's *Odyssey* states that those who seek to learn from Proteus must "grasp him steadfastly and press him yet the more." Yet Joseph Campbell offers this important detail: "This wily god never discloses even to the skillful questioner the whole content of his wisdom. He will reply only to the question put to him, and what he discloses will be great or trivial, according to the question asked."

From this perspective, each hypothesis seeking to explain the UFO phenomenon — extraterrestrial visitors, misidentification of Venus, Soviet weapons, U.S. weapons tests, products of disturbed minds, and so on — can be taken as a *particular and limited* question put to the UFO by particular observers with particular assumptions. Project Sign staffers looked at the data and "asked" the UFO phenomenon ("Proteus") whether its origins were extraterrestrial. This question was posed so as to stipulate a range of possible answers, as most questions do. ("Are you still beating your wife?")

The UFO phenomenon "answered" Project Sign's question not in ultimate or definitive terms but according to specific criteria introduced by specific observers with their own agendas. From this point it was but a short step for investigators to forget that the resulting answers came into view as a result of particular questions based on particular distinctions, and then for them to embrace the assumption that they now had a view of the UFO "as it really is." General Vanenberg asked the same question — *ET or not?* — and received a different answer, as did many other observers during the first few years of the UFO's presence at the edge of reality.

Thus, by focusing largely on the question of extraterrestrial origins — a question whose answers could only be a matter of conjecture, short of the proverbial landing on the White House lawn — it was possible for many satisfying answers to many different questions to be presented. This should never surprise us, wrote the Renaissance philosopher Giambattista Vico, "since human knowledge is nothing else than the endeavor to make things correspond to one another in shapely proportion."

It is no wonder, then, that the UFO debate that began in 1947 bordered most of the time on trench warfare in the decades to come. Proteus felt no obligation to advise his questioners about whether their question about "his" origins was futile. He seemed possessed of no great impulse to take everyone aside and suggest that focusing on other questions — such as the idea that UFOs might represent unknown dimensions of material or psychological (or both: psychophysical) reality — might ultimately prove more fruitful. Such counsel would have been more likely from Apollo, bearer of light, order, and clarity; and this god showed no sign of being anywhere near the UFO neighborhood (although the longing for his presence amid the tumult was great).

Instead, by using specific questions of his unknowing disciples to put forth aspects of his whole wisdom — "great or trivial" — Proteus remained true to the tasks necessitated by his mythic nature as a shape-shifter, as keeper of a divinely ambivalent (*ambi* = many, *valent* = strengths or powers) ground. Bearing in mind that the major players in the UFO epic were interested in *definitive* answers to their questions, we gain some understanding of the divine havoc Proteus's secret presence brought to the dialogue.

Of relevance here are the psychologist Lynn Segal's thoughts, in *The Dream of Reality*, on the enduring human wish for "reality" to have a certain shape and form:

First, we wish reality to exist independently of us, we who observe it. Second, we wish reality to be discoverable, to reveal itself to us. We wish to know its secrets, i.e., how it works. Third, we wish these secrets to be lawful, so we can predict and ultimately control reality. Fourth, we wish for certainty; we wish to know that what we have discovered about reality is true.

The wish for reality to cooperate with human intentions is not limited to UFO studies, by any means. There currently rages within the mainstream of science a fierce discussion about whether it is appropriate to continue speaking of reality as absolutely or eternally independent of our own observations and thoughts. Contrary to the longstanding, and reassuring, idea that science is growing closer and closer to knowing and mapping the exact nature of a supposedly free-standing universe, new developments in the science of cognition dictate that the active role of the observer must be included — and explicitly accounted for — in scientific explanation.

Even if we are participants in the social construction of an essentially protean reality moment by moment, still, most of the time we get along well enough on the assumption that we have a securely established place in a reality that is enduring, solid, and predictable, and most of all a reality that cooperates by remaining *out there*. But occasionally this relation reverses and we are led to question our certainty.

Many years ago the psychologist Jerome Bruner conducted an experiment designed to investigate what he called "perceptual readiness," the tendency of humans to hold expectations about their environment that predetermine to some degree what they perceive. Bruner showed subjects two sets of playing cards, one with colors reversed and one normal, at speeds of a fraction of a second.

Not surprisingly, subjects had greater difficulty identifying the color-reversed cards. But what especially interested Bruner were the lengths to which subjects went to reinterpret and "regularize" their perceptions to fit with their prior expectations about the nature of playing cards. One subject reported that the red six of clubs was indeed a six of clubs, but there was a pinkish illumination inside the tachistoscope (the instrument that presented the cards to view). There was, of course, no such coloring inside the device.

"All this is banal enough but the implications are anything but that," Bruner said. "For it means that perception is to some unspecifiable degree an instrument of the world as we have structured it by our expectancies. Moreover, it is characteristic of complex perceptual processes that they tend where possible to assimilate whatever is seen or heard to what is expected."

The analogy between this experiment and the ongoing UFO "test" seems obvious, yet there is an important difference as well. After Bruner's experimental trials, his subjects were able to examine both sets of cards and scrutinize the tachistoscope, then compare those confirmable physical parameters against their own observations. Next they could explore the implications of any variance between test constraints and their responses, no doubt thereby gaining new insights into the subtle assumptions guiding their moment-by-moment experience of living.

In contrast, after a UFO experience, what are the agreed-upon points of reference? Who will come forward with concrete criteria showing *what was really happening* during the "test" so that subjects can separate how much of "it" was really "it" and how much of "it" was really "them"? The most common response within the UFO debate is that "the facts speak for themselves." But nothing was more clear than that the "facts" (and the values disguised within) were speaking differently to different listeners, so that even the supposedly "hardest" of physical evidence (such as UFO photographs) remained open to vastly different interpretations among well-credentialed optical physicists on both sides.

Thus, by the end of the drama's first act, the intrepid UFO found itself the subject of seemingly unbounded speculation as it went about transgressing the boundaries between mind and matter, spirit and soul, stealing shamelessly from the repertoires of each. During the break before the second act, ufologists had only to get together backstage and agree on methods suited to dialogue with a phenomenon whose appearances were too compelling to be ignored, yet also too absurd simply to be taken at face value. The meeting never happened because its necessity was not apparent to the majority of UFO detectives, who, after all, were predisposed to find either evidence of metallic machines or mental malaise, nothing in between.

In the meantime, Proteus permitted himself to wonder whether those who had elected to follow his tracks — those on both sides — could be enticed to shift their *own* shape, to expand their horizons beyond the dreary one-dimensional debate that had emerged so far. He had his doubts. But in the confusion of the moment, one thing was clear: the shape-shifter would keep his own scope both broad and deep. He was finding the general pandemonium delightful.

THREE

$\times$

BETWEEN 1950 and mid-1952, when the flying saucers disappeared from the scene as remarkably as they had arrived, a new conventional wisdom took root: whatever they were and wherever they were from, UFOs were gone, probably for good. Not everyone shared this view, especially not Jim and Coral Lorenzen of Sturgeon Bay, Wisconsin, founders in early 1952 of the Aerial Phenomena Research Organization (APRO), a civilian UFO investigation group keen on a "scientific" approach to the subject. (Once incorporated, APRO in a sense *required* continuing flying saucers.) Yet for the most part, especially among pundits eager to stay ahead of trends, placing odds on UFOs as an anomaly whose time had come and gone seemed a safe bet.

In April, May, and June 1951 the air force received only seventeen sighting reports. That summer their scaled-down Project Grudge employed only one investigator. Headline writers were once again more interested in the political fortunes of President Truman than the fantastic claims of Kenneth Arnold. Writes historian David Jacobs, "It appeared that the Air Force, after eighteen months of effort, had finally succeeded in its campaign to eliminate UFO reports and reduce the mystery surrounding the phenomenon."

Then came 1952. In July and August alone of that year, Project Grudge received 862 sighting reports. As suddenly as they were gone, they were back, this time in England, France, and South America, but especially the United States.

ON THE evening of July 14, a Pan American airliner, flying at 8,000 feet, was approaching Norfolk, Virginia, en route to Miami from New York. Except for a few thin cirrus clouds above 12,000 feet, the night was clear and visibility unlimited. Shortly after 8 P.M., Captain William B. Nash and copilot William Fortenberry both caught sight of a red brilliance in the sky, apparently beyond and to the east of Newport News. "Almost immediately," they later reported,

> we perceived . . . six bright objects streaking towards us at tremendous speed . . . they had the fiery aspect of hot coals, but of much greater glow — perhaps twenty times more brilliant [than city lights below] . . . their shape was clearly outlined and evidently circular; the edges were well defined, not phosphorescent or fuzzy . . . the red orange color was uniform over the upper surface of each craft.

The single-line formation of double-DC-3-sized UFOs then suddenly seemed to slow its collective speed, with the second and third appearing to overtake the lead light. To the pilots it "looked very much as if an element of 'human' or 'intelligent' error had been introduced." Their report continues:

> All together, they flipped on edge, the sides to the left of us going up and the glowing surfaces facing right . . . they were much like coins . . . then, without an arc or swerve at all, they flipped back together to the flat altitude [sic] and darted off in a direction that formed a sharp angle with their first course . . . the change . . . was acute . . . [like] a ball ricocheting off a wall.

Captain Nash estimated that the unlighted exposed edges of each craft were about fifteen feet thick and their top surfaces flat. As two additional craft suddenly joined the six, the lights of all eight blinked off, then back on. Remaining in a straight line, the UFOs zoomed westward, climbing in a graceful arc as their lights blinked out . . . one by one. The entire display lasted fifteen seconds.

The Nash-Fortenberry sighting (as it came to be known in UFO annals) gained considerable attention quickly throughout the nation, only to be eclipsed five days later by a spectacular sighting introduced to the nation with these headlines: JET FLYERS TOLD TO SHOOT

DOWN SAUCERS and AIR FORCE WON'T TALK. Just after midnight on Saturday evening, July 19, eight unknown targets appeared on radar at the Washington National Airport. "Our shift had been on duty about forty minutes," recalled air traffic controller Harry Barnes. "The things which caused [fellow air traffic controller Ed Nugent] to call me over to the scope were seven pips clustered together irregularly in one corner. . . . We knew immediately that a very strange situation existed."

The moment he realized that the movements of these seven "pips" were "completely radical compared to those of ordinary aircraft," Barnes placed calls to radar technicians at the airport tower and at Andrews Air Force base, receiving in both cases independent radar verification that correlated with visual sightings of strange lights by local pilots and various ground witnesses. Soon radar-equipped jet fighters from a Delaware base began scouring the skies. They reported seeing nothing; this was confirmed by radar operators on the ground. Moments after the jets left the scene, the unknown targets returned to the Washington National Airport radar screens. Visual and radar sightings continued for six more hours into the early morning.

For Barnes and his beleaguered colleagues, however, the "long night" was just beginning. One week later — Saturday, July 26, near 9 P.M. — six new unexplained "pips" appeared on radar, following a southerly trajectory. As had happened the previous week, numerous radar and visual correlations were made over an extended period. Barnes put in a call to the Pentagon. Within minutes, F-94 jet interceptors moved into the target area over Washington, where visibility was excellent. Throughout the next several hours, visual sightings were made and lost several times. At one point, after three geographically separate radar units locked onto the same target just north of the city, the target suddenly disappeared from all three simultaneously. Whenever jet interceptors closed in on the lights, the UFO accelerated out of view.

All through the night, civilian pilots, ground personnel, and radar operators filed continuous reports. Finally, both visual sightings and radar blips disappeared, reports ended, and explanations began. The air force insisted that "there has been no pattern that reveals anything remotely like purpose or remotely like consistency that we can in any way associate with any menace to the United States." The radar and visual sightings were "due to mirage effects created by a double-temperature inversion."

During both weekends Harry Barnes had supervised radar tracking of the objects and remained in close communication with numerous ground witnesses. He emphatically disagreed with the air force's estimation. "There is no other conclusion I can reach but that . . . there were at least ten unidentified flying objects moving above Washington . . . [performing] gyrations which no known aircraft could perform," he wrote in a widely distributed syndicated article. Many others shared Barnes's skepticism: radar operators who had tracked the elusive lights, reporters, gung-ho Aerial Phenomena Research Organizaton members, ground witnesses, and much of the public at large. All found the air force verdict about as satisfying as that offered by debunker Donald Menzel, with his straight-faced assertion that pilots Nash and Fortenberry had mistaken lightning bugs trapped between panes of the cockpit window for something more remarkable.

Menzel soon dropped his "fireflies under glass" theory and, congratulating himself as the man "who shot Santa Claus," announced that the pilots had been deceived by the same phenomenon that had tricked radar readings and witnesses' eyes during two hot summer weekends in Washington, namely ground light distorted by different temperature layers and haze.

Jet fighters chasing temperature inversions? Maybe; maybe not. This was the problem — how, in the absence of a consensus definition for "UFO," to evaluate claims for aerial phenomena that *seemed* unconventional, nonmundane, extraordinary, fantastic. Intelligent and seemingly sincere men and women were describing and accounting for the new phenomenon in very different ways. When the Washington, D.C., sightings briefly overshadowed news coverage of the Democratic National Convention, this fact itself became news for a brief period, indicating that the very debate about the events of the two weekends — and the simmering controversy about UFOs as a whole — had captured public attention and was holding it compellingly.

It is not difficult to imagine that the official "temperature inversion" verdict momentarily settled the nerves of a postwar populace haunted by Senator Joseph McCarthy's irresponsible assertions that Communists were taking over the State Department, the Hollywood film industry, and major American universities. Even so, there is no reason to suppose that the millions of Americans who had been glued to their radios and newspapers that weekend were inclined — or even able — to simply banish from memory this widely reported news story:

WASHINGTON, July 28 (INS) — The Air Force revealed today that jet pilots have been placed on a 24-hour nationwide "alert" against "flying saucers" with orders to "shoot them down" if they refuse to land. It was learned that pilots have gone aloft on several occasions in an effort to shoot the mysterious objects to the ground, but never came close enough to use their guns.

One moment, "ground light distorted by different temperature layers and haze"; the next moment, "never close enough to use their guns." Slowly, inexorably, a chasm was widening: between sensational news accounts of UFOs and compelling firsthand testimony, on one hand, and what appeared to be convoluted disavowals by air force personnel and no-nonsense debunkers, on the other. The public — more accurately, the public's *psyche* — found itself in the middle, where it would remain for years to come, inexorably absorbing images of an evasive yet mysteriously tangible "Other."

"HAVE We Visitors from Space?" This banner title of an April 7, 1952, issue of a popular national magazine might have been greeted as yet another instance of sensational press coverage seeking to exploit UFO ambiguity, were it not for two relevant facts. The article appeared not in some supermarket tabloid but in *Life*, a magazine possessed of considerable credibility. And it followed a headline that was nothing short of extraordinary:

> The Air Force is now ready to concede that many saucer and fireball sightings still defy explanation; here LIFE offers some scientific evidence that there is a real case for interplanetary flying saucers.

The article — one of the most influential ever published about UFOs, and, surprisingly, written with the acknowledged cooperation of Project Blue Book, successor to Project Grudge — focused on ten national sighting reports that the air force had been unable to explain as psychological delusions, secret technology being tested, Russian weaponry, Skyhook balloons, or atomic test results. The article also featured testimony from two distinguished authorities who, unlike APRO, weren't perceived as having a stake in UFOs' being real.

Dr. Walther Reidel, a respected designer of German rockets and missiles, was quoted as saying: "I am completely convinced that they [UFOs] have an out-of-world basis." Dr. Maurice A. Boit, prominent in the fields of astrodynamics and mathematical physics, agreed: "The least improbable explanation is that these things are artificial and controlled. . . . My opinion for some time has been that they have an extraterrestrial origin." For the first time, authorities no less distinguished than Harvard astronomer Donald Menzel had contradicted Menzel's increasingly knee-jerk efforts to reduce the mystery of the flying saucer phenomenon.

The *Life* article offered provocative conclusions that became dinner-table discussion for millions of Americans:

> The real depths of the saucer mystery bemuse penetration, as the night sky swallows up a flashlight beam. What of the other shapes? Why do they make no sound? What power urges them at such terrible speeds through the sky? Who, or what, is aboard? Where do they come from? Why are they here? What are the intentions of the beings who control them?

No less significant than such questions being posed in the pages of *Life* was the fact that, for the first time, the air force's response fell short of a blanket denial: "The article is factual, but *Life*'s conclusions are their own." This shift was immediately leaped on by conspiracy theorists — whose numbers were growing steadily — as evidence that the air force had finally decided to "come clean" by revealing, in small doses strategically measured to avoid anticipated mass panic, that UFOs were intelligently piloted craft from outer space. (In decades to come, the prediction that *the government cover-up is going to blow sky-high any day now* would develop a life of its own, serving to rally the faithful in times when recurring doubts about the reality of UFOs threatened the *raison d'être* of flying saucer clubs and research groups.)

Indirectly, the *Life* article offered new reason for doubting a pet theory of the debunkers, namely that massive publicity about UFOs creates a contagious environment generating additional UFO reports. Even though 350 newspapers across the country mentioned the article, the Associated Press national wire carried three UFO stories during the month of the article's appearance, only one of which pertained to a sighting.

Now that a national magazine of *Life*'s stature had apparently given its blessing to the reality of UFOs, saucer advocates seemed to have carried the day — at least in a particular battle. Their victory was short-lived, however. The *New York Times* launched an immediate counter-attack challenging the article's credibility as well as the air force's analysis of the ten sightings in question, making it all too clear that the larger cultural war about UFOs and reality was far from over.

Times science writer Walter Kaempffert, pointing to inconsistencies in the reports, revived the argument that most of the sightings were in fact weather balloons. A *Times* editorial complained that even though the report of Project Grudge dismissed any factual basis for UFOs, "the idea was too fantastic to die. After all, the sea serpent was with us for decades and it took several years before the Loch Ness monster was buried."

The *Times* was partly right — Project Grudge had indeed given persuasive prosaic explanations to most sightings, and had gone on to discourage public fascination with UFOs as dangerous to the nation's morale and security. But Grudge had also listed a significant percentage of sightings as unknown, a well-publicized fact that compromised journalistic efforts to counter the effects of the *Life* article. Moreover, without intending to, the air force infuriated ally Menzel and other debunkers by continuing to issue contradictory public statements effectively undercutting efforts to reduce the "charisma" of flying saucers.

> DAYTON, Ohio, July 19 (AP) — A spokesman at Wright-Patterson Air Force Base says the Air Force still has no explanation for 15 per cent of the approximate 1,000 flying saucer reports it has received....
>
> Capt. E. J. Ruppelt, "saucer" project officer of the Air Technical Intelligence Center, said, "We are firmly convinced that persons making these reports actually see something in the skies" ...

This news report appeared near the peak of the 1952 UFO wave, at the end of which the controversy's dynamics had become notably "triangular." Occupying one point of the triangle was the air force, mired in apparent internal confusion between predictions of defeat for UFOs as a serious phenomenon and admissions that something real was being seen in the skies. The triangle's second point was held by Donald Menzel, whose no-holds-barred attempts to reduce all UFOs to mirages, reflections, ice crystals floating in clouds, light refractions, and temperature inversions, were cheered by much of the mainstream press and the academic and scientific communities. The third point belonged to Donald Keyhoe and his pro-UFO followers, whose strenuous allegations of government cover-up, like the equally predictable assertions of the air force and debunker Menzel, consistently inclined to self-parody.

The UFO phenomenon had reached its first real turning point, with a recognizable plot focused around recognizable conflicts in place. At the debate's present pitch, one of two outcomes seemed inevitable. Either tensions would rise to a point where the air force felt obliged to release its complete UFO file to the public, or else the three-way debate would continue until it exhausted itself on the shores of public disinterest.

But there was another alternative. An unexpected element, idea, or character might somehow enter the story to permit — or require — the UFO plot to unfold along very different lines. Whatever form it might take, this new factor would need to be capable of radically shifting the attentions of air force researchers, debunkers and proponents alike — capable, in other words, of undercutting the increasingly tedious triangular debate.

Which is exactly what happened. Just as Homer expanded and enriched the *Odyssey* by permitting his hero, Ulysses, to wander successively into new and significant regions, the ever-widening plot of the UFO epic was about to encompass a new adventure of events and images whose very appearance on the scene would beg the major questions of the existing debate, opening provocative new dilemmas at the same time.

Enter the contactees.

"IT WAS inevitable that someone, somewhere, sooner or later, would claim contact with the alien beings aboard a flying saucer," writes journalist and UFO historian Dennis Stacy. This dubious distinction fell to George Adamski, a Polish immigrant who had settled on the West Coast.

After a brief stint in the military and an undistinguished career as a sign painter, factory worker, hamburger flipper, and author of an unsuccessful science fiction novel called *Pioneers of Space*, George Adamski had become a luminary of sorts in the southern California occult scene by the mid-1930s, founding a religious group called the Royal Order of Tibet and lecturing on "universal law" before live audiences and on radio programs.

But it was for an incredible event — real, hoaxed, or a hybrid of both — that occurred near Desert Center, California, that George

Adamski would achieve worldwide fame, concurrently earning infamy in the eyes of UFO trackers committed to simple, nuts-and-bolts solutions to what increasingly was known as "the UFO problem."

The date was November 20, 1952. Adamski — known by his cultish followers as "professor" even though he lacked formal education — and six of his associates drove to the desert with the express hope of seeing a flying saucer and (they hoped) meeting its passengers. Soon they saw a large, cigar-shaped craft rising from behind a range of mountains, followed shortly by a second craft that appeared in the sky with a sudden flash. It was at this point that Adamski set off alone by foot, propped up the small telescope he usually carried with him, and began waiting for the contact that he felt was imminent.

Shortly, Adamski caught sight of someone waving toward him. As he walked closer, he realized he "was in the presence of a man from space — A HUMAN BEING FROM ANOTHER WORLD!" The spaceman had blond hair and an extremely high forehead, stood about five feet six inches tall, weighed about 135 pounds, wore a glossy chocolate-brown uniform, and appeared to be in his late twenties. "The beauty of this form," Adamski said, "surpassed anything I had ever seen . . . [I] felt like a child in the presence of one with great wisdom and much love."

Through a combination of sign language and telepathy, Adamski learned that the spaceman had come from Venus to warn earthlings away from their warlike ways, in particular to encourage a halt to nuclear testing, a practice that the Nordic-looking starman said was upsetting the harmony of the universe. Many Venusians already lived in disguise among humans from various walks of life, Adamski learned from this genial traveler, who allowed "the professor" to tour and photograph the landed spacecraft so long as he refrained from taking photographs of the Venusian. (One of his cameras was out of focus and the other malfunctioned, leaving Adamski with but one blurry shot.)

That Adamski was the only human witness to this alleged encounter did nothing to diminish his success on the saucer circuit, where he regaled audiences of devotees with accounts of ongoing contacts with the "Space Brothers" (as he called them), some of whom he met in Los Angeles bars and cafés. This was possible because they so closely resembled humans in appearance. Soon Adamski was the author of two best-selling books and found himself making the rounds of radio and television talk shows, being received by the Queen of the Netherlands, and, although the Vatican denied it, claiming a private meeting with the pope.

George Adamski was both one of a kind and the first of a new kind of witness who recounted personal UFO experiences not to law enforcement officials or military investigators but to hundreds of thousands of fellow citizens through books, lectures, and television and radio programs. Whereas earlier UFO witnesses typically reacted to their experiences with confusion and fear of being publicly identified with the stigma of flying saucers, David Jacobs notes that

> the contactees had no fear of ridicule and eagerly sought publicity. They often organized special flying saucer clubs based on their experiences and used the clubs to help publicize their stories. . . . Some contactees claimed to have taken a ride in a flying saucer and described the ride and the planets they visited in great detail. Moreover, most contactees reported that space people had charged them with a mission, which, they said, was why they had to seek publicity.

Seeking publicity — and receiving it — is what the first and most well known contactees did extraordinarily well. A California mechanic named Truman Bethurum followed Adamski's lead in 1954 with his book *Aboard a Flying Saucer*, a firsthand account of being awakened in the middle of the night in the California desert by "eight or ten small-sized men" with olive skin and dressed in uniforms. Unlike Adamski's telepathic Venusians, Bethurum's aliens spoke flawless English (albeit after a false start in a foreign tongue), inviting Bethurum aboard their nearby flying saucer where they introduced him to their female captain, Aura Rhanes, whom Bethurum found "tops in shapeliness and beauty." Aura Rhanes offered a thorough briefing about her home planet, Clarion, a marvelous place free of diseases (therefore doctors) and politicians (therefore taxes).

Another desert — this one in New Mexico — figured in *White Sands Incident*, Daniel Fry's account of a thirty-minute flight to New York City aboard a flying saucer where he accepted the task of helping prevent the world from falling into the "terrible abyss" of nuclear weapons. There were other famous contactees as well. Orfeo Angelucci, likewise a saucer passenger, wrote of receiving tutoring in universal truths from a spaceman named Neptune. Angelucci described a rendezvous with an alien in a Greyhound bus terminal. Howard Menger, author of *From Outer Space to You*, told of visiting the moon as a child, falling in love with a spacewoman named Marla, and discovering that he was a reincarnated Jupiterian placed on Earth to perform good deeds for the benefit of all mankind.

AND so it went throughout the mid to late 1950s. The contactees as a group might have remained little more than a curious footnote in the unfolding UFO epic but for their ability to generate publicity for their claims and their suitability as "stars" of newspaper features and radio and television programs. The nation was now familiar with the possibility that the flying saucers might be from outer space; the contactees helped release tension related to this possibility, and tensions connected with the UFO phenomenon as a whole. If the contactees provided comic relief, it was nevertheless *relief*.

In a curious sense, Adamski, Bethurum, Fry, Angelucci, and Menger (and many others like them) both hindered and helped the air force's UFO campaign — the former by generating publicity about flying saucers contrary to Project Blue Book's express effort to reduce publicity; the latter by so enhancing the aura of absurdity around flying saucers that the air force felt less pressure to take UFO reports seriously.

To Donald Menzel and other debunkers, already convinced that mundane explanations best suited claims of fantastic objects in the sky, the contactees were a godsend. Debunkers grew skilled at pointing to the self-negating nature of contactee claims ("I flew to Venus in a spaceship"), and at linking these claims with noncontactee reports of strange lights and aerial objects, aiming to cast doubts on everything connected with the acronym *UFO*. This effort proved a considerable success. It was hard enough for most witnesses to come forward to report silvery objects hovering motionless before departing skyward at fantastic speeds; now such witnesses had to be ready for the inevitable jokes about "little green men."

Donald Keyhoe, for his part, was clearly appalled by the contactees' persistent ability to garner publicity that he felt rightly belonged to "legitimate" UFO research. Yet Keyhoe met with only marginal success in his efforts to expose contactee claims as fraudulent. This was partly due to the fact that, in the public mind at least, there were parallels between the extreme *claims* of government conspiracy put forward by

Keyhoe's UFO research group, the National Investigations Committee on Aerial Phenomena (NICAP), and the extreme *behavior* of groups such as contactee George Van Tassel's Giant Rock Spacecraft Convention, an annual southern California gathering where the faithful gathered to hear interplanetary gospel (and to spend money on such items as packets of hair from a Venusian dog).

With the passage of time, owing partly to successful exposés of obvious contactee fraud, public fascination with contactees began to fade. Although in one sense this was an obvious blessing for the civilian groups eager to return to "serious" UFO research, the loss of the contactees as a focal point brought APRO and NICAP new problems. Compelling reports were surfacing concerning *apparently real* encounters with bizarre humanoid occupants of the saucers — reports bearing little resemblance to the old contactee tales and thus harder to simply dismiss out of hand.

"Ufology" (as civilian UFO researchers had taken to calling their embryonic discipline)* was now faced with the problem of deciding whether to take such reports seriously. If he had been consulted on the matter, a young Brazilian farmer named Antonio Villas-Boas surely would have voted yes.

IT WAS summer in the Southern Hemisphere. The heat was so intense that Brazilian farmers worked at night whenever possible. On the night of October 14, 1957, at approximately 1 A.M., Antonio Villas-Boas, twenty-three, an uneducated farmer, was alone tilling the field with his tractor when he saw a "luminous egg-shaped craft flying toward me at terrific speed." On previous nights, Antonio and his brother had observed a bright silvery light illuminating the corral like a power searchlight, and then sweeping the roof of their house before suddenly departing. But on this night, Antonio Villas-Boas saw more than a light.

As three metal "legs" descended from the hovering craft to support it, Villas-Boas's tractor lights failed and the engine went dead. Unable to start his tractor, Villas-Boas tried to run but was grabbed by four helmeted humanoid creatures who frog-marched him into the craft. Villas-Boas was escorted to a sparsely furnished room where the "crew" used a strange device to extract blood from his chin. Then the entities,

---

Webster's New World Dictionary contains this entry: "ufologist: a person interested in UFOs, especially as supposed craft from outer space."

who "spoke" in a series of barks similar to dog sounds, forcibly stripped him naked and sponged him down with an unfamiliar liquid.

Next a completely nude woman with bright red pubic hair entered the room as the other creatures departed. This woman, whose body was "much more beautiful than that of any woman I have ever known before," began embracing and rubbing against her confused captive, who became aroused and joined her in sexual intercourse. He described it as "a normal act . . . she behaved much the same as any woman would" (except for the decidedly repulsive barking sounds she made while having her way with him).

Afterward, while leaving the room, the woman pointed to her belly, then to Villas-Boas, then toward the southern sky, all of which he took to refer to their future hybrid alien-human child. "What they wanted of me [was] a good stallion to improve their own stock," said Villas-Boas, sounding a theme that would appear in alien abduction narratives for decades to come: human genetic material as the replenishment-of-choice for degenerate alien species throughout the known or unknown universe. After his clothes were returned and he was once again dressed, Villas-Boas was given a tour of the craft and then returned to his farm.

At the surface level, Villas-Boas's account mimics some of the more fantastic motifs of the well-known contactee stories — the quick tour of the saucer, a sense of being *needed* by the aliens — but there were important differences that made this case more interesting to ufologists. For instance, rather than seeking personal fame, Villas-Boas kept quiet about his experience until he read a newspaper notice calling for UFO reports. Also, there is no reason to believe that Villas-Boas, an uneducated South American rural farmer, had prior knowledge of UFO stories or a predisposition to concoct a hoax.

But the most suggestive evidence was physical. Olivo Fontes, a distinguished local physician, found that Villas-Boas appeared to have suffered radiation poisoning consistent with a claim of contact with a technically advanced craft. Villas-Boas also had two scars on his chin corresponding to the place where he said blood was removed. Of course, this young farmer may have had these scars prior to his alleged encounter, just as he may have fabricated — or imagined — his entire account. But what of the apparent radiation poisoning? And how to dismiss the unavoidable impression that Villas-Boas seemed to be offering a good-faith account of what, for him, was a real experience?

This case, and others involving like observations of or interactions with humanoid creatures near or in unusual craft, had the effect of highlighting already existing tensions between the two chief civilian UFO research groups, APRO and NICAP. Although originally supportive of NICAP founder Donald Keyhoe's government conspiracy theories, APRO cofounder Coral Lorenzen was becoming increasingly suspicious of Keyhoe's one-note recital. Having herself worked for the air force, Lorenzen saw the air force UFO operation less as a grand cover-up than as a moderately effective public relations endeavor.

Further, APRO was far more willing than NICAP to consider reports about UFO occupants, apparently on the assumption that the craft seen from the outside must also have an inside, along with pilots and crew — if only robots. Keyhoe would have none of these new accounts about humanoid creatures; they reminded him too much of the bogus claims of contactees.

These organizational tensions reflected a deeper strain among ufologists about how to classify reports of contact with UFO occupants. Some were skeptical of all such claims, preferring to focus their efforts on finding hard physical evidence, especially radar reports, photographs, and the occasional "landing mark." Others wanted to reject contactee claims as the sheerest nonsense and focus specifically on the provocative new descriptions of what appeared to be real interactions with real UFO occupants.

Still others, schooled in parapsychology and cross-cultural occult and spiritual traditions, had no difficulty viewing contactee encounters and abductions as equally real and equally unreal manifestations of the same complex hallucinatory process that gave rise to angelic and demonic phenomena and prophetic visionary experiences in ages past. These ufologists were primarily interested in the way these multidimensional spirit-forces skillfully manipulated the naivete of contactees and ufologists for their own mischievous ends.

To say that this minority wing of ufology was not very popular among hard-core disciples of the extraterrestrial hypothesis is a considerable understatement. Yet advocates of this provocative perspective would have tremendous influence in years to come, especially during periods when the continuing absence of concrete evidence of crashed saucers and captured alien corpses seemed to indicate that mainstream ufology had embarked on a fatally delusional wild goose chase.

For their part, air force investigators and civilian debunkers refrained from such rarefied speculations and philosophical distinctions. They were satisfied to let the whole lot — researchers, contactees, abductees, and whoever else wanted to join in — fight it out among themselves.

FOUR

———— ✕ ————

AGAINST the backdrop of the UFO's varied mid-1950s adventures, it is time to take a closer look at the dramatic structure of these events. Aristotle wrote that the essential element of drama and epic is "the arrangement of the elements" as narrative. What is it about the narrative structure of UFO events that generates such a powerful response in the collective human psyche?

According to Angus Fletcher in *Allegory: The Theory of a Symbolic Mode*, "allegory says one thing and means another. It destroys the expectation we have about language, that our words 'mean what they say.'" An allegorical work, then, goes along saying one thing in order to mean something beyond that one thing, in order to imply something or many things not stated in the primary or surface story. In the sixteenth century, the literary scholar Henry Peacham described allegory as a kind of "aenigma ... which for the darknesse, the sense may hardly be gathered." Fletcher makes a similar point when he describes allegory as "a fundamental process of encoding our speech."

The UFO phenomenon has seldom been considered a "literary problem," but let us imagine that, 200 years from now, for whatever reason, UFOs have ceased to appear. Suppose that all that is left of the phenomenon is its literature: the body of witness reports and the myriad books and magazine analyses of these. I am willing to predict that literary scholars of the twenty-second century, free of the passions associated with UFOs today, would study this vast written record as a late-twentieth-century allegory. While they would no doubt share our fascination with the physical nature of UFOs, they would probably be even more interested in how UFOs appeared to us as a form of "encoded speech" that invited — and to some extent compelled — an ongoing effort to decode the enigmatic "grammar" of this speech.

I suspect these scholars would be particularly impressed with how the UFO phenomenon held together numerous levels of meaning by implication, even as it most of the time kept the focus of observers on its surface events: flyovers, landings, encounters with occupants. One of the defining characteristics of pure allegory, says Angus Fletcher, is that its formal, or literal, surface level does not explicitly demand to be interpreted for hidden meanings, for it often makes "good enough" sense by itself. "But somehow this literal surface suggests a *peculiar doubleness of intention*, and while it can, as it were, get along without interpretation, it becomes much richer and more interesting if given interpretation" (emphasis added).

The Nash-Fortenberry sighting of 1952 offers a persuasive instance of allegory in action. Two professional pilots see "six bright objects streaking towards us at tremendous speed." In formal terms, this makes good enough sense by itself, even though of course they could not identify what they saw. But even that is comprehensible: they saw what they saw, and they were amazed. At the same time, the public's impulse to interpret, to scratch the surface of the literal sighting report, was unavoidable. The psyche — collective and personal — could not help but ask: "What *were* those things with the 'fiery aspect of hot coals, but of much greater glow'?"

A similar tension between surface and depth, text and subtext, is evident in the controversy about events that occurred the following weekend over Washington, D.C. Numerous competent observers made both visual and radar sightings of apparently unconventional aerial objects. The air force responded by scrambling jets to chase down the objects. Once again, here were events whose formal logic is clear: *something unusual seen and chased*.

It was only subsequent to these events that matters grew cloudier. Why did the jets not manage to get one of them? How could the UFOs simply "disappear" as the planes approached? *Maybe it wasn't what it seemed to be*, the psyche wondered to itself. The air force moved in to confirm this suspicion with word that the culprit was a "temperature inversion." *Good*, the psyche responded, as consistency returned to the surface story and all was once again well.

But not quite.

The air traffic controller who supervised the radar observations called the air force account nonsense: "There were at least ten unidentified flying objects . . . [performing] gyrations which no known aircraft could perform." Renewed public doubts skyrocketed when debunker Donald Menzel went "too far" by announcing that pilots Nash and Fortenberry, two weekends earlier, mistook "fireflies" for unconventional aerial objects.

Thus Fletcher's *peculiar quality of doubleness* reappeared in the narrative, with a vengeance. There was now a parallel plot: not only was something seen but, by implication, the authorities wanted to explain it away. The public at large was unavoidably moved to wonder: *Why should this be so?* Even when Menzel later dropped his luminous-insect hypothesis, even with air force assurance that temperature inversion was "indisputably" the correct explanation, still, the three most famous cases of 1952 landed in an ambiguous middle realm where, as with most well-known UFO cases, they were neither definitively confirmed as "good" UFO cases nor definitively shown to have mundane origins.

Both sides could claim "victory," but, more important, the collective psyche deeply absorbed the provocative idea that *something extraordinary had occurred*. This is also what happens in formal allegory, where a tension is held between literal events at the *surface*, on the one hand, and evocative, suggestive, implicative associations *below*, on the other. Resolution occurs at neither level; ambivalence is guaranteed. The better-known works of Franz Kafka illustrate these dynamics quite well.

"SOMEBODY must have been telling lies about Joseph K., for without having done anything wrong he is one morning arrested." Thus begins Kafka's dark novel *The Trial*. K.'s most determined efforts to learn why he has been arrested, to learn of the charges against him, consistently meet with failure; he is supposed to *know*. Through the course of this enigmatic novel it becomes clear that K. is neither incarcerated nor free. Indeed, he never meets the Court, only its agents, messengers, and henchmen. His trial never takes place, yet its invisible presence pervades his entire life.

It is not necessary for Kafka to announce to readers that Joseph K. is Everyman, that we are all under an unspecified sentence, all in effect waiting on death row; in fact, the rules of allegory forbid such an overt disclosure. "By having a surrealistic surface texture allegory immediately elicits an interpretive response from the reader," Fletcher notes, adding: "The silences in allegory mean as much as the filled-in spaces, because by bridging these silent gaps between oddly unrelated images we reach the sunken understructure of thought."

Thus *The Trial* stands as masterful art in large part because Kafka maintains a surrealistic surface story that consistently *points*, rather than *forces*, the reader's attention to implicit, more global meanings. If Kafka had sought to drive home the point that it is Everyman who is on trial, then the surface story would probably have gone the route of much classical allegory, becoming little more than a mechanistic, ritualized vehicle for an abstract truth. The essential tension between the life of one man, Joseph K., and the implications of this life for the rest of us would have been lost.

In a similar sense, because the events of UFO encounters are typically surrealistic — dreamlike, fantastical, at once less than and more than real — the psyche reaches for interpretations in order to bridge the gaps. Some UFO researchers seek exhaustive answers by focusing entirely on the surface events, trying to prove that it's all happening just as it appears to be happening. These are ufology's "surface literalists." Others look beneath the surfaces for the exhaustive truth, trying to prove that nothing is as it seems in UFO encounters, that truth lies never in the events themselves but only "elsewhere." These are ufology's "depth literalists."

Both sides appear equally committed to a single definitive solution. To that extent, both positions are mechanical and ritualistic, although in different ways. (Literal materialists reduce downward, literal symbolists upward. The result is effectively the same: a flattened worldview.)

The continuity of the overall UFO mythology is maintained through a curious dialectic between these extremes. Just when those who favor a purely symbolic approach seem to carry the day, the phenomenon appears in the form of new sightings with a strong physical-reality component, thus supporting the position of those who say UFOs require no "secondary intepretation" whatever. But just as this side is most confident that it has finally uncovered hard and final patterns, the phenomenon renews itself with striking new developments: the emergence of the alien abduction motif in 1957, for instance.

It is as if, each time the collective mind approaches boredom with redundancy, the UFO retires to its thematic greenhouse to sprout new forms and faces, tactics and temperaments, motives and motifs. These in their own turn become standardized, ritualized, and overelaborated, which tips the allegorical scale once again in favor of the idea that none of it is as it seems, therefore the UFO phenomenon's most significant meanings must reside below the surface.

Thus in an overall sense the UFO phenomenon keeps its face pointed in two directions at once: toward events in time and space that seem to defy conventional explanations, and toward the symbolic/mythic milieu arising in and around these events — just as Kafka's *The Trial* reads like a surrealistic documentary of one man's nightmarish encounter with living hell *and* as a parable about the more general nightmare of human existence.

Jacques Vallee, who formally enters our story in chapter nine as a leading analyst of UFO patterns, has speculated about the symbolic meaning of the contradictions within the larger body of witness reports. "If you strive to convey a truth that lies beyond the semantic level made possible by your audience's language," Vallee observes, "you must construct apparent contradictions in terms of ordinary meanings." This, Vallee suggests, is what the UFO phenomenon accomplishes by speaking a "double language."

By projecting images just beyond the belief structure of the target society, the phenomenon "manages to disturb and reassure at the same time, exploiting both the gullibility of the zealots and the narrow-mindedness of the debunkers," says Vallee. A constant factor of absurdity "leads to a rejection of the story by the upper layers of the target society and an absorption at a deep unconscious level of the symbols conveyed" by UFO encounters, he adds.

Back in the domain of literary criticism, Angus Fletcher concluded that because allegory manifestly has two or more levels of meaning, "the apprehension of these must require at least two attitudes of mind." The doubleness of intention in an allegory requires a *double attention* to the narrative events at the surface and to their psychic effects and hidden depths — this to preserve the *tension*, and to honor the *intention*, of the allegorical form.

As of the mid-1950s, the notion that it might be fruitful to hold two or more attitudes of mind toward the UFO phenomenon had not even entered the dialogue as a possibility. Given the polarized tenor of the controversy, the idea that UFOs could be mythic and real at the same time was unimaginable. So was the idea that someone from outside the UFO debate might suddenly arrive, as if from nowhere, make a few poignant comments, refocus the entire dialogue, and retire to his home in the Swiss Alps.

That was before Carl Gustav Jung appeared on the scene.

WHEN Jung published a short book entitled *Flying Saucers: A Modern Myth of Things Seen in the Sky* in 1959, UFO partisans had little idea what to make of it. Proponents, ever in search of elusive extraterrestrial hardware, were suspicious of psychological and mythological perspectives toward UFOs. Debunkers, on the other hand, were interested in psychological explanations only to the extent that they faciliated the dismissal of UFO sightings as hallucinations and misidentifications of planets and airplanes.

Even so, Jung's influence on the imagination of UFOs easily rivals that of any other serious thinker on the subject. This is not because he provided an account of origins — he didn't even try — but rather because he opened up an entirely new horizon on the subject, one that fostered vast creativity in the decades to come.

The debate that Jung entered was widely perceived to be populated by monomaniacal cultists who differed only in the content of their beliefs. Thus the very willingness of an eminent philosopher-psychologist to consider UFOs as a problem with depth had the effect of uplifting the ongoing dialogue. An early protégé of Sigmund Freud, Jung had gone on to study religion, philosophy, mythology, and mysticism in a dozen languages, and had traveled in Asia, Europe, India, and North America. Although he saw himself as a medical doctor and scientific empiricist first and foremost, he considered this no reason to preclude turning his prolific pen to subjects including the workings of the unconscious mind, the work of James Joyce and Pablo Picasso, spiritualism and séances, fairy tales and astrology, alchemy, and the doctrine of the Assumption of Mary. There is simply no doubting that Jung was one of the great minds — and spirits — of his age.

As early as 1946, a year before the Kenneth Arnold sighting in the United States, a seventy-one-year-old Jung turned his attention to reports of unidentified flying objects in Europe. Over a period of several years, he collected and studied newspaper clippings; statements from scientific, military, and governmental establishments; and the reports of civilian UFO research groups. In early February 1951, Jung wrote to a friend that he had not been able to determine whether UFOs were best considered rumors related to mass hallucination or "a downright fact." Either case would be interesting, he said.

> If it's a rumour, then the apparition of discs must be a symbol produced by the unconscious. We know what such a thing would mean seen from the psychological standpoint. If on the other hand it is a hard and concrete fact, we are surely confronted with something thoroughly out of the way.... The phenomenon of the saucers might even be both, rumour as well as fact.... It's just too bad that we don't know enough about it.

"Something is seen, but one doesn't know what," Jung stated. "It is difficult, if not impossible, to form any correct idea of these objects, because they behave not like bodies but like weightless thoughts." At the very least, it appeared to Jung, "this obviously complicated phenomenon had an extremely important psychic component as well as a possible physical basis." What remained unclear in his mind was "whether a primary perception was followed by a phantasm or whether, conversely, a primary fantasy originating in the unconscious invaded the conscious mind with illusions and visions."

In the first case, a physical process provided the basis for an accompanying myth; in the second case, a psychic process created a corresponding vision. Jung also considered a third possibility: UFOs could be *synchronicities*, or meaningful coincidences of events separated by time and/or space, happenings that suggest unseen links between consciousness and matter. This hypothesis reflected Jung's lifelong interest in paranormal phenomena and unusual states of consciousness. Yet as much as such speculation interested Jung, he felt himself qualified as a psychologist only to comment on the psychic component, or the UFOs as "rumors."

Perhaps the rumors of UFOs were not mundane but rather "visionary rumors" of the same order as religious visions. Such visions are experienced in times of personal and collective distress or danger, or in response to "vital psychic need," Jung noted. Perhaps the collective unconscious was sending forth such visions, just as individuals experience abnormal convictions, visions, and illusions at times of dissociation between conscious and unconscious attitudes.

With a certain somberness, Jung noted that he was not pleased to conclude that the appearance of UFOs clearly indicated "coming events which are in accord with the end of an era." Such large-scale anomalies typically arise when wholesale changes are under way in the balance of forces in the collective unconscious — that vast repository of images and motifs common to the myths and dreams of peoples throughout the world, all connected as a complex matrix transcending time and space. Jung had no doubt that humanity was entering a time of profound transition from one set of ruling images — those of the Piscean Age coinciding with the rise of Christianity — to a new collective disposition of psychic elements related to the era of Aquarius.

The frequently reported round shape of the objects suggested to Jung the *mandala*, a recurring image of psychic totality found in mythologies throughout the world, with names such as the "sun wheel" or "magic circle." UFOs might represent a mythological concept of the soul, which was said in ancient times to assume the form of a sphere. Jung found it interesting that an image expressing order, wholeness, and salvation should "now take the form of an object, a technological construction," to bypass the disadvantages of mythological associations in an age where magic had been supplanted by machines (but only apparently so, Jung added, for humanity's hunger for "salvation from above" had found a new focus in UFOs).

Jung was the first reputable scholar to observe parallels between the motifs of UFO events and a variety of religious and mythological motifs throughout recorded history. As a primordial image of the Self, the round form of the UFO is "an Elijah who calls down fire from heaven, rises up in a fiery chariot, and is a forerunner of the Messiah." Religious experience brings human beings "face to face with a psychically overpowering Other," Jung said, adding that on the antique level, UFOs "could easily be conceived as 'gods'."

While Jung offered no solution to the mystery of origins, he went into considerable discussion of the relation between UFOs and parapsychology and psychokinesis — mental influence on inanimate objects.

Jung considered the possibility that UFOs might be "materialized psychisms," that is, actual physical or paraphysical materializations formed out of the collective unconscious. His statement that this very idea "opens a bottomless void under our feet" indicated that he appreciated the challenges that such thinking posed to ordinary views of reality.

Yet the idea of a shifting rather than absolute dividing line between mind and matter, spirit and nature, was not new to Carl Jung, originator of a provocatively wide-ranging doctrine about the fundamental structures of existence. Based on his intellectual and cultural journey through the social and political histories, religions, mythologies, folk and fairy tales, and dreams and fantasies of myriad cultures, Jung turned his attention to the underlying patterns of the human psyche. He called these patterns *archetypal*, from the Greek word for "original pattern or stamp." Archetypes are the invisible collective patterns underlying form, the primordial images that perform and continually influence our thoughts, feelings, and actions.

Although archetypes cannot be known in themselves, Jung said, we recognize archetypal experience whenever we are in the presence of that which speaks to us as *deep, necessary, universal, basic, fundamental*. Biological archetypes include Woman, Man, Mother, Father, Brother, Sister; psychological archetypes include Good or Terrible Mother; Tyrant Father; professional archetypes include Scientist, Healer, Dictator, and Capitalist. Archetypes "hold whole worlds together and yet can never be pointed to, accounted for, or even adequately circumscribed," writes psychologist James Hillman, who received training in the Jungian tradition.

Jung originally conceived of archetypes as the deepest patterns of psychic functioning, the root patterns of instinctive behavior. As his thinking developed over time, however, he came to see archetypes as the immaterial potentials inherent in *all* structure, as fundamental to the existence of all living organisms. Eventually the archetype became, in his own words, "the bridge to matter in general." In volume nine of his *Collected Works*, Jung wrote:

> The deeper "layers" of the psyche lose their individual uniqueness as they retreat farther and farther into the darkness. "Lower down" . . . they become increasingly collective until they are universalized and extinguished in the body's materiality, i.e., in chemical substances. The body's carbon is simply carbon. Hence, "at bottom" the psyche is simply "world."

With these words it was clear that, for Carl Jung, the distinction between organic and inorganic matter — and the distinction between mind and body — is not static or absolute but dynamic and protean. Thus we begin to grasp why a new generation of researchers, not wedded to the nuts-and-bolts school of ufology, came to value the richness of Jung's thinking about archetypal reality as they wrestled with the fundamental nature of the events called UFOs.

If the relation between mental and material reality is in some sense reciprocal, then perhaps there are intermediate states of reality — subtle matter, perhaps many different grades of it. Perhaps some UFOs are temporary formations of psychic or quasi-physical material independent of individual psyches, originating from corridors beyond our time-space coordinates yet in effect "right here."

Such a hypothesis is not inconsistent with characteristic UFO behaviors: apparent craft executing remarkable changes of direction, coming to a complete stop, hovering, changing color and shape, disappearing and reappearing on the spot, then accelerating at extraordinary speeds within seconds, typically without a sonic boom; accompanying electromagnetic effects, including the failure of nearby automobile engines and farm machinery (such as Villas-Boas's tractor); and the ability to be unambiguously recorded on radar while remaining peculiarly localized and selective in their appearances.

Nor is the "paraphysical hypothesis" inconsistent with reports of mysterious Men in Black (MIB). Beginning in the late 1950s, reports surfaced of strange men arriving, unannounced, sometimes alone, sometimes in twos or in threes, at the homes of particular UFO witnesses usually before they had reported their sightings to anyone. Often seeming to know more than a stranger should know about the witnesses, MIB caution against reporting their sightings or close encounters. MIB typically walk with a strange limp, speak in mechanical monotones or annoying sing-song tones, wear black suits and black shoes, often arrive driving black cars, and convey an overall eerie "otherworldly" aura.

Pure fantasy? If so, a strangely coherent, collective fantasy. Social contagion? UFO researchers independently came across many such consistent reports from a wide variety of credible witnesses prior to their public dissemination. Professor Peter M. Rojcewicz, a folklorist well versed in the literature of UFOs and cross-cultural accounts of nonordinary experiences, found impressive parallels between reports of MIBs in ufology and reports from various traditions of ominous "dark men" in contexts having nothing to do with UFOs. Rojcewicz takes the parallels as evidence of the protean adaptability and real-world vitality of the archetype of the Devil.

Veteran ufologist John Keel reported disturbing personal encounters with MIB within a year of beginning full-time UFO investigation. Keel reported keeping rendezvous with black Cadillacs that disappeared on back roads, checking into motels at random and finding reservations made in his name and accompanying nonsense messages, awakening in the middle of the night with a dark apparition standing over him, and nonstop telephone calls featuring strange clicking and humming sounds, with disembodied voices delivering messages from "the space people." It was as if he had fallen into a demonic fantasyland nestled within the ordinary and sharing common boundaries with UFO phenomena.

On discovering that many UFO witnesses reported similar experiences, Keel subsequently lost faith in the extraterrestrial visitation hypothesis and concluded that the flying saucer legend is but one thread in a larger thematic quilt:

> The real UFO story must encompass all of the many manifestations being observed. It is a story of ghosts and phantoms and strange mental aberrations; of an invisible world which surrounds us and occasionally engulfs us; of prophets and prophecies, and gods and demons. It is a world of illusion and hallucination where the unreal seems very real, and where reality itself is distorted by strange forces which can seemingly manipulate space, time, and physical matter — forces which are almost entirely beyond our powers of comprehension.

Jung came to believe that archetypes are not purely psychic but rather possess an inherent impulse to transgress their psychic frames and materialize in visible forms. *The archetypes of the collective unconscious tend toward manifestation.* He did not develop this idea with respect to UFOs, but a new generation of investigators did, many of whom, like Keel, recognized what they considered severe limitations in the extraterrestrial visitation hypothesis in addressing the full range of UFO data. The new school looked to parapsychology, religious studies, folklore, and mythology for new kinds of insights into a phenomenon whose effects called into question where mind leaves off and matter begins.

By and large, mainstream ufology saw such associations as unrelated to the truly important UFO-related questions facing the modern world: *from which galaxy do the saucers come, and what do they want with us?* Although the organizational behavior of 1950s ufology was more masonic than scientific, its practitioners nevertheless saw themselves as "scientists" and insisted that evidence of apparitions taking on convincing physical forms be left to university folklore departments. The new school of researchers, perceiving the fallacy in this perspective, correctly argued that science is a method of observation and evaluation, not (at least officially) a religion that places whole areas off limits for study.

Thus began a whole new chapter in UFO research, focused around the question of the true scope of the phenomenon. In essence, the old school was interested only in aliens; the new school saw parallels between angels and aliens, and wanted to follow these leads toward larger psychological, mythological, and religious conclusions. Whether such parallels were substantive or simply coincidental was to become a point of enormous contention within the cosmos of ufology.

Proteus, for his part, saw no need to make such fine distinctions. He was as amenable to being linked to origins in outer space as to origins in parallel dimensions beyond our formulations of time and space (neighboring "twilight zones"). He was equally at home with aliens in a decidedly modern mythos involving saucers and abductions, and with angels in a continually expanding mythos involving the full spectrum of human encounters with anomalous phenomena.

Who could blame ufologists for trying to cure Proteus of his apparent multiple personality disorder? Joseph Campbell had already presented the encouraging news that "the life-voyager wishing to be taught by Proteus must 'grasp him steadfastly and press him all the more,' and at length he will appear in his proper shape." *Proper shape* — this phrase echoed in the minds of mainstream ufologists, who took it to mean they had only to keep asking their determined questions in order to secure the simple, hard-edged answers to which their dreams had already given shape.

Proteus, for his part, would keep providing answers — many different answers to many different questions. The word *allegory* was not in his vocabulary, but he knew its meanings well. This polyphonous (*poly* = many, *phonous* = voiced) divinity had as many songs as voices, and he had barely begun to sing.

FIVE

———— ✕ ————

IN LATE 1957, Donald Keyhoe agreed to appear on a popular CBS television program, "Armstrong Circle Theater," in an episode called "UFOs: Enigma of the Skies," along with other key players in the flying saucer controversy: Kenneth Arnold (the man who started it all), Eastern Airlines pilot Clarence Chiles, former air force Project Blue Book head Edward Ruppelt, and astronomer and no-holds-barred debunker Donald H. Menzel. Although originally reluctant to participate, because the format wouldn't allow him to put hard questions to the air force, Keyhoe agreed to join in when CBS agreed to let him prepare his own script.

Keyhoe submitted a statement repeating his familiar litany against air force credibility, citing the rumored existence of a top-secret 1949 "Estimate of the Situation" memorandum that concluded that UFOs were interplanetary, intending to contrast this memo with later air force statements denying the reality of UFOs. A CBS official edited this part of Keyhoe's script, claiming it made his portion of the program too long. Keyhoe was expressly forbidden to say anything about documents whose existence was denied by the air force, even though the "Estimate" document had been discussed in detail in Edward Ruppelt's 1956 book, *The Report on Unidentified Flying Objects*.

By the day of the program — January 22, 1958 — Ruppelt, Arnold, and Chiles had all withdrawn from participation. Arnold left because he felt the show was rigged in favor of the air force. "I will not be a participant on any program that obviously misrepresents the facts," he wrote in a telegram to CBS. Keyhoe shared Arnold's feelings, but decided not to drop out when he learned that with fewer participants he would have more time to make his presentation. The program began with Lieutenant Colonel Spencer Whedon reciting the air force catechism that all UFOs are either hoaxes, hallucinations, or cases of mistaken identity. UFO historian Jerome Clark describes what happened next:

> A thoroughly frustrated Keyhoe came on and dutifully read his script for a few minutes, then shocked everyone present by abruptly departing from it. He began, "And now I'm going to reveal something that has never been disclosed before. For the last six months we have been working with a Congressional committee investigating official secrecy about UFOs. If all the evidence we have given this committee is made public in open hearings, it would be proved . . ." At this juncture program engineers stopped his microphone, though the picture continued, with Keyhoe's lips moving silently. Unaware of what had just happened, he continued to speak, finishing his sentence with these words: ". . . that it will absolutely prove that the UFOs are real machines under intelligent control."

Keyhoe would later write that he immediately regretted his decision to override the program's agreed constraints. His outraged colleagues (and, increasingly, competitors) in the other leading civilian UFO group, APRO, went considerably further, suggesting that Keyhoe's move may have been "calculated to insinuate censorship, whether or not it actually existed." CBS responded to the debacle with a surprisingly candid admission that, in effect, it had censored Keyhoe — at the air force's direction. The program had been cleared in advance for security reasons, stated the network's director of editing. "Any indication that there would be a deviation might lead to statements that neither this network nor that individuals on the program were authorized to release." CBS insisted that its decision had served the public interest.

The air force, for its part, appeared to side with Keyhoe, maintaining that by cutting off the audio CBS had "enhanced rather than detracted from Major Keyhoe's . . . sensational and unsupported claims." Even so, the air force saw the program as a net win for its aims because Keyhoe had alienated himself from the nation's news media by appearing to continue a personal vendetta against the air force. An amazingly resilient Keyhoe took the incident in stride and quickly returned to his larger strategy: a campaign to force congressional hearings on UFOs.

Soon Keyhoe and his comrades in NICAP, along with the entire civilian saucer research community, suffered a far more important setback when Edward Ruppelt recanted his longstanding commitment to the view that UFOs constituted a true unknown. In a letter to an inquirer dated May 6, 1958, Ruppelt wrote: "I have visited Project Blue Book since 1953 and am now convinced that the reports of UFO's are nothing more than reports of balloons, aircraft, astronomical phenomena, etc. I don't believe they are anything from outer space." This was an amazing admission for a man who, a few years earlier, had complained about an air force intelligence director

> taking the old ostrich approach to keeping his head in the sand thinking [they] will go away. He is wrong. . . . They claim they have gotten the unknowns down to about 10% but from what I saw this was just due to a more skeptical attitude. The reports are just as good as the one we got and their analysis procedures are a hell of a lot worse.

Shown a copy of Ruppelt's letter contradicting his earlier position, Keyhoe concluded that his old friend — then working for an aircraft corporation with air force contracts — was "under pressure directly or indirectly . . . to reverse his position." A year later, Ruppelt told Keyhoe that he was planning to issue a new edition of his classic book *The Report on Unidentified Flying Objects*. When word got around that Ruppelt had embraced the air force's anti-UFO position, Keyhoe said this meant that Ruppelt would be in the strange position of "debunking his own book."

In an open letter in the *APRO Bulletin*, meant to be read not only by Ruppelt but by the larger UFO community, Keyhoe implored Ruppelt: "Don't let them trick you. If you try to retract, you will be bitterly attacked by many readers, including influential book reviewers, for daring to put the record straight." Keyhoe's efforts to keep his friend on board were of no avail. The revised edition of Ruppelt's book appeared with three new chapters in which Ruppelt played up wild contactee stories; stood behind the air force's dismissal of several recent sightings believed by many ufologists to be "good"; and wrote patronizingly about Keyhoe and NICAP.

Ufology was clearly crestfallen. "It seems odd," a dispirited NICAP writer remarked,

> that while active in the Air Force as the Project Blue Book Chief, Ruppelt could find no explanation for . . . good cases; but now that he no longer has access to all of the sources of information necessary to check a UFO sighting, he has been able to find answers.

Ruppelt died in Long Beach, California, in 1960 of a second heart attack. Modern conspiracy buffs continue to insist that Ruppelt was "forced" by the air force to disavow his prior stance, although there is no documented evidence to this effect. His widow told interviewers that her husband's continuing exposure to the wild claims of southern California contactees "soured" him on the UFO phenomenon. Edward Ruppelt would not be the last thoughtful individual to find the social tensions of being perceived to be in favor of UFOs too much to bear.

DURING the very month that Keyhoe was publicly urging Ruppelt not to sell his soul, one of the most spectacular sightings in UFO history was unfolding a thousand miles away on the small island of New Guinea.

After dinner on June 26, 1959, at 6:45 P.M., the Reverend William Booth Gill, an Anglican priest, walked outside the mission house after finishing his evening meal. Looking to the sky he "saw this sparkling object, which to me was peculiar because it sparkled, and because it was very, very bright, and it was above Venus, and so that caused me to watch it for awhile; then I saw it descend toward us." Soon Father Gill was joined by Stephen Gill Moi, who tried to measure the size of the object by holding his arm straight out and his fist closed. Moi found that his fist covered "about half of the object." Shortly, some thirty parishioners joined the two missionaries in gazing at the remarkable sight.

Unlike George Adamski, Father Gill had not gone in search of something remarkable in the skies. In fact, Gill had been particularly skeptical of the UFO sightings that had been occurring during an island wave for almost a year, sixty of them during the ninety days of Southern Hemisphere winter alone. When a colleague mentioned seeing a UFO during the previous fall, Gill suggested that he had actually seen the

Soviet satellite Sputnik. But they were not staring at Sputnik on the evening of June 26.

Gill and his audience watched in amazement as the "bright light" resolved into a huge, four-legged, disk-shaped object hovering at about 500 feet overhead. The onlooker could distinguish the illuminated forms of four humanlike figures moving about on top of the craft, apparently working at some unknown task requiring leaving the deck and reappearing again, sometimes individually, other times as a group. At 7:30 P.M., the object, which had a large base and smaller upper deck, ascended into the gathering clouds, which Gill estimated to be at 2,000 feet. A little over an hour later, the craft returned to view and descended again to a slightly lower altitude where, hovering silently, it was joined by three more UFOs (which Gill later speculated might be satellite craft from the larger vehicle, or the "mother ship" as he would call it). Just short of 11 P.M., the UFOs disappeared when clouds covered the view.

At 6 P.M. the next evening, Gill and his associates were treated to a repeat performance of the previous day's display — the mother ship with its four occupants and two of the smaller craft. Once again, the occupants appeared to be working on a project, "as though adjusting or 'setting up' something," as Gill would recall. One of the occupants stood with his hands on what appeared to be a rail not unlike that of a ship.

"I stretched my arm above my head and waved," Gill said. "To our surprise the figure did the same. Ananias [one of Gill's parishioners] waved both arms over his head; then the two outside figures did the same. . . . There seemed to be no doubt that our movements were answered." As darkness fell, Gill used a flashlight to signal the crew. "After a minute or so of this, the UFO apparently acknowledged making several wavering motions back and forth," Gill said. As waving and flashlight signaling continued, the UFO slowly began getting bigger, as if heading toward its observers. Then the movement stopped and didn't start up again. Soon the figures seemed to lose interest in Gill and company and disappeared below deck. At 6:25 P.M., two figures reappeared and seemed to continue with their unknown tasks on deck.

At 6:30, Gill went to dinner. Thirty minutes later the smaller UFOs had disappeared; the original vehicle was still present but at a greater distance. Gill went indoors to preside over a church service, after which (at 7:45 P.M.) the sky had clouded over and there were no UFOs in sight.

Amazingly, the "fleet" showed up for a third and final performance on the next evening, Sunday, July 28. This time there were eight craft, one hovering at low altitude with no occupants in view. When news of this extraordinary case later reached the world through a British publication, *Flying Saucer Review*, a more familiar kind of spectacle immediately began — another battle to set the definitive terms of the UFO phenomenon.

The Royal Australian Air Force declared the sighting as astronomical and meteorological in origin, yet this explanation fell considerably short of the collective testimony of twenty-five witnesses who signed a detailed sighting report prepared by Father Gill. Debunker Donald Menzel insisted that the New Guineans who signed the report did so only to please "their great white leader . . . I doubt very much that they knew what they were signing."

Gill found Menzel's assertion amusing. "That 'great white leader' business might happen in Hollywood movies about African missionaries, but certainly not where I was." Gill noted that the New Guineans who observed the hovering objects were both fluent in and educated in English, and that many of them had assumed leadership positions in nearby communities.

Trying another tack, Menzel wondered why Gill had failed to mention Venus as a point of reference, suggesting Gill had mistaken the planet for a spaceship. This attack proved fruitless, for Gill's account specifically stated: "I saw Venus, but I also saw this sparkling object [the large UFO] . . . above Venus." Then Menzel adopted a hypothesis that rivaled his earlier statement that two experienced airline pilots had mistaken fireflies caught between windshield panes for flying saucers. Menzel proposed that Gill, who suffered from myopia and an astigmatism, had mistaken an out-of-focus, elongated image of Venus for his mother ship. "The slight irregularities on the 'hairs' of the lashes, perhaps dust or moisture, could easily be interpreted as activity of the 'beings' inhabiting the saucer," he wrote.

Later it was revealed that Gill was wearing a properly corrected lens at the time of the sighting. Besides, Gill reasoned, what of the corroborating testimony of Stephen Gill Moi, a respected and intelligent native teacher in the mission? Philip J. Klass, who would eventually succeed Menzel as the world's foremost UFO debunker, found Stephen Gill Moi's "independent" testimony next to worthless. Klass wrote that

Moi's name "suggests his close friendship with Gill," which would foster an understandable desire to go along with his superior's hallucination — or worse, his hoax.

Father Gill responded that he had known Stephen Gill Moi for only nineteen months prior to the sighting. "When I arrived on the scene, Moi was a man well into his thirties, and he had that name [Gill] since he was a baby. How could he have been named after me?"

Klass saved his best shot for last. "I simply could not believe my eyes" when he read Gill's statement that he had gone in to dinner in the midst of the second night's sighting. Why had Gill not been willing to delay his meal in order to keep pace with the spectacular events he was watching? "Actions speak louder than words," Klass insisted. Gill responded: "Having had about four hours of this sight on Friday night, we were not nearly so interested when it returned on Saturday night after we were unable to persuade it to land." He added that "there was nothing eerie or otherworldly about any of this . . . I took it to be some kind of hovercraft the Americans or even the Australians had built. . . . It was only in retrospect that the whole thing seemed really extraordinary."

Years later, UFO investigator J. Allen Hynek, after meeting with Gill, concluded that the smaller UFOs were attributable to bright stars and planets. As for the original object, the "mother ship," Hynek said that "any astronomical object would have had to move through forty-five degrees of arc in that time," whereas the object reported was stationary for long periods.

As with most classic UFO sightings, the Gill report led to different conclusions among different researchers. Menzel and Klass saw it as a typical folly of errors compounded by a need to believe in extraterrestrial visitation. Hynek and his young associate, astrophysicist Jacques Vallee, considered it one of the most convincing on record, in part because it was one of more than sixty sightings over a one-year period, but also because it seemed unlikely that Gill would fabricate such a fantastic story out of sheer intent to deceive.

The Gill story lives on, each side of the larger, ongoing UFO war reciting those details that most affirm one or another unwavering position about UFOs in general — thereby proving neither the reality nor unreality of UFOs but rather, in the words of Randall Fitzgerald, showing "how one can prop up any theory imaginable, utilizing the available 'evidence' so abundantly generated by the history of human endeavor."

• • •

NINE thousand miles away, in Washington, D.C., the debate continued about what the air force knew concerning flying saucers. Donald Keyhoe continued to insist that a cover-up of epic proportions was under way. University of Arizona physicist and UFO researcher James McDonald thought "foul-up" was a better word for the air force response to UFOs, but he and Keyhoe were in complete agreement on another issue: the time had come for full-scale congressional hearings, which, they and many others felt, were the only way to get to the proverbial bottom of the simmering UFO quandary. According to historian David Jacobs, the air force's decision to actively prevent — or at the very least to limit — congressional hearings reflected its belief that it had nothing to gain from opening its UFO file to public scrutiny:

> Congressional hearings presented a serious threat to the Air Force. They might imply that the UFO phenomenon was vitally significant and that the government was very interested in it. This might lead to another "flying saucer scare," threatening to the national interest. Hearings might force the Air Force to declassify its files, contradicting Air Force claims that its files were open already. Hearings might prompt criticism of the Air Force's UFO investigation, criticism that would harm its public relations program. Therefore, preventing or limiting congressional hearings became a major objective for the Air Force from 1957 to 1964.

The ensuing debate was largely one in which NICAP made well-publicized calls for congressional hearings and the air force responded with numerous private attempts to head them off. The air force scored an opening victory in August 1958 when military witnesses appeared in executive session before the House Subcommittee on Atmospheric Phenomena to present the air force's best case, which was based on numerous factual errors.

Captain George T. Gregory maintained, for instance, that Blue Book *Special Report Number 14*, a statistical study of UFOs released to the public in 1955, found a "total lack of evidence" for extraterrestrial visitors. Gregory neglected to mention that the *Report* had termed the evidence "ambiguous." He also cited air force consultant J. Allen Hynek as representative of the quality of scientists who had found nothing unusual about UFOs — but he didn't add that Hynek in fact had made clear that UFOs deserved systematic study. Gregory made particularly effective use of the contactee phenomenon, telling the committee that

the air force would be more impressed with their claims if the contactees weren't so obviously in the money-making business and so eager
to use their newly-found fame to level unwarranted charges against the
air force. The very mention of George Adamski's name was sufficient
to remind committee members of the kind of circus that congressional
hearings might precipitate. All in all, Gregory's testimony helped diffuse the drive for congressional inquiries — but only temporarily.

Air force credibility was poorly served in May 1958 when retired
air force Major Dewey J. Fournet, Jr., confirmed in a letter to Donald
Keyhoe the existence of two secret documents that Keyhoe had tried
to discuss during his ill-fated appearance on CBS's "Armstrong Circle
Theater" program. Previously, the existence of both documents (the
1948 Top Secret "Estimate of the Situation" concluding that UFOs
were from outer space, and a 1952 intelligence analysis concluding that
UFOs were intelligently guided) had been denied categorically by air
force spokesmen.

Keyhoe embraced this new admission as still more evidence of a con-
certed (rather than incidental) government cover-up. Yet he was still
at a loss to explain the ultimate logic of the air force's actions. Writes
David Jacobs:

> On the one hand, Air Force public policy statements about UFOs seemed
> to him contradictory, confusing, and sometimes erroneous. On the other
> hand, Keyhoe thought there was overwhelming evidence for the exis-
> tence of extraterrestrial vehicles. Given this situation, Keyhoe reasoned
> that the only explanation to reconcile the two sides was his conspiracy-
> to-avoid-panic theory, with minor variations. *Keyhoe tried to deal with
> an illogical situation in a logical manner* [emphasis added].

In his 1960 book *Flying Saucers: Top Secret*, Keyhoe removed any
remaining doubts about his mastery in exploiting rumors when he recited
undocumented reports that air force pilots had heard that UFOs had
caused mysterious plane disappearances. Although some observers
viewed such remarks as evidence of Keyhoe's desperate attempts to play
a weak hand, NICAP's systematic presentation to congressional members
of "good" UFO sightings had begun to pay off. In a letter to Keyhoe,
House Majority Leader John McCormack stated that following several
recent private congressional study sessions, "it was pretty well established by some in our minds that there were some objects flying around

in space that were unexplainable." Minnesota representative Joseph E. Karth went further:

> Despite being confronted with seemingly unimpeachable evidence that such phenomena exist, these [high air force] officers give little credence to the many reports on the matter. When pressed on specific details the experts refuse to answer on grounds that they are involved in the nation's security and cannot be discussed publicly. . . . I will continue to seek a definitive answer to this most important question.

By the early 1960s, the air force found itself at a crossroads. Whereas a decade earlier proponents of the extraterrestrial visitation theory held considerable influence among military investigators, now most inside observers had concluded that extraterrestrial vehicles did not exist and that UFO sightings deserved conventional explanations. Yet to simply disband the UFO project and release all files to the public would be to reveal that the air force's primary aim since the 1950s was to decrease the number of UFO *reports* by downplaying the subject. This in turn could only play into the hands of Keyhoe and NICAP, always eager for additional confirmation of their near-religious faith that something important was being hidden. The air force — like the civilian UFO groups — had too much at stake to simply quit. Writes David Jacobs:

> The public relations problem had assumed a life of its own. The Air Force, highly sensitive to bad publicity, looked at the conflict with civilian groups as it would a war. Each attack was a battle; to declassify its files, stop its debunking campaigns, or close down operations in the field of attacks was tantamount to surrender.

It was equally true that the civilian groups viewed the contest with the air force in martial terms; "surrender" was unthinkable. This reciprocal mind-set did nothing to lessen the classic Catch-22 situation in which the air force found itself: the policy of secrecy must continue, if only to prevent future bad press about past secrecy. Yet in Keyhoe's eyes this policy would simply confirm the irrevocable truth of something that would be expressed with compelling simplicity over twenty years later, by the young girl portrayed in the popular film *Poltergeist*. Her unforgettable words: "They're here."

• • •

No DISCUSSION of the effects of UFO reports on the mythic imagination can get very far without recounting the famous case of Betty and Barney Hill.

On the clear, bright night of September 19, 1961, sometime after 10:30, Betty and Barney Hill turned their Chevrolet off Route 3 beneath Cannon Mountain near Lancaster, New Hampshire. Betty had been watching a bright, moving starlike object, which, through her 7 × 50 binoculars, resembled the fusilage of an airplane but without wings. Betty became agitated by the object, although Barney was sure they were seeing nothing more than an airplane on its way to Montreal. But when the object began curving around toward the west and then heading eastward in their general direction, Barney, too, became concerned.

Peering through the binoculars, Barney saw red, amber, green, and blue flashing lights. The craft's motion was "eerie." It had "a step-like flight pattern, tilting vertically as it climbed each step, leveling off, dropping vertically, leveling off, tilting upward," rather like a falling leaf except spinning constantly. The Hills continued driving slowly along Route 3 toward Cannon Mountain, catching occasional glimpses of the object through the windshield. Just south of Franconia Notch and Indian Head in the White Mountains, the UFO came within a few hundred feet of their car.

The craft appeared huge as it hovered 80 to 100 feet above the ground. Through one side of the object a cold blue-white light shone, and there was a red light on each side of the object. The saucer had stopped spinning.

Leaving the car headlights on and the engine running, Barney got out and walked to within 50 feet of the object. Through what seemed to be a row of windows, Barney saw strange faces staring down at him. Inside the car, Betty could hear her husband exclaiming, "I don't believe it! I don't believe it! This is ridiculous!" Panicked, Barney jumped back into the car and began speeding down the road.

Their car had not gone far when the Hills heard a series of beeping sounds seemingly coming from the trunk, causing the car to vibrate. Then a strange drowsiness fell over them; things grew hazy. Later, when they heard two more sets of beeping sounds, they realized they had traveled thirty-five miles since the first set of beeps, with no memory of the trip. Betty and Barney glanced at their watches and found they had stopped running.

Something was wrong — they both knew it. Within ten days Betty began having dreams in which she and Barney were taken aboard a flying saucer and medically examined. Barney suffered from apprehension, insomnia, and a duodenal ulcer. While talking with civilian investigators one month after the incident, the Hills realized that the trip from Montreal to their home in Portsmouth, New Hampshire, had taken two hours longer than it should have. The investigator urged the Hills to be hypnotized to find out what had happened during the "missing time." (In years to come, the use of hypnosis to recover so-called missing time would become a standard ritual in ufological circles, convincing pro-UFO researchers of an alien abduction epidemic, persuading debunkers of the power of self-fulfilling delusions.)

Through a referral, Barney and Betty arrived in the office of a prominent Boston psychiatrist, Dr. Benjamin Simon, who placed them under hypnosis independently during a series of visits. In these sessions, what the Hills believed to be memories of the "two lost hours" were unlocked through time-regression inductions. On later listening to tape recordings of their accounts, their conscious memories were supposedly restored.

Barney recalled standing on the road, peering through binoculars and seeing (through portholes in the hovering craft) eight to eleven illuminated humanoid figures staring back at him. Their frightening machinelike motions reminded him of Nazis. Then he remembered being captured by the aliens, carried inside the ship, and subjected to a physical examination during which his fear was so great that he kept his eyes tightly closed. Barney communicated with his captors via telepathy, as did Betty, whose "medical" examination included the piercing of her navel with a long needle — a "pregnancy test," the aliens let her know.

Before being released, Betty was shown a chart of dots joined by lines that her captors said represented where they were from. Betty's subsequent drawing of her memories of this chart would become famous in ufology as the "Star Map." She was also told she would forget the entire experience, but she was determined to remember. On being returned to their car, where their frightened dog lay curled under the seat, the Hills watched as the craft first increased in brilliance and then resembled a glowing orange ball as it departed.

The bizarre experience of Betty and Barney Hill became legendary as the first reported — and the most exhaustively publicized — alien abduction in the United States. For over thirty years, various ufologists have championed the credibility of the case, pointing to the fact that an unknown aerial object was tracked on radar at the same time and in the same area as the Hills' sighting. As for the Star Map that Betty saw in the saucer and later sketched from memory, independent tests based on an analysis of a scale model of the drawing confirmed for some that the map accurately represented the home of the skyfaring aliens: Zeta Reticuli 1 and Zeta Reticuli 2.

Debunkers had different ideas. Astronomer Carl Sagan, who had thus far approached flying saucers with an air of genteel derision, argued that the patterns of at least three other constellations matched Betty's map. The Hills' claims of "missing time" were equally open to suspicion. Because Betty and Barney variously offered 11 P.M., 1 A.M., and 3 A.M. as the time of capture, debunkers were able to make a persuasive case that this four-hour discrepancy accounts for the missing time. Others were quick to note that there were more details of the "abduction" in Betty's account than Barney's, suggesting that the story of capture and examination by aliens was a fantasy unknowingly absorbed by Barney as he listened to Betty recount her dreams in the first days following their strange drive home.

Dr. Simon, who spent many hours with the Hills and came to know them well, speculated that as an interracial couple (Barney was black, Betty white), the Hills may simply have been dramatizing deeply embedded, unresolved conflicts relating to racial difference. Dr. Simon admitted that he couldn't prove this hypothesis, but he was considerably less tentative in challenging the notion of UFO researchers that the results of hypnotic induction deserve to be taken at face value:

> The charisma of hypnosis has tended to foster the belief that hypnosis is the magical and royal road to TRUTH. In one sense this is so, but it must be understood that hypnosis is a pathway to the truth as it is felt and understood by the patient. The truth is what he believes to be the truth, and this may or may not be consonant with the ultimate nonpersonal truth.

Yet most observers, including Dr. Simon, agree that the Hills saw *something*. The question is what.

One of the most interesting aspects of this case is the way certain debunkers have attempted to diminish the Hills' extraordinary narrative by making counterclaims, which, although intended to settle the case in mundane terms, required leaps of logic exceeding those of Betty and Barney. For example, setting aside details of the case as reported, California debunker Robert Schaeffer insisted that what Barney saw when he looked through his binoculars at alien faces was in fact the planet Jupiter. Not to be outdone, Philip Klass offered the theory that the Hills had been frightened — indeed, *mesmerized* — by a kind of freak "plasma" that somehow jettisoned from nearby high-voltage power lines.

Scientists agree that plasma exists as an extremely short-term and highly localized phenomenon similar in some respects to ball lightning, but these characteristics bear little resemblance to what the Hills actually reported. Science writer Ronald Story challenges the accounts of Schaeffer and Klass as species of pseudoscience:

> The main problem with both of these attempts to explain the sighting is that the theoretical constructs which are inserted in the UFO's place simply do not match the reported features of the observed object. . . .
> If the sighting is accepted by the theorist as a genuine event (i.e., external to the observer), it is simply against the scientific method to deviate very far from the reported characteristics, in the absence of specific evidence to the contrary. And when one does operate within the methods (and limits) of science, one simply must regard the Hills' sighting as a genuine "unknown."

Story adds that he himself suspects that the abduction portion of the Hills' experience was a psychological response to a real physical stimulus. But *what* stimulus? Story admits he doesn't know. "That is why . . . the famous Hill abduction has remained a subject of controversy."

SIX

—————— ✕ ——————

WHAT stands out about the Hill abduction case so many years later is its continuing vitality within the cosmos of ufology. Like Kenneth Arnold's sighting fourteen years earlier, the legend of Betty and Barney Hill became timeless from the moment its images entered the collective imagination. The Hill case stands as a primordial precedent — the mythic First — for future alien abductions, just as much as Arnold's sighting represents the mythic Origin of flying saucers.

The scholar Karl Kerenyi reminds us that in mythology *origin* refers to a kind of archetypal grounding that *once was* and *continues to be.* "All the institutions of mythological times are founded on and illuminated, that is, hallowed, by a mythologem of origination, the common divine origin of life whose forms they are," Kerenyi writes. This grounding and founding is maintained through the elaboration of particular ceremonies and rituals, especially the repetition of the content of the myth: the creation story. Each repetition of the foundational myth re-creates those primary distinctions (such as "flying saucer" or "alien abduction") that bring a particular world into view; each succcessive re-creation *holds the world in place.*

As we discovered in chapter two, over time this primal ground becomes synonymous with authenticity. Ufology maintains an ongoing pilgrimage to the Kenneth Arnold sighting report, in the service of elaborating — hence perpetuating — ufology's founding myth. Likewise, ufologists continue to return to the Hill sighting report as the unspoken prototype for the world of events and images known by the phrase "alien abduction." But the importance of the Hill abduction is not simply taken for granted in ufology, as UFO investigator Budd Hopkins showed when he stepped forward to state the logic behind the Hill case's *ideal* status in explicit terms.

Hopkins is a UFO investigator who emerged in the 1980s as mainstream ufology's designated alien abduction specialist. He is perhaps the foremost advocate of the view that, indisputably, alien abductions are hard-edged, real-world events. In his book *Missing Time*, a study of several alien abduction cases, Hopkins confirmed the primordial necessity of the Hill case when he said that he adopted it as a model and primary reference point for his research with abductees. If a particular case followed the basic outlines of the Hill encounter, according to Hopkins, it thereby merits designation as either a likely or a definite abduction.

It is here that we approach a new level of complexity — and danger. For as Kerenyi takes great pains to point out, the "authenticity" that a particular originating myth holds for a particular "tribe" (past or contemporary, rural or urban, oral or literate, Third or First World) is not necessarily synonymous with *real-world* authenticity. That is, a myth may powerfully inform the imagination and actions of a particular community, may provide a conceptual framework for bringing order to a particular stream of experience, and may speak to deep aboriginal truths in the nature of psyche and the psyche of nature. A myth may also provide a compelling model for research, as Budd Hopkins demonstrated. But this is all very different from saying that any myth *necessarily* provides an accurate map of historical events in time and space.

In his second book about alien abductions, *Intruders*, Hopkins urged his readers to put aside their prejudices and bear in mind that "if any aspect of the UFO phenomenon is true, then any of the rest of the reported phenomenon may be true too." This statement holds a particular appeal in mythic terms as a primordial or founding judgment, in its insistence that once a precedent of apparent authenticity is established, more authenticity may follow. But there is a catch. The converse of Hopkins's theory is necessarily invoked: If any aspect of the UFO phenomenon is *not* true, then any of the rest of the reported phenomenon also may be not true.

In other words, once the Hill case is established as primordial precedent or mythic forerunner, thus providing a model to guide future abduction research, then all of its complexities, paradoxes, crosscurrents, and unresolved questions — like those of the Arnold sighting — can be expected to be carried forth and to live on. In both cases they do.

We recall Martin Kottmeyer's assertion that a *foundational* confusion in interpeting Kenneth Arnold's 1947 experience shrouds all future sightings of *saucers* in doubt. At the time, Arnold used the phrase "flat like a pie-can" to describe the objects he saw, but this phrase was not widely quoted. If it had been, would people around the nation have begun reporting seeing "flying pie-cans"? As we discovered in chapter two, there is an unavoidable human impulse to shape our perceptions along the lines of expectancy. It is difficult to doubt that Kenneth Arnold and Betty and Barney Hill were amazed — to say the least — by what they saw. Perhaps their observations were largely accurate. In any case, important questions present themselves: What constitutes a *true precedent*? Were the Arnold and Hill sightings unparalleled in human history, or were their "visions" (in the broad sense of the word) consistent with a broader tapestry of mysteries, marvels, and miracles throughout human history?

These are thorny questions. If the Hill case is the primordial abduction, we should expect to find the case free of meaningful precedents, in Aristotle's sense of a beginning as "that which is not itself necessarily after anything else, and which has naturally something else after it." Thus we are obliged to ask what prior events or preexisting images — general or specific, near or distant, modern or archaic — may have influenced the Hill case and the course that it followed as one of the premier sagas of UFO mythology.

Antonio Villas-Boas's extraordinary experience in Brazil took place four years prior to the Hills' experience in the White Mountains of New Hampshire. There are remarkable parallels between the two cases. Villas-Boas saw a bright object descend toward the field where he was working late at night; the Hills saw a light descend toward their car along a country road. Villas-Boas's tractor died and a being appeared next to him; the Hills' car stopped of its own accord and beings walked toward them. Both cases involve witnesses being carried into landed UFOs by creatures less than five feet in height and being taken into rooms and subjected to quasi-medical procedures. On leaving, Villas-

Boas tried to take a "clock" as evidence of his experience but was rebuffed; Betty Hill hoped for a book but was shown a map instead.

There are specific differences between the two cases as well. Villas-Boas remembered the experience consciously afterward, whereas the Hills' recollections began as a series of nightmares for Betty and led to hypnosis sessions during which the abduction narrative came forth. Villas-Boas was carried against his will into the UFO, whereas the Hills were floated into the waiting spaceship. The important point for our present discussion is that there is no way the Villas-Boas case could have influenced the Hills' sighting because the Brazilian farmer's sighting report was not made public until four years after the Hill abduction occurred. Both cases were publicized in 1966 after separate independent investigations.

From the archetypal perspective pioneered by Carl Jung, it could be argued that each case was a specific instance of an emerging shift in the collective structure of reality. Perhaps some entirely new, or latent, dimension was beginning to "bleed through" into collective consciousness, via particular individuals in particular places. Or perhaps something quite ancient from the world soul was making its periodic return, in a novel form, as part of a larger cycle or spiral of manifestation. Although fascinating, such speculations must stand outside our present focus: whether it can be shown that cultural influences played a significant role in predisposing the Hills to have such a bizarre experience and/or in shaping their subsequent "memories."

After the abduction experience but before her nightmares began, Betty read Donald Keyhoe's *The Flying Saucer Conspiracy*, a book that discusses Venezuelan UFO cases in which a man is dragged to a luminous UFO by four small men, and another man is found unconscious after being abused by a hairy dwarf. In Betty's later dream, she was dragged along by four little men while barely conscious and later subjected to "medical tests" consistent with Keyhoe's speculation that her ufonaut captors were conducting a probe of Earth out of neutral scientific curiosity or as a prelude to a mass landing.

There are as well certain motifs in Betty's report that bear some resemblance to motifs in the 1953 alien invasion film *Invaders from Mars*. Betty said that her captors "looked like mongoloids" with noses as big as that of the entertainer Jimmy Durante. This description is not inconsistent with the large-nosed mutants who appear on the *Invaders from Mars* poster. (Barney, who said he peeked only occasionally during the abduction ordeal, didn't recall seeing noses, "there just seemed to be two slits that represented nostrils.") Betty found herself on an operating table inside the UFO as needles were placed on the back of her neck, as well as in her abdomen.

In the same film — which became an instant classic — a female abductee is placed on an operating table and a needle is used to implant a device in the back her neck. Earlier in the film the protagonists are shown a large star map by Dr. Kelston in an observatory discussion about the proximity of Mars to Earth. When he points to the map, the moviegoer may or may not notice the fact that Earth isn't shown on the map. Betty was shown a star map by her abductors, who asked her if she knows where Earth is on the map. Betty did not.

One could assume that the likenesses between Betty's experience and the classic film are purely coincidental. Or one could assume that Betty didn't know where Earth is because she was correctly following the missing-Earth motif from the script of *Invaders from Mars*. Martin Kottmeyer, a self-admitted "badfilm buff," argues for the latter proposition, pointing to another feature film, *Killers from Space* (1954), as the likely source for the "amnesia with recoverable memory" motif that emerged in the Hill case and became a stock theme of abduction narratives.

Kottmeyer has made it his business to look for parallels between UFO events and motifs from films and television episodes. While watching an old episode of "The Outer Limits" entitled "The Bellero Shield," he became convinced that he had found a cinematic solution to Barney Hill's abduction memories as well. In this episode, an alien is featured with "wraparound" eyes. Being very familiar with the Hill case, Kottmeyer recalled that Barney had described his alien kidnappers as having "wraparound eyes." Then he realized that "The Outer Limits" played in the mid-1960s, well after the Hill abduction had occurred. Efforts to connect the two seemed absurd.

However, additional research completed the loop to Kottmeyer's satisfaction. In an unpublished paper entitled "Gauche Encounters: Bad-films and the Ufo Mythos," he writes:

Barney Hill said or drew nothing about "wraparound" eyes until a hypnosis session dated February 22, 1964. "The Bellero Shield" aired on

February 10, 1964. As if this was not sufficient proof, I further learned Barney said, "the eyes are talking to me." The Bifrost alien of this show, perhaps unique among science fiction celluloid creations, explicitly claims to speak through its eyes.

"These cases demonstrate the cultural transmission of error and form an object lesson in being wary of similarities among UFO cases," he says, adding: "Ufo abductions only became popular after a decade of alien invasion movies. There is a visible borrowing of conventions including fogs, one-piece foil suits, macrocephaly [aliens with large heads], dying worlds, and mind control." Kottmeyer goes on to argue that ufologists systematically edit out such cultural sources for UFO reports, not because they are trying to hoodwink the public but because of their own unconscious biases as investigators.

He cites the example of a leading abduction researcher who came across a reference to a saucer being propelled by lithium crystals. Recognizing "Star Trek" as the source for the image, the ufologist discounted that part of the abduction claimant's account. Likewise, according to Kottmeyer, details of another UFO case never made it into UFO literature because late night TV–viewing ufologists recognized that it had its genesis in a "Saturday Night Live" Coneheads sketch.

"The only [Star Trek and other similar] influences to pass through this sieve of scrutiny are going to be arcane or ambiguous ones," Kottmeyer argues. "Only when the influences come from esoteric or forgotten sources will the cultural material sneak into the ufo literature. The badfilm buff thus has an advantage in recognizing the wellsprings of certain details of ufo experiences."

Recently the French sociologist Bertrand Meheust made an important discovery that further clouds the question of what counts as a "UFO precedent." Meheust came across an abduction report involving a Belgian citizen named Mr. Belans. The event took place in a remote area near Brabant where farmers had reported suspiciously crushed vegetation in their wheat fields. While walking in this area, Belans noticed a man dressed in black under a tree, apparently waiting for something. His curiosity aroused, Belans waited and watched. Soon an unusual feeling of fatigue came over him, as if some force had taken control of his actions. This was followed by a strange buzzing sound, then by a very bright light, as an elongated craft landed nearby. When a door opened over a barely lit rectangle, the man in black stepped into the object. Belans felt compelled to follow.

The interior of the craft was evenly illuminated but without an apparent source of light. Momentarily, the craft took off with a faint vibration, after which a tall man entered through a wall of the room. This man seemed to know Belans's every thought. Speaking in French, the tall man revealed that he hailed from a faraway star.

"Why don't you establish open contact?" asked Belans.

"Because we do not wish to force the rapid evolution of elements that are foreign to our own civilization," the ufonaut answered.

When Belans was later returned to Earth, he discovered a significant period of amnesia, missing time, a theme known to those familiar with abduction narratives.

This abduction case is dated *1934*, twenty-seven years prior to the Hill abduction. More precisely, the case appeared in a science fiction story entitled "Hodomur, Man of Infinity," published that year by Ege Tilms. By combing a vast amount of science fiction literature dating back to before World War I, Meheust found stories of strange aerial objects stalling cars, chasing trains and automobiles, zapping people with strange beams, and abducting them into spherical structures. Meheust also found the alien abduction motif central to hundreds of stories, most in French and English, published between 1880 and 1940.

In light of these developments, the plot of the UFO epic thickens considerably. Kottmeyer and Meheust succeed in calling into doubt efforts to take modern abduction narratives at face value. But it is important to note that neither researcher goes so far as to suggest that the science fiction literature and films of the 1950s and 1960s simply planted their ideas in the collective psyche, thus entirely creating the close encounter phenomenon. Such a conclusion is unwarranted in light of several considerations, including the emergence of close encounter cases among witnesses in populations largely unexposed to science fiction motifs. Antonio Villas-Boas is one such witness; there are many others like him.

Questions remain about "UFO precedents" on a much larger scale of time. We discovered in chapter three that by the late 1950s and early 1960s, ufologists were divided about whether to focus their investigations on so-called "hard" evidence (photographs, landing marks, and so on) or whether to consider reports of encounters with UFO occupants.

We also discovered that a third wing of ufologists had decided to take seriously the idea that modern UFO reports were continuous with reports of human encounters with extraordinary beings throughout human history.

At the heart of UFO accounts, a relatively small number of interactions are consistently described. An object or a light appears in the sky or, less specifically, in the spatial environment of a witness or witnesses. This object or light (or combination) affects people, animals, machines, or the physical surroundings in an unusual way. Frequently, but not invariably, some form of interaction occurs between human witnesses and occupants of apparent craft or beings that appear out of vast luminosity. Sometimes communication takes place, verbal or nonverbal; occasionally the beings perform "operations" on the human witness; often a voyage to "other realms" takes place inside a strange craft.

We recall from chapter two that the shape-shifting god Proteus doesn't place much stock in *either/or* as a fundamental distinction. He claims to feel just as much at home when identified as "UFO," the star player in a distinctly modern and unique drama set against the backdrop of outer space, as when he is identified as the hero of a far older epic featuring a vast assembly of spiritual beings known by different names in various cultures throughout the world.

In light of this, and bearing in mind the preceding summary of characteristic UFO interactions, let us turn back the clock and take inventory of various precedents to the modern age of flying saucers.

BETWEEN 1946 and 1948, cigar-shaped objects called ghost rockets were seen in Finland and Sweden close to the Soviet Union. These were assumed to be Soviet military devices, but this was never confirmed. Throughout World War II, Allied bombers over Germany and Japan reported odd balls of light ("foo-fighters," a pun on the French word for fire, *feu*) flying off the wingtips of their planes. After the war, it was learned that Japanese and German pilots experienced the same phenomenon and assumed, as did Allied pilots, that the lights were enemy devices. (These balls of light were reported by pilots during the Korean War, as well.)

In November 1896, in California, the first of many "mystery airships" was seen in the sky. Over a period of two years, several thousands of people reported seeing strange craft assuming a variety of forms: cigars, cylinders, barrels, globs, eggs, pears, V-patterns, but most often resembling a dirigible from which a railroad car seemed to be suspended. Witnesses reported colored or white lights on the objects, including red or white searchlights. As with later flying saucer reports, the objects anticipated feats of technology not yet possible, although not beyond the range of imagination. This prompted some UFO researchers to speculate that a vast paraphysical metaphenomenon lay behind all human visionary experiences, aimed at slowly and imperceptibly expanding human consciousness.

A publication prepared by the German scholar Hartmann Schaeden, dated 1493, describes a remarkable sphere of fire following a straight path through the sky from south to east, then turning toward the setting sun. An illustration depicts a cigar-shaped form surrounded by flames against a blue sky. In Nuremberg (1561) and Basil (1566), witnesses reported seeing large aerial "tubes" from which spheres and disks emerged and appeared to "fight" with each other in aerial dances.

Fiery aerial phenomena bearing the distinct shapes of military shields appeared during the battle between the Saxons and the Franks at Sigisburg in the year A.D. 776. In A.D. 1118, the emperor Constantine witnessed a fiery cross suspended in the sky, accompanying the message "In this sign you shall conquer." Agobard, Archbishop of Lyons, an eminent rationalist scholar of the Middle Ages, wrote of coming upon a mob in the process of lynching three men and a woman accused of landing in a "cloudship" from the celestial region known as Magonia. W. R. Drake, in an article entitled "Spacemen in the Middle Ages," writes: "The belief of Beings from the skies who surveyed our Earth persisted in human consciousness throughout the Middle Ages."

An important Western religious figure of the nineteenth century offered this report: "I saw a pillar of light exactly over my head, above the brightness of the sun, which descended gradually until it fell upon me. . . . When the light rested on me I saw two personages, whose brightness and glory defy all descriptions, standing above me in the air. One of them spoke unto me." These are the words of Joseph Smith, founder of the Mormon Church.

Since there was no "machine" involved in Smith's report, does his sighting belong in the same category as modern UFO sightings? Let us hold this question in mind as we consider the following account of the prophet Ezekiel, who received his spiritual call one day by the river Chebar while he was among a group of captives. Ezekiel reports that, suddenly,

> ... a whirlwind came out of the north, a great cloud, and a fire unfolding itself, and a brightness was about it, and out of the midst thereof was the color of amber, out of the midst of the fire. Also out of the midst thereof came the likeness of four living creatures. And this was their appearance; they had the likeness of a man. And every one had four faces, and every one had four wings. And their feet were straight feet; and the sole of their feet was like the sole of a calf's foot; and they sparkled like the color of burnished brass.
>
> As for the likeness of the living creatures, their appearance was like burning coals of fire, and like the appearance of lamps: it went up and down among the living creatures; and the fire was bright, and out of the fire went forth lightning.
>
> Now as I beheld the living creatures, behold one wheel upon the earth by the living creatures, with his four faces. The appearance of the wheels and their work was like unto the color of a beryl: and their work was as it were a wheel in the middle of a wheel. When they went, they went upon their four sides: and they turned not when they went.

Joseph Blumrich, a National Aeronautics and Space Administration (NASA) engineer, wrote a book, *The Spaceships of Ezekiel*, interpreting Ezekiel's experience in technical terms and came up with a great metallic spaceship with whirling fan wheels, rocket exhausts, and portholes. As an alternative to "technocentrism" of this sort, could it be that Ezekiel's report and modern UFO witness accounts are equally "accurate" versions of an essentially protean technology whose mastery of dimensions beyond space-time far surpass exhaustive human description?

Should modern "UFO" sightings be considered a distinct, discrete, historically specific phenomenon? Or are we bound to widen our perspective and consider these sightings in the larger context of human encounters with a shape-shifting *Other* that appears in forms suited to the collective attitudes and beliefs of particular eras?

Proteus had already stated his view: "*Call me alien, if you wish, or angel, if that suits you better. Or call me both, or place me somewhere in between. Above all else, you will not be able to ignore me.*" Most of his human observers, however, proved not quite so adaptable. This was, and is, understandable, since the significance of the UFO phenomenon changes considerably when its images and events are framed in two such differing contexts.

The debate about where to *place* the remarkable events known as UFOs continued well into the 1960s, along with a fierce controversy about whether the phenomenon "began" in the late 1940s or in ages recalled only at the depths of the world soul.

SEVEN

— ✕ —

J. ALLEN HYNEK, astronom-
ical consultant to Project Blue Book,* went to Socorro, New Mexico,
aiming to find contradictions in Lonnie Zamora's account of what he
saw on the outskirts of Socorro on April 24, 1964. Instead he discovered
"one of the soundest, best substantiated cases" in UFO history. Philip
Klass, aviation journalist and determined flying saucer debunker, went
to Socorro expecting to find more evidence for his legendary "plasma
UFO" theory, a hypothesis still in search of convincing evidence. Like
Hynek, his longtime adversary, Klass would change his mind — but
in a very different direction.

At 5:45 P.M., Deputy Marshal Lonnie Zamora was chasing a speeding driver on the outskirts of town. His attention was suddenly diverted
by a roar and a descending orange and blue flame in the southwest
sky at 4,000 feet. Breaking off his chase, he made his way up a nearly
impassable incline, where, to his amazement, about 800 feet away he
saw what appeared to be an upside-down car with two men standing
nearby. Then he realized it was an elliptical object, standing on two
legs, with a strange, two-foot-high red insignia on its side. The two men,

---

*Blue Book was the code name of the air force's UFO investigation from March 1952
to December 1969, after which date the air force maintained no "official" interest
in the subject.

dressed completely in white, seemed startled to see Zamora watching. By the time the officer had driven within 100 feet, the men were no longer visible. As he stepped out of his car to get a better look, he suddenly heard a loud roar. Zamora feared an imminent explosion and ran for cover behind his car. Turning to look back, his arms covering his face for protection, he

> looked up, and I saw the object going away from me, in a southwest direction. When the roar stopped, [I] heard a sharp tone whine from high tone to low tone.... The whine lasted maybe a second. Then there was complete silence about the object.... It appeared to go in a straight line and at [the] same height — possibly 10 to 15 feet from ground.... Object was traveling very fast. It seemed to rise up, and take off immediately across country.

As with most of the increasing numbers of such strange sightings, the aftermath was as complex, contradictory, and strangely compelling as what Zamora originally reported. After radioing for a backup officer, the shaken officer noticed charred greasewood brushes and four indentations (or "pod marks," as they would later be called in the press), indicating the spot where the *thing* had landed and apparently scooped up some dirt. When Sergeant Sam Chavez arrived on the scene, he found his colleague pale and sweating. Before Zamora would allow his report to be released to authorities, he insisted on seeing a priest.

That the strange craft was no experimental lunar module was confirmed through contact with NASA, the Jet Propulsion Laboratory (JPL), and fifteen industrial firms with military connections. From this point on, myriad conjectures began to appear, but even more important, began to be publicized, fostering the familiar aura of contentious ambiguity that had come to characterize the periods following major UFO sightings.

A local gas station attendant reported having been told by a motorist that he had seen a strange craft in the same area at about the same time. When the motorist and his companion were finally located and interviewed separately fourteen years after the fact, their reports corroborated Zamora's report on some details and departed from it on others. Debunkers claimed this effectively maintained Zamora as the only witness; proponents responded that the variations between their testimony and Zamora's was simply a measure of the amount of time that had passed before they were found.

The insignia on the craft described by Zamora (and by one of the other witnesses) became a focal point of the controversy. Astrophysicist and computer scientist Jacques Vallee pointed out that the insignia was the same as a medieval Arabic sign for Venus, proving to some (but not to Vallee) that the craft was from Venus, and causing others (including Vallee) to wonder why extraterrestrials would adopt a Middle Eastern logo for their vehicular decal. As if to save the day, a debunker showed up to offer the most imaginative hypothesis of all.

An engineer named Leon Davidson attempted to show that by maneuvering the lines of the insignia, the initials CIA and AD can be formed. Davidson theorized that the latter represented the initials of Central Intelligence Agency director Allen Dulles. Pressed to explain why the CIA — a top-secret organization that doesn't even list its phone number — would place its initials on a crude saucer hoax, Davidson insisted that "Dulles had enough 'chutzpah' to order such a stunt." (As if to cover himself, Davidson offered an alternative hypothesis: A rival agency — perhaps the FBI in concert with the DIA (Defense Intelligence Agency) — staged the event in order to downgrade the CIA's public image. In this scenario, the speeding driver was but a decoy to lead Zamora to the landing sight.)

Soon Philip Klass arrived in town. After first considering the event as yet another instance of rogue plasma, Klass settled on a hoax explanation quite different from Davidson's: one perpetrated by Zamora himself. In examining the Socorro case, Klass brought an investigatory style that would bedevil pro-UFO researchers for many years to come: a fine-toothed attention to selected details pressed in support of subtle theories implicitly offered as "obvious facts." Klass began his attempted demolition of Zamora's credibility by raising several apparently relevant questions:

Why had Zamora specifically requested that Sergeant Sam Chavez, rather than a local police officer or someone from the sheriff's office, be sent to the scene? Since a Mr. and Mrs. Phillips lived only 1,000 feet from the site, why had they not heard the loud roar reported by Zamora? Why were the pod marks different from each other? Why was it so easy to create new indentations with a shovel that were indistinguishable from the original ones? What credibility should be attached to Zamora's sketches of the craft, when these "resembled drawings made by a young child"? Is it not relevant to note that, in attempting to flee an expected explosion, Zamora admitted that he knocked his glasses off? If Zamora's story was true, why did local scientists at the New Mexico Institute of Mining and Technology exhibit no interest whatever in what would have to be "the most exciting scientific event of all time — a visit from an extraterrestrial spacecraft?"

Some of Klass's questions were relevant, others sheer rhetoric. But by raising these concerns in terms conveying a dispassionate attempt to get at the *simple facts*, Klass was in a position to drive home his own hypothesis: the entire Lonnie Zamora affair was concocted to whip up tourism in Socorro, a town by Klass's assertion "sorely in need of a tourist attraction to stop passing motorists." As evidence, Klass allowed his imagination free rein concerning the possibilities for commercial exploitation of the Socorro affair:

> The property where the UFO reportedly landed had, prior to the inci-
> dent, been next to worthless "scrub land." But now, if the site became
> a long-lived tourist attraction, there could be need for refreshment
> stands, perhaps even a motel for those who might like to spend the night
> near the spot where an extraterrestrial spaceship had seemingly landed.
> By a curious coincidence, the property where the UFO reportedly landed
> was owned by Mayor Bursum, officer Zamora's boss! The mayor's prin-
> cipal business? He is the town banker and as such would not be unhappy
> to see an influx of tourist dollars.

Klass's exquisite scenario lacked only one element: a modicum of supporting evidence to make it more than a likely story. Perhaps Socorro was indeed "sorely in need" of a tourist trap, but Klass neglected to provide convincing documentation. Twenty-five years after Lonnie Zamora filed his report, there is no hint of vendors hawking "It Landed in Socorro" T-shirts or buttons, nor of paved roads leading up to the alleged landing sight, nor of plans for full-color "Hometown of Lonnie Zamora" billboards — just as there were no hints of any of these when Klass published his speculative account ten years after the Socorro incident.

In fact, one year after his sighting, a statement by Zamora seemed at odds with Klass's later theory: "I wanted to keep it to myself," Zamora said. "But Chavez . . . made me report it. . . . If something like this should happen again, I'll know what to do." (Extending Klass's logic, a vigilent debunker might say Zamora's later statement was a hoax designed to provide additional cover for the original fraud. The pathos of a beleaguered visionary might have been contrived to foster a local flying saucer cult, one with potential for catching on. Such circular speculation is characteristic of both sides of the UFO debate.)

But even if Klass was partly or even completely correct in his tourist-attraction hypothesis, and in his earlier plasma-UFO thoery, it is unlikely that he appreciated the extent to which his attempted debunkings (and those of his role model Donald Menzel) played into a growing conviction among the public at large that UFOs could not be explained away, especially not through byzantine theories requiring the seeming unlikely convergence of numerous ideal factors. Likewise, even if Davidson was accurate about an FBI/DIA conspiracy to discredit the CIA, and Menzel correct about fireflies and stray eyelashes being mistaken for strange aerial events, these explanations nonetheless seemed to many ordinary observers to be as nonsensical — if not more so — as the details of the original UFO sightings to which they referred.

As a result, by the mid-1960s the UFO phenomenon was rapidly attaining a curious kind of credibility among an increasing number of individuals who showed no signs whatever of being "flying saucer cultists." This is not to say that most people had decided with certainty that UFOs were real (although a 1966 Gallup poll indicated that 46 percent of Americans were inclined to take UFOs quite seriously). Rather, a stalemate was emerging in the public mind, a deadlock over claims of unlikely celestial events, on one hand, and unlikely alternative explanations, on the other.

The result was a vacuum in which magic — and considerable mischief — were bound to unfold.

THE Socorro affair pumped new life into the UFO phenomenon at a time when its continuity as a modern marvel seemed in doubt. In 1963, Donald Menzel's second book, *The World of Flying Saucers: A Scientific Examination of a Major Myth of the Space Age*, although essentially a rehash of his previous thoughts, offered renewed (and vitriolic) condemnation of the extraterrestrial visitation theory, thus providing new ammunition for skeptics to direct against the claims of contactees, abductees, startled radar scanners, and ordinary witnesses of silvery aerial disks and strange nighttime lights, all at once.

NICAP's drive for congressional hearings had pretty much failed, raising new doubts about whether the organization would remain intact. Matters weren't helped when APRO cofounder Coral Lorenzen, in a bid to boost her organization's membership, wrote an editorial to her newsletter readers dismissing NICAP as a mere lobbying group (as opposed to an effective research-based body, like APRO). This move catapulted longstanding tensions between the groups into open warfare, ensuring that the two organizations would never be able to cooperate again.

Despite this ufological malaise, the UFOs themselves continued their "real or not, here we come" approach with a flurry of impressive sightings following the Socorro affair and continuing well into 1965.

JUNE 29, 1964. Businessman Beauford E. Parham of northeast Georgia, while driving home in the late evening, caught sight of a bright light in the sky heading directly toward his car. The next thing he knew it was directly in front of his headlights — top-shaped, spinning, emitting a hissing sound "like a million snakes," amber colored, six feet tall and eight feet wide, with something like a mast on top and small portholes around the bottom through which "flames" were apparent. The object performed maneuvers around Parham's car, leaving a strong smell like embalming fluid and a gaseous vapor before suddenly disappearing. Federal Aviation Administration officials later detected radioactivity on the car, although no formal report was made. The car hood was warped and its paint bubbled, and the radiator deteriorated soon thereafter.

July 3, 1965. At a Chilean scientific station in Antarctica, a "curious celestial body" was observed for about twenty minutes. Commander Mario Jahn Barrera of the air force described it as "something that moved at a frightening speed, zigzagging and giving off a blue-green light . . . it was something solid, which caused interference in the base's electromagnetic equipment . . . no apparatus constructed by man to date has anything like this, either in shape, speed, maneuverability, or other characteristics." Ten color photographs were allegedly taken of the lens-shaped UFO, which registered on magnetograph tapes and caused strong radio interference. Although there were supposedly multiple scientific witnesses and simultaneous photographic and instrumental confirmation, UFO researchers continue to maintain that official secrecy prevented them from being made public. There was news coverage of the sightings at the time, however.

August 19, 1965. Harold Butcher, age sixteen, was milking cows on his parents' farm in Cherry Creek, New York, with a tractor-powered milking machine, when his transistor radio was suddenly interrupted with static, the tractor motor stopped, and a bull tethered in the barnyard bellowed, reacted violently, and bent a metal stake. Butcher looked out the window and saw a large elliptical object landing about a quarter mile away, emitting a beeping sound and a red vapor around its edges. After the UFO shot straight up into the clouds and disappeared, family members detected a strange odor in the air, and found a purplish liquid, damaged grass, and two depressions in the ground near the apparent landing sight.

SIGHTINGS of this sort, reported in daily and weekly newspapers and on radio and television throughout the United States, contributed to a new shift in the ever-changing "social balance of power" regarding UFOs. Having remained mostly on the sidelines for the first seventeen years, the public, members of Congress, and the scientific community demonstrated a new willingness to become involved in the vigorous debate. Influential editorial writers stepped forward with voices remarkably free of the ridicule that had marked early media coverage.

The *Denver Post* of August 3, 1965, editorialized that "maybe it's time for more people to get serious about the UFO question.... If we still choose to be skeptical, we nevertheless are not nearly so ready as we once were to dismiss all reports of variously shaped but elusive flying objects as products of midsummer night dreams." The next day, the Fort Worth, Texas, *Star Telegram* took an even bolder stand:

> They can stop kidding us now about there being no such thing as "flying saucers...." Too many people of obviously sound mind saw and reported them independently.... Their descriptions of what they saw were too similar to one another, and too unlike any familiar object....

Even the science editor of the conservative *Christian Science Monitor* joined the growing chorus: "Flying saucers are all but literally knocking on the laboratory door.... Something definitely is going on that cannot be explained."

But the most significant shift of opinion in the wake of Lonnie Zamora's sighting was the one that took place in the mind of longtime air force consultant J. Allen Hynek. Invited in 1948 by the air force to use his expertise an an astronomer to weed out obvious cases of natural phenomena, the thirty-eight-year-old Hynek was certain that whatever cases remained could be easily explained as a "psychological postwar craze" sweeping the nation. Over the years, however, his doubts began to grow, especially as a result of his close personal and professional relationship with a young graduate student named Jacques Vallee, whom he met at Northwestern University when Hynek took a teaching position there in 1960.

Hynek's extensive familiarity with UFO cases, joined with Vallee's considerable skills as a computer scientist, made a formidable combination. By the mid-1960s, together they had reached a conclusion whose effects would be felt in UFO research for many years to come, namely that while the data refused to conform to the air force's robotic denials of UFO reality, neither did the data lend much credence to the extraterrestrial visitation theory. Rather, there appeared remarkable parallels among UFO phenomena and descriptions of human encounters with *spiritual entities* throughout history.

"It began to seem to us that rather than being 'extraterrestrial' in any simple sense, UFOs could well be part of the same larger intelligence which has shaped the tapestry of religion and mythology since the dawn of human consciousness," Hynek said in 1985, a year before his death. The challenge he faced, twenty years earlier, was to keep his growing doubts to himself and a few close associates, and to remain a part of the air force investigation. Thus he could retain access to UFO case reports that Vallee could continue to subject to the kind of systematic computer analysis that the air force had refused to undertake.

This meant Hynek faced a considerable personal and professional challenge: to maintain an increasingly strenuous tension between his private suspicion that UFOs posed a fundamental challenge to prevailing notions of reality, and his public position that UFOs could and would be explained in mundane terms. But it would take being at the center of one of the most infamous debacles in UFO history to convince Hynek of the terrible costs of deliberately splitting his public and private stances. Until the day he died, Hynek would recall the agonies of his decision each time he heard two simple words: *swamp gas.**

ON MARCH 14, 1966, citizens and police officers in three western Michigan counties reported that they had seen strange lighted objects flashing across the predawn skies. "These objects could move at fantastic speeds, make very sharp turns, dive and climb and hover with great maneuverability," according to a local deputy sheriff. Three days later, yet another predawn performance was offered over another part of the same Michigan county.

On Sunday, March 20, near the town of Dexter, twelve miles from Ann Arbor, a forty-seven-year-old farmer named Frank Mannor stepped outside at about 8:00 P.M. to quiet his dogs. "When I turned my back I saw this meteor," he said later. "It stopped and settled to the ground, then rose again. It was about a half mile away. I called my wife and kids out, and we watched it for fifteen minutes." Mannor and his son Ronnie approached to within about 500 yards of an object that was "sort of shaped like a pyramid, with a blue-green light on the right-hand side and on the left a white light," Mannor said, adding: "I didn't see no antenna or porthole."

After the Mannors reported the object, a crowd of more than fifty persons — including police officers — gathered to watch the same object cavorting in the skies and on the ground near Dexter. As several of the evasive objects were chased by police in six patrol cars, a circus atmosphere was building on the Mannors' front lawn — to their great dismay.

The high point of this UFO fantasia came on the following night, March 21, in Hillsdale, twenty miles west of Dexter. There, eighty-seven female students, along with the local civil defense director and college dean, watched a football-shaped, car-sized object perform incredible gyrations, which included veering toward a dormitory window before coming to a sudden halt. The curtain came down on this four-hour performance when the mysterious object maneuvered over a swamp near the Hillsdale College campus.

---

*J. Allen Hynek talked in detail about his gradual awakening during the early and mid-1960s when I met with him at his home in Scottsdale, Arizona, in 1985. When I spoke with his longtime colleague Jacques Vallee in Palo Alto, California, in 1991, Vallee independently confirmed the details of Hynek's account.

Enter J. Allen Hynek. Had these Michigan sightings not received nonstop national media coverage, Hynek and his boss, Major Hector Quintanella, head of Project Blue Book, might not have been sent in at all. But the demand for an official explanation was overwhelming, and this task fell to Hynek — although the sightings were history by the time he arrived. Compounding matters was the fact that he was expected to find answers for phenomena ranging from apparently hard-edged objects to faint, flickering lights, as if they were all the same thing. Hynek wasn't at his best in any event, his jaw wired from a recent fracture.

"The situation was so charged with emotion," Hynek said, "that it was impossible for me to do any really serious investigation." One night he rode in a squad car with officers whose radios crackled with excited messages such as, "There it is!" or "I see it!" At one point, several squad cars converged at an intersection and officers spilled out, pointed frantically at the sky, and shouted: "There it is! It's moving!" (No, it wasn't moving, Hynek realized, wearily. "It" was the star Arcturus.)

Four short days after the Hillsdale College sighting, Hynek found himself facing a crowded news conference. He would later say that the air force assigned him to face the press; the air force would claim Hynek insisted that he be allowed to. (Given the outcome, it is hardly surprising that no one coveted the dubious distinction.) In any case, Hynek didn't feel ready to meet the press; the idea of facing a crowded den of news-hungry reporters was antithetical to what he loved most about science: its slow, methodical deliberation; its embrace of complexity; its freedom from political pressures (at least theoretically). Now Hynek was expected to provide instant answers.

Facing reporters a mere four days after the Hillsdale sighting, Hynek felt he had nothing to go on except a phone call from a colleague who had called his attention to the rare phenomenon of burning swamp gas: methane rising from rotting vegetables in marshlands, capable of igniting spontaneously and casting a brief, flickering light. It occurred to Hynek that *some* of the sightings — especially those that centered around local swamps — might be attributable to swamp gas. It didn't occur to Hynek that the very mention of this phrase in the current context would be a mistake of epic proportions.

Quickly emphasizing that he was not offering a blanket explanation for all the recent sightings did Hynek very little good; the damage was done. "I watched with horror as one reporter scanned the page, found the phrase 'swamp gas,' underlined it, and rushed for the telephone," Hynek recalled. Within a matter of hours, Hynek's swamp gas theory had become as famous as the Michigan sightings themselves. As he continued in the days that followed to clarify his position (to no avail whatever), Hynek felt the noose further tighten around his neck when his air force superiors pronounced themselves satisfied with his explanations and placed the Michigan sightings in the "explained" category.

While much of the nation's press responded with amused detachment, the hundreds of people who had seen the UFOs or knew people who had were outraged about what to them was the obvious implication that they were backwoods morons incapable of discriminating between amorphous will-o'-the-wisps flickering at the edge of swamps and clearly defined objects executing sharp turns, hovering, diving, climbing, and traveling at remarkable speeds. Gerald R. Ford, congressional representative for the the Hillsdale-Dexter area, received so many angry letters and telephone calls from his constituents that he appeared in the House chambers to call for a congressional study of the UFO phenomenon.

With one innocently uttered phrase, Hynek had achieved a result he had once helped oppose, a result that, ironically, Donald Keyhoe's most determined efforts had not been able to accomplish: congressional hearings. On April 5, 1966, a one-day open session of the House Armed Services Committee was held in Washington. The hearing ended with a plan for the air force to establish an independent scientific study of UFOs under the auspices of a respected American university. Seven months later, the air force publicly announced that the University of Colorado had accepted the UFO study project and that prominent physicist Edward Condon would be in charge.

Although its decision to inaugurate an independent study constituted a tacit admission that its nineteen years of investigation and analysis had been found inadequate, the air force was nevertheless delighted to be rescued at last from "the unenviable position of having to pass judgments on every report of an unusual occurrence in the sky," as David Jacobs puts it in *The UFO Controversy in America*.

Allen Hynek likewise felt liberated — deeply embarrassed by the Michigan fiasco — but liberated all the same: "It wasn't until after the 'swamp gas' incident that I said, 'I've had it! This is the last time

I'm going to try to pull a chestnut out of the fire for the Air Force!'"
Just as Saul had become Paul through a momentous epiphany on the
road to Damascus, Allen Hynek in his tortured rite of passage was able
to recapture his integrity after a long period of indenture to a cause
that was never really his: the military's futile effort to explain unidentified flying objects out of existence.

Frank Mannor of Dexter, Michigan, on the other hand, was decidedly
not satisified with the outcome. When CBS News asked him whether
he was "sorry now that you did tell people" what he had seen, Mannor
responded in no uncertain terms:

> Yes, I am. I am sorry because — not that it's not the truth, but it's
> just the idea of the reaction of the people. They think you're a nut:
> to tell the truth, that's just what they figure you are. And I'm not going
> to take it no more. I don't want nobody down here. I just — leave me
> alone. And if the thing lands right here, right there by that pump, I'd
> never say a word . . . I wouldn't tell nobody. That's just the way I feel.
> . . . What would you think if somebody was throwing beer bottles at
> your house, standing out in the middle of the road screaming "you nut,
> you fanatic," and all that? What would *you* think?

Reaction to the news that UFOs would be the subject of a credible
nonmilitary investigation brought mixed reviews. A New Jersey columnist called the Condon committee an intolerable example of one branch
of the government investigating another: "the most insulting thing that
has happened to one of our armed forces in some time." Hollywood
columnist Austin Cooper criticised the enterprise from a different perspective, saying that the air force would continue to withhold the most
sensitive UFO reports for legitimate security reasons, effectively ensuring an irrelevant committee report. An editorial in *Nation*, playing on
the standard need-to-believe theme, expressed the hope that the study
would shed light on why people "must look to beings from beyond the
earth as the only hope for escape from the tensions, dangers and boredom of everyday life." The editorial warned Condon to expect to be
"crucified" by UFO cultists if he failed to find convincing evidence
of "little green men."

Donald Keyhoe, on the other hand, said that putting the UFO problem in the hands of civilian scientists "where it belonged" constituted
"the most significant development in the history of UFO investigation."

Allen Hynek said he felt a "sense of personal triumph and vindication" because now the UFO question would get the attention it deserved. Writing in the *Saturday Evening Post*, Hynek reported on a dinner meeting with several members of the new Condon committee. "What a pleasure it was to sit down with men who were open-minded about UFOs, who did not look at me as though I were a Martian myself."

There was every reason to believe that Condon, former director of the National Bureau of Standards and recognized as one of the most distinguished scientists of his day, could bring the stature necessary to ensure that if there was anything behind UFO sightings, the committee would ferret it out. Yet in the months preceding the committee's formal start, there came to be doubts about Condon's objectivity — or more accurately, there came to be *no* doubts, for Condon elected to make his views unmistakably clear:

> It is my inclination to recommend that the government get out of the UFO business. My attitude right now is that there's nothing to it, but I'm not supposed to reach that conclusion for another year.

Some ufologists entertained the hope that Condon's public statement of his bias might ultimately serve to make the committee's deliberations ultimately more fair. With Condon's views well known in advance, they reasoned, there could be no basis — especially among conservative scientists — for believing him to be any kind of a closet "UFO buff." This would thus give additional credibility to the committee when it finally came forward with its considered evaluation of the most puzzling and compelling UFO sightings — those cases for which conventional explanations had not been found after the air force's supposed best efforts to do so.

The first assumption — that no thoughtful person would ever mistake Edward Condon for George Adamski — was irrefutable. But the idea that the committee's leadership ever intended to examine the "best" UFO sightings fell into doubt when, three months prior to the formal start of the project, Condon's chief lieutenant, Robert Low, who held the title of project director, wrote a confidential memorandum. In it, Low recommended to his boss that the project follow a covert course:

> Our study would be conducted almost exclusively by nonbelievers who, although they couldn't possibly prove a negative result, could and prob-

ably would add an impressive body of evidence that there is no reality to the observations. The trick would be, I think, to describe the project so that to the public, it would appear a totally objective study, but, to the scientific community, would present the image of a group of non-believers trying their best to be objective, but having an almost zero expectation of finding a saucer. One way to do this would be to stress investigation, not of the physical phenomena, but rather of the people who do the observing — the psychology and sociology of persons and groups who report seeing UFOs. If the emphasis were put here, rather than on examination of the old question of the physical reality of the saucer, I think the scientific community would quickly get the message. ... I'm inclined to feel at this early stage that, if we set up the thing right and take pains to get the proper people involved and have success in presenting the image we want to present to the scientific community, we could carry the job off to our benefit....

When project members David Saunders and Norman Levine came across this incriminating document, they sent off a copy that eventually reached Donald Keyhoe. Those who had any remaining doubts about Condon's loyalties were stripped of their illusions when, on learning of the matter in February 1968, Condon immediately fired Saunders and Levine for insubordination rather than dismissing (or at least reprimanding) Low. Condon appeared mostly amused by the episode.

Two weeks later, Low's administrative assistant resigned, maintaining that the project members had little confidence in his leadership and, more, that they had reached decidedly different conclusions from those reached by Low, who had spent practically no time reviewing the details of actual sighting reports. NICAP and APRO withdrew their cooperation from the project, which in one sense satisfied Condon, who had made no secret of his contempt for the civilian UFO research community. Yet Condon recognized that the loss of their cooperation left the committee facing a loss of considerable credibility and prestige, which he attempted (with some success) to counteract by securing for the project's final report the stamp of approval from the respected National Academy of Sciences.

Published in 1969 with the title *Scientific Study of Unidentified Flying Objects*, the project report ranks as one of the most curious publications in all of UFO literature. It opens with Condon's unmodified assertion that UFO reports can be explained in conventional terms, followed by several chapters explaining such matters as how radar works, concluding with analysis of fifty-nine cases, approximately 25 percent of which are listed as *unsolved*. In effect, Condon's opening statement is contradicted by the report's specific findings — almost as if Condon had not read the case studies before writing his conclusions, which, oddly, appeared at the front of the report.*

Overall reaction to the report followed predictable lines. The *New York Times* praised Condon and his staff for making "a careful and extensive investigation" of UFOs, predicting that the report would gain "wide acceptance" except for hard-core "true believers" who were "committed" to the extraterrestrial visitation hypothesis. Donald Keyhoe faulted the project for focusing on what he called "kook cases" while ignoring numerous "top cases" involving credible witnesses who fit the committee's criteria for witness reliability. Citing those sections of the report that seemed to affirm the reality of UFOs, Keyhoe did what he did best: appealed to his followers to open their checkbooks in support of a "full-scale campaign to bring the UFO subject out in the open."

Allen Hynek's cogent response removed any remaining doubts that the former air force consultant left the swamp gas fiasco a defeated man. Writing in the *Bulletin of Atomic Scientists*, Hynek argued that for a scientist of Condon's caliber to place his distinguished name on the 1,485-page report was comparable to "Mozart producing an uninspired pot-boiler, unworthy of his talents." Condon had "grossly underestimated the scope and nature of the problem he was undertaking," Hynek stated. But the report's most glaring and inexcusable error was *philosophical*, Hynek insisted.

> Both the public and the project staff, apparently, have confused the UFO problem with the ETI (extraterrestrial intelligence) hypothesis. This may hold the greatest popular interest, but it is not the issue. The issue is: Does a legitimate UFO phenomenon exist? . . . It may be that UFO phenomena are . . . inexplicable in terms of twentieth century physics. From this point of view, how does the Condon Report serve science

---

*Jacques Vallee later commented that the order should have been reversed. Rather that being tucked away in the back, the case analyses should have preceded the conclusions so as to give a clearer idea of Condon's intractable bias.

when it suggests that a phenomenon which has been reported by many thousands of people over so long a time is unworthy of further scientific attention?

Condon responded by calling Hynek "sort of nuts" and saying the air force would have done well to fire him early on. Then he labeled as "kooks" many others who considered the UFO phenomenon worthy of further study. When the prestigious American Association for the Advancement of Science planned a scientific symposium on the UFO phenomenon, Condon appealed to U.S. vice president Spiro Agnew to stop the meeting. Agnew declined, no doubt sensing a battle he didn't need.

Many who knew Condon well were pained to watch his initial skepticism toward UFOs and those who "favored" them shift to unbridled ridicule, and to see a fine scientist eventually teeter on the brink of the very fanaticism that, ironically, Condon had attributed to the two groups he considered equally contemptible: ufologists, with their boundless claims of government conspiracy; and contactees, whose tales of travel to distant planets with "the space people" (even after George Adamski's death in 1965) held a persistent corner of the universe called ufology.

Over a decade earlier, Edward Ruppelt had authored a classic book about UFOs that he later rewrote, reaching entirely different conclusions. Edward Condon had just now midwifed a classic UFO report that effectively challenged its own conclusions; no sequel was necessary. Both men had encountered UFOs in similar ways: as investigators. By the end of their lives, both had good reason to wish they had never gotten involved with the subject in the first place.

EIGHT

———— ✕ ————

MANY UFO researchers point to the disparity between what government officials say in public about UFO reports ("nothing to be taken seriously") and what their once top secret documents indicate they say in private ("we've got a real problem on our hands with these flying disks"). Others propose that UFOs are manifestations of an essentially mischievous, deceptive, shape-shifting intelligence that directs cultural evolution by sustaining approved beliefs (fairies and angels then, saucer-shaped spacecraft now). Debunkers, in insisting that UFOs are not real, maintain that flying saucers are nothing more than a surrogate religious movement.

All three perspectives indicate the presence of allegorical structures in the UFO epic. "Allegories are based on parallels between two levels of meaning," Angus Fletcher writes, "the one supposed by the reader, the other literally presented in the fable." No ideas appear more often in ufology than *deception* and *disguise, conspiracy* and *cover-up,* accompanied by an impulse to get to the "real truth" (the deep structure) beyond "mere appearances" (the surface structure).

Attempts to line up the two levels, to find correspondences between *what seems to be happening* and *what is really happening* are to be found at every level of what we can call "the UFO allegory": among field investigators searching for UFO landing traces; among researchers using hypnosis to recover "blocked memories" of UFO witnesses; among conspiracy theorists scrutinizing released government memoranda; among debunkers trying to dismiss UFOs once and for all; among proponents trying to prove the reality of UFOs once and for all; and, not least, among close encounter witnesses and the observing public, struggling in their own ways to reconcile the mundane and fantastic elements of UFO experiences, seeking *once and for all* to separate fact from fiction.

The complexity of these efforts is compounded because, according to Fletcher, allegory "seems to aim at both clarity and obscurity together, each effect depending upon the other. Enigma, and not always decipherable enigma, appears to be the allegory's most cherished function, and who will doubt that confusion in the symbolism will aid this function?" Fletcher adds: "The more metaphors, the more epigrams, the more 'well-constructed riddles,' the greater the amount of liveliness."

Given the UFO epic's two-leveled structure — and the tendency towards polarization between thematic extremes — it seems wise to suspect that there are players in this epic who, like Proteus, made their original entrance through side doors while our attention was fixed on players we meet from chapter to chapter: skeptics, debunkers, proponents, disciples, charlatans, would-be scientists, and so forth. By entering covertly, these actors have been shaping our plot all the more because they perform at the periphery of the stage.

It is time to welcome them by name: Hermes, Trickster, and Dionysus, three actors from the timeless annals of mythology. In the decisive break in narrative action provided by the Condon fiasco, let's get to know these players directly, so we might better recognize them in the shadows of scenes to come.

Hermes

Born the son of Zeus (considered by the Greeks the father of gods and men, the ruler and preserver of the world) and Maia (one of Zeus's many mistresses), the god Hermes (known as Mercurius to the Romans) appears in many different aspects and plays numerous roles in the Greek pantheon. He is the swift-footed messenger of the gods between heaven and earth, from which derives his character as a god of oracles. As a messenger or herald, Hermes has access as well to the underworld, guiding the souls of the departed to rest across the threshold of life and death. From the shadowy realms of spirits it is but a short step — especially for one so nimble as Hermes — to the realm of dreams and sleep, where he serves as guide and mediator between conscious and unconscious, surface and depths.

Hermes also came to be known as guardian of commerce and trade, and as god of "persuasive speech" or oratory — all consistent with his gift as a spanner of boundaries, mediator, and ambassador between domains whose thresholds Hermes instinctively recognizes as doorways. Because none of these professions is pure or unmixed, Hermes came to be known both as god of communication and as patron saint of liars and thieves.

Hermes was born in the darkness of night in a lonesome, seldom frequented cave on Mount Kyllene, in Arcadia. Barely a day old, he stole a herd of cattle belonging to his half-brother Apollo. Hermes tried to cover his tracks — and those of the cattle — by fastening bunches of broom to their hooves and driving them backward into a cave, striving to create the impression that the cattle had departed rather than entered the crevice. Hermes' act was noted not by radar but by a yokel named Battos, who reported the theft to an appropriately indignant Apollo, who in turn dragged Hermes off the couch where he pretended to be asleep and delivered him to their father, Zeus, for the certain punishment he deserved.

Without a hint of shame, Hermes immediately denied the charge of cattle rustling. *The Homeric Hymns*, translated by Charles Boer, offers this account of Hermes' audacious performance:

> "If you want,
> I'll swear a great oath
> on the head of my father:
> I declare that I am myself
> not guilty,
> nor did I see any other thief
> of your cattle,
> whatever cattle are, anyway —
> I've only heard about them."
> And while he said this,
> he peeked out
> from under his bright eyelids,
> looking here and there.

And he whistled too,
for a long time,
like somebody listening to a lie.

"*Whatever cattle are, anyway,*" Hermes throws in, seeking to convey an innocence more endearing than simple absence of guilt. Then Hermes proceeded to pick up a lyre and make music, to the delight of Zeus and Apollo, both of whom found his account unbelievable and its teller irresistible in telling so blatant a falsehood.

Hermes further ingratiated himself with Apollo by giving him the lyre. By way of showing his own good faith, Apollo gave Hermes a divining rod and along with it the power of prophecy. There was one condition: Hermes was to communicate his revelations not by words (this was Apollo's domain) but by signs and occurrences. The knave and cunning, the same good humor that he showed in the cattle escapade, Hermes displayed many times over: stealing the sceptre of Zeus, the sword of Ares, Apollo's bow and arrows, Aphrodite's girdle. In each instance, this brash young god managed to smooth the indignation of his victims.

Mythology scholar Ginette Paris finds no contradiction whatever in Hermes' combined role of tradesman, guide, thief, orator, messenger, diplomat, and mediator. "Hermes knows better than to collide head-on with authority; it has to be outsmarted, turned aside, turned into laughter," she writes in her fine book *Pagan Grace*. "Knowing how to distract, amuse or ridicule authority can be just as effective as heroic confrontations." The proverbial landing on the White House lawn in a flying saucer wouldn't be Hermes' style, which is much more suited to appearing as suggestive blips on radar. (By the way, such blips are typically designated by radar operators as "uncorrelated targets." Thus Hermes' presence is noted, but ambiguously; perfect for a god that Paris describes as "multi-faceted, shimmering, impossible to pin down.")

Hermes can preside simultaneously as god of commerce and god of thieves because, Paris notes, both involve acts of *displacement* in which "goods" pass from one owner to another. That there is not always a clear defining line between theft and trade suits Hermes all the more, for he is always most at home "somewhere between the explicit and implicit and never tires of inventing nuances of voice, tone or gesture to place his message in the right context." Whereas Apollo insists on single meanings, clear and straight like an arrow, "communication under the sign of Hermes borrows from twisted pathways, shortcuts and parallel routes, it makes many round trips and ends up sometimes in meaningful dead ends. The paths of Hermes are multiple."

Yet if Hermes the liar were *merely* a liar, no one would listen to his stories, Paris observes. This is a crucial point for the UFO phenomenon as well. If each and every sighting invited a definitive explanation, there would be no controversy about *meanings*. Inherently ambivalent, leaning to this side and that, hermetic intelligence operates through analogy, intuition, and association, always seeking the larger pattern in the small isolated event. Ufologists (pro and con), like Apollo, are interested in *proving* things. Hermes (like UFOs themselves?) "wants to win over the audience and get the applause, even if it means twisting the truth," Paris writes.

Paris adds that Hermes "seems fascinated with a specific form of magic: binding and unbinding, tying and untying, attaching and detaching." When a situation — a debate over a particular UFO sighting, for instance — becomes rigid and bound, Hermes arrives to dissolve the stuck-point. Yet, as with all gods, his magic works both ways: "Hermes can hold, hypnotize, and put to sleep as well as untie, wake up, and break the bonds." Thus, when the UFO scene periodically becomes too fluid — with angels, poltergeists, elves, dwarves, and leprechauns threatening our sense of the phenomenon's coherence — a single myth (such as the extraterrestrial visitation theory) usually casts its allure over the field again, recementing conventional preoccupations.

The poet and mercurial storyteller Robert Bly captures the duality of Hermes beautifully in psychological terms in his book *Iron John* when he notes this god's "part in hermetically sealing off certain interior space, keeping out what needs to be kept out, and holding in what wants to be held in." Certain magical events take place inside such a "walled space." Even so, Bly notes, "when we are in Hermes' field,

> messages pass with fantastic speed between the brain and the fingertips, between the heart and the tear ducts, between the genitals and the eyes, between the part of us that suffers and the part of us that laughs. Hermes is Mercury, and we know that mercury cannot be held in the hand — it rolls everywhere, separates into tiny drops, joins again, falls on the floor, rolls under the table, moves with amazing quickness. It is correctly called quicksilver.

At last — a word that might equally please nuts-and-bolts and angel-oriented ufologists: *quicksilver!* There is much more to be said about Hermes in pages to come. For now, Karl Kerenyi deserves the final word with an observation well suited to the perspective of this book: "If we are to have success in reviving [Hermes'] image in its fullness, *we must be prepared not only for what is immediately intelligible, but also for what is strangely uncanny*" (emphasis added).

Trickster

In mythologies ranging from the North American Indians, the Greeks, the Chinese, the Japanese, and the Siberian and Semitic peoples, a figure known as the Trickster appears again and again in characteristic adventures and ordeals. Although often personified as specific animals — raven, coyote, hare, spider — Trickster has no well-defined or fixed form. Indeed, this mythic person appears to correspond to an undifferentiated form of consciousness prior to the emergence of more developed mental functions although remaining active in the most archaic recesses of the collective mind.

The complexity of Trickster is given in his capacity to manifest at the same time as creator and destroyer, giver and negator, one who dupes and is always himself duped. "Laughter, humour and irony permeate everything Trickster does," writes the anthropologist Paul Radin in his classic account on the subject, *The Trickster.* We find remnants of Trickster motifs in medieval jesters; in the modern clown and Punch-and-Judy plays; in the carnival festival where for a specific period of ritual time the hierarchy of social roles reverse (mayor and garbage collector, prince and pauper); and most assuredly in the modern debate about unidentified flying objects.

Jung finds in the Trickster figure "a forerunner of the saviour, and like him, God, man, and animal at once. He is both subhuman and superhuman, a bestial and divine being, whose chief and most alarming characteristic is his unconsciousness." On the one hand, in his aspect as a creator he embodies many original possibilities that far exceed human powers: removing his anus and entrusting it with a special task, turning himself into a woman and bearing children, bringing forth useful plants from his penis. On the other hand, Trickster "is in many respects stupider than the animals, and gets into one ridiculous scrape after another, [doing] the most atrocious things from sheer unconsciousness and unrelatedness," Jung adds.

Yet each time Trickster gets himself into some abysmal jam, his ability to turn the tables restores him to his savior nature. Jung warns that modern consciousness has for the most part lost touch with Trickster, but Trickster has not forgotten how to find us. He makes his disturbing presence felt in phenomena ranging from frustrating "accidents of fate," to "the malicious tricks played by the poltergeist" to the uneasy coexistence of angelic and demonic potentials within both individual and collective consciousness.

Like Proteus and Hermes, Trickster is indeed a shape-shifter, but he is also less well defined and lacking in the overall order that characterizes the domains of full-fledged divinities. Kerenyi notes that where Hermes conducts the souls of the dead to rest, Trickster is to be found "playing tricks in the ghostly regions of the psyche, where spirits and poltergeists reign." From this perspective, the ominous apparitions of Men in Black (see chapter four) might well be laid at the doorstep of Trickster. Longtime UFO researcher John Keel urges his colleagues to wake up to what they are dealing with:

> Obviously there is some kind of intelligence behind all these manifestations. It is very mischievous, with a great sense of humor. Would beings from some distant galaxy travel hundreds of light years to play such tricks on us? . . . In my own peculiar adventures with people claiming to be in contact with the UFO entities, I found that the representatives of that superior technology in the sky were astonishingly stupid, had a wild, even vicious sense of humor, and also had furious tempers like the devils, demons, and valkyries of old. . . . If the source is crazy for teasing us so pointlessly, what are we who allow ourselves to be so easily teased?

Dionysus

Born of Zeus and Semele (yet another of his mistresses), Dionysus is the Greek god of fertility, wine, and theater. It is in this third role — patron of dramatic arts — that Dionysus is of particular interest to our unfolding story. Dionysus secretly slipped into the UFO play alongside the first hints of concern about the *disclosure of true identity*, one of his all-time favorite themes.

Although associated by Nietzsche with the birth of tragic themes, Dionysus is more accurately linked with the emergence of tragedy as a dramatic form, and with the appearance of drama in general. Dionysus goes by many names and moves in many roles. He has been called the "masked god" or the "god of masks." It is this god's genius that he does not, strictly speaking, disguise himself through his many masks; rather he *reveals* himself through them. By focusing so much on the motif of deception through disguise, perhaps mainstream ufology misses the larger point. Could the UFO's behavior, which fits our *fantasy* of secrecy, constitute its own particular style of revelation?

Ginette Paris makes the point that to act untroubled while feeling panicked might appear a lie. Yet this assumes that any behavior that is not an expression of the "one deep true emotion" is dishonest. In his book *The Presentation of Self in Everyday Life*, Irving Goffman defines sincerity as "trust in our own performance." A good actor, Paris notes, "puts all of himself into his role and tries to be for the audience the character he pretends to be." He is not worried about whether he is being consistent with or true to his "real self," for he is an *actor*. As we all are, writes Paris, adding: *"Dionysus is not the God behind the mask. He is the mask."*

There is an important parallel to be noted between the desire to find a single all-encompassing identity behind UFO reports and modern psychology's curious assumption that there exists a necessary separation between True Self (which is deep, good, abiding, and authentic) and False Self (which is a "mere" social role, a mask). Karl Kerenyi, who studied cultures in which personality is not conceived as a consistent singular substance, nor naturally moving toward such a goal, found moderns peculiarly obsessed with the notion that if we could take off all of our masks, the original, authentic, good, true man would emanate forth from the depths. Writes Paris: "This negative definition of the mask as something behind which one hides is just the opposite of the ancient concept of mask as a link between the person and the archetypal animal, ancestor, or divinity it embodied."

Here we come upon a splendid circularity. Conventional thinking holds that masks *conceal*. Dionysus teaches that masks also *reveal*. Efforts to "get beyond" the mask, typically framed in terms of revelation, also serve to conceal — especially assumptions, which, if revealed, might lead to doubts about the solidity of the patterns and regularities which *seem* to belong to a supposedly independent "reality."

Certainly the distinction between interior and exterior represents a deep-rooted habit of our thinking. Dionysus arrives on the scene not to reveal this distinction as false, but rather to turn our gaze on the extent to which the distinction — when taken literally — forces dichotomies (*inside vs. outside, idea vs. form, truth vs. appearance*) that have not been shown to exist in nature. The philosopher Gaston Bachelard, in a book called *The Poetics of Space*, notes that because the distinction between inside and outside has the same sharpness as the distinction between *yes* and *no*, "which decides everything," there is constant danger that the dichotomy will be "made into a basis of images that govern all thoughts of positive and negative."

From this vantage point, the disguise-as-deception motif in the UFO epic is seen to have a sort of necessity different from that commonly perceived. Ufologists must necessarily proceed with urgency to *unmask* and *get inside* the UFO phenomenon, not least so the drama can move to the next act. There is a "mythic necessity" to the mantralike pronouncements about imminent disclosures: "Any day now, the lid on the government cover-up's gonna blow sky-high." (In a domain where anything can be made meaningful, the fact that ufologists have been repeating this unfulfilled prophecy for over four decades does nothing to dampen the zeal of today's researchers, for whom the accumulation of past predictions curiously affirms their view that "it's only a matter of time... *any day now....*")

None of this is to suggest that military and civilian government officials have been forthcoming with information about their interest in or knowledge of UFOs — clearly much indicates otherwise. Alleged top-secret government UFO documents, anonymously released with whole sections tantalizingly blacked out, have the effect of affirming the disguise-as-deception myth with all the more vigor, thus fostering new efforts to reveal. So the spiral continues: masking, unmasking, displaying, concealing, always in the context of *getting closer to the deeply hidden truth*.

IT BEARS emphasizing that these figures — Hermes, Trickster, Dionysus, like their colleague Proteus — are ultimately neither more nor less real than those with human names. In the imagination of ancient

Greece, where mythic sensibility reigned with extraordinary depth, the gods were not considered at odds with, or disruptive of, the natural order of things. Rather, specific gods were understood to be present when particular kinds of events (protean, hermetic, dionysian) took place — present *in* and *as* the events.

The ancient gods who operate tacitly within the UFO epic do not ask to be worshipped in a conventional religious sense, nor do they seek to lead us "away from the real issues." Instead, the characteristic adventures of divine persons — tricking, cheating, contending, concealing, bargaining, blaming, conspiring, aspiring, longing, and so forth — symbolize the actual situations of our lives, including in the field of endeavor known as ufology.

Myth offers a background of images through which the UFO phenomenon might gain the deeper, richer, wider volume to which its events so consistently aspire. The fact that, for the most part, UFO researchers continue to seek precisely the opposite — a reduction of the phenomenon to a literal (singular, flat, unambiguous) understanding — doesn't mean the gods will go away. To the contrary: They will simply continue to play, *in disguise*, wrapping ufology all the more in their many and varied spells.

For as Joseph Campbell wrote: "The latest incarnation of Oedipus, the continued romance of Beauty and the Beast, stand this afternoon on the corner of Forty-second Street and Fifth Avenue, waiting for the traffic light to change."

NINE

———— ✕ ————

AS THE defining event of the fly-
ing saucer mythos, Kenneth Arnold's 1947 sighting in a very real sense
set the stage for everything to come connected with the term *UFO*.
Yet Arnold's legendary experience was not to be ufology's only defining event, just its first: a milepost that fostered a preliminary set of
assumptions ("they're either from outer space or they're not real") and
rituals (an ongoing debate ending in successive stalemates over particular sightings). These assumptions and rituals would, over the next two
decades, permit something called "the UFO phenomenon" to become
recognizable as a social and cultural fact.

But after the Condon committee debacle, the predictable speculations
and ceremonies of the UFO debate had grown both stale and sterile.
A new generation of researchers said it was time to refocus the debate
and thereby to revision UFOs, and vice versa. No one understood this
better than the young computer specialist and astrophysicist after whom
the character of the French scientist in the film *Close Encounters of the
Third Kind* was modeled. Jacques Vallee's defining moment had come.

In the mid-1960s, Vallee had authored a book called *Anatomy of a
Phenomenon*, still recognized by many as the most sophisticated scientifically based book exploring the origin, behavior, and physical nature
of UFOs. Vallee set out to transcend the prevailing emphasis on *explaining* — equally the pitfall of civilian UFO groups and debunkers, the

air force and conventional scientists — and instead turned to *analyzing* UFOs. Vallee's initiation into this perspective came about in 1961, during his work with the French Satellite Tracking Program, part of a worldwide research network that reported to the Smithsonian Astronomical Observatory.

One evening he and his coworkers tracked an elusive object that behaved abnormally for a satellite yet seemed not to be an airplane or a lighted balloon. Vallee felt the excitement of knowing he and his colleagues were *on* to something. But before they could feed their data on this object into the computer for analysis, their supervisor confiscated and erased the tape. The object no longer existed, for all intents and purposes.

For Vallee, the unknown (and now forever lost) object on the radar screen immediately paled in significance compared to the deliberate suppression of scientific evidence he had just witnessed. It was in trying to understand the reflexive action of his supervisor — who saw himself as a scientist no less than Vallee and his colleagues saw themselves as scientists — that Vallee became truly interested in the UFO phenomenon. As his study continued, he came to believe

> that one should not try to prove that UFOs constitute a new phenomenon of an unknown, possibly artificial nature before one has made an attempt to understand why such violent reactions are provoked by the thought of . . . contact with our civilization by nonhuman knowledge for nonhuman purposes, possibly prompted by nonhuman emotions and perceptions.

In 1969, Vallee the consummate scientist surprised many of his colleagues with his suggestion that UFOs may not be a "scientific" problem after all, for "modern science rules over a narrow universe, one particular variation on an infinite theme." Likewise, Vallee said, "ufology has become such a narrow field of specialization that the experts have no time left for general culture." He called on his colleagues to join him in moving beyond the limited — and increasingly obsessional — concern with whether UFOs are extraterrestrial in origin, and to begin probing the UFO phenomenon's impact on culture and our collective psyches.

For Jacques Vallee, this decision marked a fateful turn away from the hope of finding simple, uncomplicated answers about UFOs — and thus away from the mainstream of UFO research. He turned his attention to exploring historical, anthropological, and mythic literatures throughout the world and throughout history, there discovering remarkable parallels between religious apparitions, the fairy-faith, reports of dwarf-like beings with supernatural powers, the Great Airship sightings of the nineteenth century, and the modern events called UFOs. In one sense, Vallee reached a conclusion similar to that of debunkers — *UFOs are mythic*. But unlike debunkers, for whom myth is synonymous with falsehood and delusion, Vallee came to believe that the parallels among UFOs and these realms are real, and profound, because behind them all lies an extraordinary mechanism that shapes consciousness and culture in complex and substantial ways.

In a book called *Passport to Magonia*, Vallee journeyed well beyond the specific frame of reference involving UFOs and probed the larger mechanism that generates religious visions, mystical raptures, appearances by supernatural creatures, and flying saucers — all relying on the same processes and mechanisms, all sharing similar characteristics and effects on the human observer, *depending on the predominant belief structure of a given culture*. Ezekiel saw a burning wheel. In the Middle Ages, angels and fiery crosses and shields appeared in the sky, and a legendary celestial region called Magonia was said to be inhabited by extraordinary beings who traveled in aerial "cloud ships," sometimes descending to abduct unsuspecting humans. In nineteenth-century America, people saw airships resembling zeppelins. Since 1947, we have seen flying saucers.

Summarizing his extensive familiarity with modern UFO sightings and his growing understanding of parallels from history and myth, Vallee put forth five self-evident "principal facts":

1. Since the middle of 1946, among the public in nations throughout the world, "an extremely active generation of colorful rumors" has emerged, centering on "a considerable number of observations of unknown machines close to the ground in rural areas, the physical traces left by these machines, and their various effects on humans and animals."
2. The underlying archetypes of the saucer myth "coincide to a remarkable degree with the widespread belief among all peoples concerning entities whose physical and psychological descriptions place them in the same category as the present-day ufonauts."

3. The entities reported fall into various biological types, including "beings of giant stature, men indistinguishable from us, winged creatures, and various types of monsters."
4. The absurd behavior of the entities, the ludicrous appearance of their craft, and the typically misleading nature of their pronouncements are consistent with reports of human encounters with extraordinary entities throughout history, and serve both to keep professional scientists from taking such reports seriously and to give the saucer myth its religious and mystical overtones.
5. "The mechanism of the apparitions, in legendary, historical, and modern times, is standard and follows the model of religious miracles."

In light of these five principles, Vallee cautioned, "it is quite conceivable that nature should present us with circumstances so deeply organized that our observational and logical errors would entirely mask the pattern to be solved." With this remark, Vallee became one of the first of a long line of researchers to challenge the assumption — dear to proponents and debunkers alike — that the mere cataloging of sighting reports would necessarily and inevitably bring about a definitive resolution of the UFO phenomenon. In fact, the collection of cases by true believers on both sides, in the name of finding *"the answer,"* was just as likely to obscure the phenomenon further as to clarify it.

This was not a possibility to which members of the Condon committee or leaders of the civilian research groups had given much consideration, understandably. The presumption that the UFO phenomenon can and would be "cracked" — reduced to a pattern accessible to human comprehension — was an article of faith for both sides, as it remains today. Without the defense that this assumption provides, how could determined efforts to find answers not seem comic? (Apart from all apparent disagreement, civilian ufologists and debunkers shared one plot of common ground: neither group wished to appear ridiculous.)*

---

*Ironically, the effort to avoid appearing ridiculous, when pursued as an end in itself or as an obsession, almost always appears ridiculous. The philosopher Henri Bergson defines an object or situation as laughable when it gives the appearance of "something mechanical in something living." By so often seeming to be little more than an arena for habitual, predictable stances ("UFOs *must* be real" versus "UFOs *can't* be real"), ufology consistently slips into the kind of unconscious self-parody familiar to audiences of absurdist theater. (In Samuel Beckett's play *Waiting for Godot*, for instance, the

But Vallee was not calling for UFO investigation simply to be abandoned. Rather, he urged his fellow researchers to delve even more deeply into the phenomenon, realizing all along

> that the universe might contain intelligent creatures exhibiting such an organization that no model of it could be constructed on the basis of currently classified concepts.... The behavior of such beings would then necessarily appear random or absurd, or would go undetected, especially if they possessed physical means of retiring at will beyond the human perceptual range.

No matter whether the phenomenon is natural or artificial in nature, Vallee concluded, "we are presented with the dual possibility of long-term unsolvability and of continued manifestation." That a new myth should be nourished on this duality is entirely predictable, he added. Indeed, the consistency of UFO observations, combined with their apparent irreconcilability with scientific knowledge, creates a logical vacuum that the human imagination cannot but seek to fill with its own fantasies.

Unlike the report of the Condon project or the writings of Donald Keyhoe, *Passport to Magonia* did not create large waves at popular levels. Instead its impact was felt especially among a new school of thinkers and researchers for whom the redundant one-dimensional debate about UFOs consistently negated the phenomenon's thematic richness. Vallee's message was also heard by general readers who would never join the ranks of active investigators, but who longed for ideas and images capable of releasing greater significance from the phenomenon's fertile depths.

AT ABOUT 10:30 on the night of October 18, 1973, a four-man army reserve helicopter left Columbus, Ohio, for its home base of Cleveland Hopkins airport. Captain Lawrence J. Coyne, with nineteen years of flying experience, was sitting in the right-hand seat. Next to him, at the controls, sat First Lieutenant Arrigo Jezzi, behind whom sat Sergeant John Healey, the flight medic. Sergeant Robert Yanacsek, a computer technician, was behind Coyne. The night was calm, clear,

---

characters wait expectantly, with "robotic" enthusiasm, for the arrival of Monsieur Godot, never realizing what is unmistakably clear to the audience: their waiting is in vain.)

and filled with stars. The copter was cruising at 2,500 feet, at a speed of ninety knots.

About ten miles south of Mansfield, Yanacsek alerted Captain Coyne to a red light on the southeast horizon. Coyne glanced over, noticed the light, took it to be distant traffic, and told Yanacsek to "keep an eye on it." Thirty seconds later, Yanacsek announced that the light had banked toward the helicopter and appeared to be closing in. To avoid a collision, Coyne immediately put the craft into a twenty-degree dive at 2,000 feet per minute. After initial contact with the Mansfield tower, the radio went dead. As they neared 1,700 feet, the object was still heading straight for the helicopter. The crew braced for impact.

Just as a collision seemed inevitable, the object stopped about 500 feet above and in front of the helicopter. "It wasn't cruising, it was *stopped*. For maybe ten to twelve seconds — just *stopped*," Yanacsek reported. The crew stared in amazement at what was in front of them: a sixty-foot-long gray metallic object resembling a streamlined fat cigar delineated against the background stars. At the front end was a red light, at the rear a green spotlight that had swung around to envelop the cockpit in green light.

After about ten seconds of hovering, the object began to accelerate off to the west-northwest, with only a white "tail" light visible. As the object made a climbing turn and disappeared, Coyne caught sight of his altimeter. To his surprise, the needle was rising. All controls were set for a twenty-degree dive, but the copter was *rising* at 1,000 feet per minute. The helicopter reached nearly 3,800 feet before Coyne regained control of his craft. The crew had watched the unknown object continuously for a period of four to five minutes. Radio contact was achieved at 2,500 feet, and the flight proceeded uneventfully.

Five witnesses on the ground (identified as Mrs. E.C. and four adolescents) had pulled their car to the shoulder of the road and watched both the helicopter and the object ("like a blimp . . . as big as a school bus . . . sort of pear-shaped"). They saw the object hover over the helicopter, then cover the area with green light. "It was like rays coming down," the witnesses said. "The helicopter, the trees, the road, the car — everything turned green." The frightened kids jumped back in the car and Mrs. E.C. drove on. Their subsequent report of their continuing observations squared with the object's motions as described independently by the crew.

Philip Klass determined (or simply asserted, said his detractors) that the Mansfield UFO was really a large fireball of the Orinoid meteor shower, which would have appeared red as it entered the atmosphere at high speed. The blue-green color of the meteor (characteristic of the Orinoid shower) then reflected off the overhead portion of the helicopter's green-tinted canopy, creating the mere impression of a green light flooding the cockpit. The meteor's "hovering" was likewise illusory: nothing more than the long, luminous tail of the meteor passing over the helicopter. The men were so understandably frightened by the meteor that their observations — individual and collective — were fundamentally mistaken, said Klass. It only *seemed* that they watched something "hovering" for several minutes, for even the most spectacular meteors are relatively short-lived phenomena.

All four crew members insisted that the duration of the event was approximately five minutes. They all saw a precisely defined metallic gray object come to a nearly complete stop and maneuver at a hard angle. UFO researcher Jennie Zeidman ruled out the possibility of a high-performance airplane as being at odds with the characteristics of the unusual object as reported by crew and ground witnesses. Once again, the public was presented all the details of the event and heard the debate about the details, and was left to decide for itself. The legend that a flying saucer had rescued an army helicopter caught in a dangerous dive proved ultimately more compelling in the public mind than the mundane alternatives, although indeed the facts of this case made conventional explanations seem forced.

Over the years, Klass attempted to diminish Coyne's credibility through a strained guilt-by-association strategy. On November 27, 1978, Coyne was invited to speak before the United Nations Special Political Committee, along with Allen Hynek and Jacques Vallee, on the subject of UFOs. Klass cited this as evidence that "Coyne has become an international celebrity in the world of UFOlogy." Klass then noted that the U.N. presentation had been arranged by the prime minister of the island Grenada, Sir Eric Gairy, who (on being toppled from power) was accused by his successor of practicing witchcraft during his term as prime minister. After thus linking Coyne (and, by extension, Hynek and Vallee) with an alleged occultist, Klass let the matter drop.

NASA consultant James Oberg has dismissed as many UFO claims as Klass, earning his own stripes in the halls of debunking. Yet Oberg called the army helicopter case "truly spectacular and unexplainable." Said Oberg:

> Something that behaved like an alien spaceship might be expected to behave was reported by four credible witnesses; the stimulus must have been something truly extraordinary. Such reports in the past have turned out to have been honest misperceptions, but there are features of this case much harder to explain. The Coyne UFO flies on, one of the best on record.

IT IS Thursday, October 11, 1973, one week prior to the Mansfield helicopter incident. Charlie Hickson, forty-five, and Calvin Parker, eighteen, of Pascagoula, Mississippi, are fishing in the Pascagoula River somewhere between 7 and 9 P.M. Charlie snags his line, and starts cussing because he's lost his bait. He leans back to his tackle box. That's when he sees *it*, over his shoulder: a blue light about two miles away approaching very quickly — how fast he has no idea — to within about forty yards in front of him and his pal Calvin. There an oblong-shaped object hovers eight to ten feet above the ground.

Hickson later said it made a "little buzzin' sound — *nnnnnnnn, nnnnnnnn* — just like that, that's all. . . . We was right on the river. It didn't hit the ground. It hovered. And all of a sudden — right in the end of it — this opening was laid up there, and three of them just floated out of the thing," moving toward Hickson and Parker, who simply sat and stared, too terrified to even jump into the river, as both considered doing. Parker passed out from fright; Hickson was picked up by his arms and carried inside the hovering craft.

Thus begins one of ufology's most fantastic cases.

On the following day, news media throughout the world picked up the following story from the wire services of United Press International:

PASCAGOULA, Miss. — Two shipyard workers who claimed they were hauled aboard a UFO and examined by silver-skinned creatures with big eyes and pointed ears were checked today at a military hospital and found to be free of radiation. . . .

Jackson County chief deputy Barney Mathis said the men told him they were fishing from an old pier on the west bank of the Pascagoula River about 7 P.M. Thursday when they noticed a strange craft about two miles away emitting a bluish haze.

They said it moved closer and then appeared to hover about three or four feet above the water, then "three whatever-they-weres came out, either floating or walking, and carried us into the ship," officers quoted Hickson as saying.

"The things had big eyes. They kept us about twenty minutes, photographed us, and then took us back to the pier. The only sound they made was a buzzing-humming sound. They left in a flash."

"These are reliable people," Sheriff Diamond said. "They had no reason to say this if it had not been true. I know something did happen to them."

The sheriff said the "spacecraft" was described as fish-shaped, about ten feet square with an eight foot ceiling. The occupants were said to have pale silvery-gray skin, no hair, long pointed ears and noses with an opening for a mouth and hands "like crab claws."

Parker had remained unconscious throughout the ordeal and remembered nothing after seeing the creatures coming toward him. Hickson said he was taken into a brilliantly lit, circular room where, after being suspended in midair in a horizontal position, a free-floating object, resembling a huge eye, scanned up and down his body as part of an examination of some sort. Soon both men were returned to the riverbank, and the creatures floated back inside the UFO and left immediately. It was then that Parker came to.

Two days later, Allen Hynek arrived in Pascagoula to investigate the sighting — this time not for the air force (those days were over for good) but as director of his own new civilian research group, the Center for UFO Studies, headquartered near Chicago. Ralph Blum, an investigative journalist who had hopped the same flight as Hynek, turned to Sheriff Diamond and asked about Hickson and Parker. Diamond looked very hard at Blum and answered:

"First thing they wanted to do was take a lie detector test. Charlie — he was shook bad. You don't see a forty-five-year-old man break down and cry from excitement unless it's something fierce that happened. He said to me, 'After what I already went through on this earth, why did I have to go through this?' " The sheriff added: "Charlie, he said inside the spaceship he was laid down on *nothing* — he was weightless. He floated! And Calvin — I'm not easily convinced, but I heard that boy pray when he was alone and thought that nobody could hear. That was enough for me."

The sheriff's deputy said they had done all they could to find holes in the two men's story, even leaving them alone in a room where a hidden tape recorder had been left running. Here is an excerpt from the secretly recorded conversation between the two men:

CALVIN: I got to get home and get to bed or get some nerve pills or see the doctor or something. I can't stand it. I'm about to go crazy.

CHARLIE: I tell you, when we through, I'll get you something to settle you down so you can get some damn sleep.

CALVIN: I can't sleep yet like it is. I'm just damn near crazy.

CHARLIE: Well, Calvin, when they brought you out — when they brought me out of that thing, goddamn it I like to never in hell got you straightened out.

CALVIN (his voice rising): My damn arms, my arms, I remember they just froze up and I can't move. Just like I stepped on a damn rattlesnake.

CHARLIE: They didn't do me that way.

CALVIN: I passed out. I expect I never passed out in my whole life.

CHARLIE: I've never seen nothin' like that before in my life. You can't make people believe it —

CALVIN: I don't want to keep sittin' here. I want to see a doctor —

CHARLIE: They better wake up and start believin' . . . they better start believin'.

CALVIN: You see how that damn door come right up?

CHARLIE: I don't know how it opened, son. I don't know.

CALVIN: It just laid up and just like that those son' bitches — just like that they come out.

CHARLIE: I know. You can't believe it. You can't make people believe it —

CALVIN: I paralyzed right then. I couldn't move —

CHARLIE: They won't believe it. They gonna believe it one of these days. Might be too late. I knew all along they was people from other worlds up there. I knew all along. I never thought it would happen to me.

CALVIN: You know yourself I don't drink.

CHARLIE: I know that, son. When I get to the house I'm gonna get me another drink, make me sleep. Look, what we sittin' around for. I gotta go tell Blanche. What we waitin' for?

CALVIN (panicky): I gotta go to the house. I'm gettin' sick. I gotta get out of here.

Police captain Glen Ryder said: "If they were lying . . . they should be in Hollywood."

On Sunday, October 14, Hickson and Parker agreed to be hypnotized by California UFO researcher James Harder, who placed considerable weight on the testimony recovered through hypnosis in UFO cases. (Debunkers claim that the process creates false memories and, worse, further victimizes witnesses by subjecting them to pro-UFO researchers' preconceived conclusions about invaders from outer space. Proponents say hypnosis unlocks authentic memories buried either by fear or by alien-induced amnesia, sometimes both.) Not surprisingly, Harder, a strong advocate of the extraterrestrial visitation hypothesis, emerged from the session with an unambiguous assessment: "There was definitely something here that was not terrestrial, of the earth."

Hynek refused to join Harder's instantaneous interpretation. "Terrifying experience of some sort, yes. But captured and taken aboard a strange craft from another planet? It's premature to say anything like that." For his part, Philip Klass found Hynek's statement as misleading in its own way as Harder's because the idea that the two men's *experience* was real effectively conveyed to the public that a real *event* had taken place. And the evidence that a real event had transpired was decidedly weak, according to America's premier UFO-basher.

Why, Klass demanded to know, were there no other witnesses to so spectacular an event occurring only a few hundred yards from heavily traveled Highway 90? Klass located a bridge attendant from whose post the abduction site was plainly visible. Wouldn't he have seen something? Hickson responded that the attendant usually sat with his back to the abduction site. As for motorists, Hickson claimed that high bushes, weeds, and the bridge railing probably obscured the area from view. In Hickson's defense, Sheriff Diamond revealed that three unnamed motorists — including a minister and a former Pascagoula city councilman — had seen a UFO "flying low in the direction where the men were." Two days later, a meteorologist from nearby Columbia, Mississippi, reported picking up "what I thought to be an aircraft" on his radar screen. "It got rather close to the station, about three miles, then it became stationary and all of a sudden my radar just completely jammed."

Irrelevant hearsay evidence, Klass retorted, insisting that the question of the two men's credibility had gotten buried by a pro-UFO stampede. Not so, responded proponents, who reminded Klass that

Hickson had passed a lie detector test, a fact that trumpeted in national headlines such as UFO STORY STANDS UP TO LIE TEST." Klass was unimpressed. He claimed that the operator who administered Hickson's polygraph test was neither licensed to do so nor experienced enough to be taken seriously. Besides, Klass added, a lie detector test indicates only that the subject being tested believes his story — it can't prove objective truth.

From this point, the Pascagoula case degenerated rather quickly into the kind of shouting war familiar to viewers of televised wrestling matches. If Klass was so skeptical about the value of polygraph tests, *why was he so insistent that Hickson be tested a second time?* If Hickson's devotees were so confident of his credibility, *why did Hickson decide at the last moment not to take a second test?* Even the appearance of the creatures generated controversy.

Researchers increasingly inclined to take abduction reports seriously were disturbed that the creatures seen by Hickson and Parker were "too fantastic" — that is, they didn't fit the emerging profile of alien anatomy emerging from other such reports. An Ohio ufologist named Leonard Stringfield took exception to this point, saying that the creatures seen in Pascagoula bore a strong resemblance to aliens reported by a Cincinnati man in 1955. So what? responded skeptics. Hickson and Parker may have seen Stringfield's book containing an illustration and description, and unknowingly adjusted their riverside perceptions in accordance.

Even though no one had alleged that these two residents of a small Mississippi bayou town had delved into the literature of UFOs, this claim — while probably false — seemed right at home in a debate whose limits were as ambiguous as the debate's subject: what had happened to Charlie Hickson and Calvin Parker that night by the river. The affair slowly faded from view with Hynek terming the case one of the most compelling on record and making his familiar call for an international group of scientists to seriously investigate the UFO problem. Philip Klass continued making the most of discrepancies in Hickson and Parker's accounts of the time of the abduction and the size and shape of the craft.

Today both sides continue to cite the case as a classic instance of their (diametrically opposed) overall positions on UFOs. In fact, the case became a classic not because it was airtight from an evidential standpoint but rather because it was *not*. For either side of the ongoing argument to truly win would violate one of ufology's unspoken rules: *the debate must continue*. The Incident at Pascagoula, as it came to be known in UFO annals, left an indelible impression in the American psyche at the height of the 1973–1974 UFO wave and was reinforced in its "charisma" by the much-publicized Coyne helicopter sighting a week later.

Certainly the whole nation would not recall all the details of the arguments and counterarguments in the Pascagoula debate; these tended to overload even ufological advocates seeking to prove one outcome or another. Instead it was the specific images of the "claw-men," the "silvery-skinned creatures," and the "pointy-eared saucer folk," along with Hickson and Parker's obviously sincere attempts to make sense of their experience, that most people would recall when they thought of this case — just as images of Betty and Barney Hill's terrifying roadside capture, and of Captain Coyne's helicopter being sucked upward by a UFO, would stand out for most people who followed the events of this period.

Charlie Hickson, by contrast, would remember *everything*. As he told journalist Ralph Blum:

"You know at night, I lie in bed and think about them."

"Are you still afraid?"

"No, the fear's gone," Charlie said gravely. "If I can, I think I'd like to get in touch with them. I mean it. Every night when I'm in bed, it's almost a picture that comes into my mind. Just the same way every time."

"Are you reliving what happened?"

"No. I'm not inside the ship, they're just there. All I have to do is close my eyes."

THE fact that the appearance of the creatures seen in Pascagoula resembled accounts of remarkable beings from myth, legend, and fairy tales did nothing to dampen the recurring suspicion that the flying saucer phenomenon far predated Kenneth Arnold's 1947 sighting near Mount Rainier. Throughout this period, a Swiss former hotel manager, bartender, and waiter named Erich von Däniken tapped into this sentiment by proposing that between 10,000 and 40,000 years ago superintelligent astronauts arrived on Earth, mated with early humans, and produced *Homo sapiens*.

Von Däniken's first and most successful book, *Chariots of the Gods?*, achieved enormous success in Europe before being published in the United States in 1970. Looking to Nazca on the plains of Peru, von Däniken was moved to pose compelling rhetorical questions: Who else but ancient astronauts could have "induced the pre-Incan peoples to build the fantastic lines, the landing strips" visible only from the air? How else but from ancient astronauts did semisavages in the Fertile Crescent "suddenly" give birth to a culture comparable in majesty to that of the Sumerians, with mathematics, astronomy, and a written language? Are we really to believe that the awesome stonework of the Bolivian city of Tiahuanaco was fashioned by people who had "nothing better to do than spend years — without tools — fashioning conduits of such precision that our modern concrete conduits seem the work of mere bunglers in comparison?"

The response to the exposition of these ideas in a total of six books was instantaneous — and extremely mixed. Sales approaching 50 million copies (continuing into the 1990s) indicated an unprecedented public welcome for von Däniken, who appeared at a time when debate about ambiguous encounters with strange saucers and their occupants had reached a tendentious stalemate. There was a certain irresistible appeal for many in his provocative nonstop questions. Instead of sending radio telescope signals into space, "why don't we first or simultaneously seek the traces of unknown intelligence on our earth?" Tired of ufology's debate about evidence, and suspicious of science's unwillingness to take UFO reports seriously, the public mind was primed for a writer who "seizes upon every megalith, every seemingly technical vestige of lost civilizations, practically every known myth or religious tale that mentions gods from the heavens, to make the case that conventional theories of history and archeology cannot explain the evolution of human intelligence," as science writer Randall Fitzgerald put it.

For once, ufologists and mainstream scientists had something to agree on: opposition to what they considered von Däniken's outrageous metaphysical assumptions disguised as empirical research. In response to von Däniken's claim about ancient Peruvian landing strips, astronomer (and UFO skeptic) Carl Sagan snorted: "The space vehicle sets down on the ground, the great bay opens, and out wheel what? B-24 Liberators, Spitfires? Most remarkable that they need airfields." Others scoffed at many hundreds of obvious factual errors, including von Däniken's assertion that Sumerian culture simply appeared *tout ensemble* rather than — as archaeological records clearly demonstrate — over a period of 6,000 years.

Many ufologists feared that von Däniken's theories, which resembled those of contactee George Adamski and of occult philosophers through the ages, would further damage efforts to build a scientific basis for UFO research. But two of ufology's leading voices saw deeper significance in von Däniken's success, even as they criticized his cavalier scholarship and unfounded claims. Allen Hynek suggested that von Däniken had "touched a sensitive nerve in our collective unconscious." Jacques Vallee agreed: "There's a big credibility gap between the scientist and the public. . . . von Däniken just dramatized the existence of the gap."

BY THE mid-1970s, another kind of gap was in effect: a new clearing within which UFOs could suddenly flourish with unforeseen respectability. Between 1973 and 1974, during one of the biggest waves in UFO history, thousands of people across the United States reported *happenings* of various types: distant and high-level silvery disks, nocturnal meandering lights, car-chasing incidents, instances of UFOs interfering with mechanical and/or electromagnetic equipment, UFO landings leaving traces behind, frightening animals, and having physical and psychological effects on humans; and of course more occupant sightings, often featuring monsters who refused to conform to Hollywood's portrayal of the "classic outer space alien."

The most significant shift in the UFO plot was the absence of official involvement by the air force. As of December 17, 1969, Project Blue Book became history, ending the air force's twenty-two year study of unidentified flying objects. A new social and political context could now emerge, writes David Jacobs, who noted that in all previous UFO sightings,

> the Air Force had acted as the official body that made pronouncements and judgments about the reports. . . . Through its press releases, its system of classifying reports, and its assumed authority and expertise on the subject, the Air Force had pushed public opinion toward disbelieving and ridiculing UFO witnesses. . . . Without an official government body assuring the public that it had found no evidence to suggest that UFOs were extraterrestrial, or even anomalous or extraordinary, the American people for the first time in twenty-five years could indulge in unrestrained interest in the phenomenon.

The 1973–1974 wave was all the more remarkable given that it followed on the heels of the Condon committee's "official" declaration that UFOs did not exist (except for the 25 percent termed "unsolved" in the back pages of its report). Many younger scientists who noted the discrepancy in the Condon project's verdict quietly began studying the phenomenon during the mid-1970s, making good use of the air force's release of accumulated sighting reports.

And, of course, they could look with respect to ufology's elder statesman, Allen Hynek, whose Phoenixlike rise from the ashes of the swamp gas fiasco was nothing short of spectacular. In 1973, at age sixty-four, Hynek realized a longstanding dream when he founded the Center for UFO Studies (CUFOS) in Northfield, Illinois, the first UFO study group under scientific direction. His new position as chair of Northwestern University's astronomy department signaled to scientists still on the sideline that keeping company with flying saucers would not necessarily prove to be the kiss of death.

In 1969, a group of APRO members, dissatisfied with what they saw as the increasing dogmatism of its founders, walked away from the organization and started one of their own: the Mutual UFO Network, led by Walt Andrus of Seguin, Texas. By the mid-1970s, Donald Keyhoe's NICAP held the least stature of all the civilian UFO groups, largely because its leaders had placed all its eggs in a small basket: habitually pressing demands for congressional hearings and an end to the alleged massive government conspiracy witholding truth about UFOs. (Now in retirement, Keyhoe spent his final political capital championing a plan to build a large model of a UFO on a vast parcel of vacant land. This, he hoped, would attract the aliens' attention and entice them to stop to get to know us. Keyhoe's project provided ample grist for satirists.)

A new attitude of fair-mindedness became apparent in news media coverage after the Condon catharsis, a shift that bore some relation to the sudden absence of the air force as final arbiter of the phenomenon's reality. Where in previous waves the media took pains to highlight the incredible claims of contactees, the television networks now seemed to compete in proving their absence of bias. NBC's "Today" show featured conversations with UFO witnesses and astronauts on the same panel; other programs offered enthusiastic free-for-alls between proponents and debunkers. NBC reporter John Chancellor captured the new spirit of openness best with a commentary clearly departing from the "silly season" editorializing of years past:

> Many people would like the UFOs to go away. But the UFOs won't go away, and many scientists are taking them very seriously. It's likely that we will hear more and more about the UFOs.

Likely, indeed; the epic was far from finished. With the air force no longer the official bogeyman (temporarily), civilian ufologists had what they wanted: free access to the UFO phenomenon. But there was a dark side to the victory: the new populist spirit of UFO research meant that anyone could get into the act — and "anyone" did, simply because the qualifications to be a ufologist were finally as vague as the definition of UFOs themselves.

For those who tracked these elusive events, the compelling new question concerned the phenomenon's origins: remote galaxies in outer space versus extraordinary dimensions closer than we dare imagine. The debunkers, as always, listed three other options: hoax, hallucination, misidentification; *only* these. Inevitably, most players would bring to the coming round the same gnawing hunger for *unambiguous* answers. Divisive new battles loomed.

TEN

—————— ✕ ——————

APPRECIATING the decisive
nature of Jacques Vallee's contribution to the unfolding UFO epic is
easier when he is compared to other equally defining personalities within
the drama. Vallee belongs in the same category as Kenneth Arnold,
Carl Jung, Betty and Barney Hill, and Allen Hynek — all appearing
at crucial turning points, their individual and collective presence permanently altering the course of the plot.

Kenneth Arnold's 1947 encounter with nine aerial objects undulating
"like saucers" ranks with other great opening moments in narrative —
even if it lacks the literary polish of the *Iliad*'s "Sing, goddess, of the
wrath of Achilles." All emerges out of Arnold's initial situation, focused
around an amazing sighting, "the coming into being of a deed and its
consequences on the human soul," as Gustav Freytag described the
focus of true drama. A playwright would do well to invent a character
like Arnold and place him so squarely within a conflict that would remain vital long after he was gone from the stage.

Does Jung belong in the same category, but not Donald Keyhoe?
I believe the answer is yes. Keyhoe, although influential, remained active
at one only plane, the plot's horizontal surface. Defining characters are
here presented as those whose actions significantly touched both surface
and depth, who turned our attention — deliberately or not — to the

vivid doubleness of our plot. Jung, the Swiss-born son of a Protestant minister, understood that the seemingly new events in the sky mirrored important changes in the human soul. Some of his UFO ponderings seem tenuous, even forced, in retrospect; and his soliloquy came during an unexpected brief walk-on appearance that provoked little response at the time. But the lines Jung spoke *mattered*, especially "We have here a golden opportunity of seeing how a legend is formed." This from one for whom *legend* and *myth* were never spoken dismissively.

Betty and Barney Hill became legendary exemplars of Woody Allen's maxim "Ninety percent of life is showing up." Although not actually the first to be abducted by aliens, they continue to hold that ceremonial title, and rightfully, for their experience instantly became the one against which all others of that genre would be measured, correctly or otherwise. Betty Hill retains an active interest in UFOs, and is never shy about challenging latter-day efforts to dismiss the experience she shared with husband Barney, who died in 1969.

Allen Hynek showed himself to be one of the few characters in the entire epic to grow, in a dramatic sense, according to Aristotle's time-honored criterion: gaining crucial recognition through experience. Hynek's ordeal over swamp gas recalls tragic Othello's awakening, at the end, to himself as "one that loved not wisely but too well." Yet Hynek was not to be a tragic figure, in the classic sense of awakening too late to avoid death, or a deathlike condition like Oedipus's blindness. Instead, like the heroes of Shakespeare's comedies, Hynek opened his eyes to the big mistake of his life (running errands too long for the air force in the name of "science"), discovered his better nature, found "enlightenment," and began all over again as a member of a reformed social order. (His fellow ufologists enthusiastically welcomed their chastened elder hero.)

Each of these players increased the tension between the story's surface and its depth, if only by virtue of raising questions about what *could* be going on with the events called UFOs.

Enter Jacques Vallee. In 1969, young (he was thirty at the time) and clearly gifted, he appeared on stage in a limelight all his own for the first but not the last time. Like the shakers and shapers named above, Vallee directed attention to the disparity between appearance and reality in the UFO controversy. But he did so in an original way. This French-born astrophysicist and computer specialist did not say simply that the hidden mythic underpinnings of the phenomenon deserved attention; this had been done well by Jung and sensationally by von Däniken. Vallee went considerably further, reversing the playing field itself by saying that what is below their surface — *the symbolic* — is actually more significant than the UFOs themselves, whatever they may actually be.

This point merits elaboration. The literary scholar Angus Fletcher, our authority on the ways and means of the genre, had already noted that "allegories are based on parallels between two levels of being that correspond to each other, the one supposed by the reader, the other literally presented in the fable." The reader of Orwell's *Animal Farm*, for instance, comes to recognize that the tale about barnyard animals presented literally corresponds to a secondary plot about the dangers of authoritarian forms of governance. In a strict sense, the surface story of any allegory, although apparently *primary*, is actually *secondary* to the deeper meanings below. "Allegorical stories exist, as it were, to put secondary meanings into orbit around them; the primary meaning is then valued for its satellites," Fletcher wrote.

Vallee made it clear that he understood this relationship through and through. Although he himself began studying UFO sightings for their own special relevance, over time he concluded that these modern events (flyovers, landings, occupant interactions) were but a formality — a kind of "front" — for a larger, fundamentally *disguised* interaction between humankind and a parent source engaged in slowly (over a period of centuries) and largely *imperceptibly* shaping human imagination by offering displays of image-events coherent enough to be noticed but too fundamentally complex to be grasped in their entirety.

Citing case after case, Vallee insisted that the events called *UFOs* and *flying saucers* are "nothing but a resurgence of a deep stream in human culture known in older times under various names," a continuum that "leads directly from primitive magic, through mystical experience, the fairy-faith, and religion, to modern flying saucers," even to the practice of witchcraft through the ages. Vallee went beyond naming thematic parallels among these realms (although he did this masterfully) to argue that "the mechanisms that have generated these various beliefs are identical."

The surface phenomena of these domains vary, he said, "as a function of the cultural environment into which they are projected." But behind the flux were "stable, invariant features" of a larger phenomena-generating technology. *This* was the context that Vallee wished to explore, not the meanings of flying saucers in a category by themselves.

Here are the kinds of correspondences that interested young Jacques Vallee. Because the time span to be covered is vast, we will have to move quickly, establishing a thematic tapestry, a motion picture of sorts.

ON JUNE 15, 1952, a team of archaeologists led by Alberto Ruz Lhuillier made a remarkable discovery in the jungles of the Yucatan, in the state of Chiapas at the site of a well-known Mayan city then undergoing systematic restoration. Inside an enormous construction known as the Pyramid of Inscriptions lay a splendid crypt, which, despite the high temperatures and constant humidity of this area of the world, had not deteriorated. On a single carved stone measuring twelve by seven feet was depicted a sophisticated and complex device, with a man operating an elaborate piece of machinery. The man's knees were brought up toward his chest and his back turned toward a mechanism trailing flames.

The Mayan civilization is widely held to have vanished without having discovered the basic principles of technology — including the wheel, say some archaeologists. Had the Mayans encountered spaceship-faring visitors from a superior civilization, as speculated by Soviet science writer Alexander Kazantsev? Such an interpretation is not easy to prove, Vallee notes. He adds, however, that "the only object we know today closely resembling the Mayan design is the space capsule."

THE Jomon Era of ancient Japan, ending around 3000 B.C., mastered the art of making earthen statues. The earliest such artifacts were quite simple, yet by the middle of the period, artisans began making larger statues featuring a markedly different design: large chests, arc-shaped legs, abbreviated arms, and large heads clearly covered with round helmets. Some archaeologists proposed that the headgear was actually a mourning mask used at burials. However, some of the statues uncovered in the Tohoku area of northern Japan "show something like a pair of 'sunglasses': huge eyes with an insectlike slit — a truly remarkable design," Vallee states. Other designs carved on soft stone feature costumes with large goggles and one-piece suits with wide collars.

*O*CTOBER 27, 1180. A remarkable luminus object characterized as an "earthenware vessel" soars from a mountain in the Kii Province of Japan beyond the northeast mountain of Fukuhara at midnight, gradually changing its course until the only sight left is its luminous tail.

September 12, 1271. The famous priest Nichiren is about to be beheaded at Tatsunokuchi, when suddenly there appears in the sky a bright, shiny object like a full moon. Officials panic; the execution is canceled.

March 8, 1468. A dark object making a "sound like a wheel" flies from Mount Kasuga westward at midnight. Its sound and color are difficult to explain in natural terms.

A.H. CLOUGH, in his book *Introduction to Plutarch's Lives*, recorded the details of an event that foreshadows Betty and Barney Hill's experience centuries later:

> One day, among other instances, it chanced at Lyons that three men and a woman were seen descending from . . . wonderfully constructed aerial ships, whose flying squadrons roved at the will of the Zephyrs. . . . The entire city gathered around them, crying out that they were magicians. . . . In vain the four innocents sought to vindicate themselves by saying that they were their own country-folk, and had been carried away a short time since by miraculous men who had shown them unheard-of marvels. . . . The frenzied populace paid no heed to their defence, and were on the point of casting them into the fire, when the worthy Agobard, Bishop of Lyons . . . came running at the noise, and having heard the accusations of the people and the defense of the accused, gravely pronounced that . . . it was not true that these men had fallen from the sky, and that what they said they had seen there was impossible.

Shall we name Bishop Agobard the first "UFO debunker"? If we incline to dismiss this account as "mere folklore," we are then obliged to similarly reject myriad reports through the Middle Ages of people consistently encountering beings they called the Elementals. And if we do that, we must then ask why we should take similarly consistent modern UFO reports as "fact" rather than "folklore." For *the same mechanism is in place now as it was then,*" Vallee insists.*

IN WALTER Evans Wentz's classic book *The Fairy-Faith in Celtic Countries,* Patrick Water gives this description of a "fairy-man": "A crowd of boys out in the fields one day saw a fairy-man with a red cap. Except for his height he was like any other man. He was about three and a half feet tall. . . . And he disappeared as he walked away in the direction of the old fort." A local citizen gave this account of the fairies, or the Gentry:

> They are not a working-class but a military-aristocratic class . . . a distinct race between our race and that of spirits, as they have told me. Their qualifications are tremendous: "We could cut off half the human race, but would not," they said, "for we are expecting salvation." And I knew a man three or four years ago whom they struck down with paralysis. Their sight is so penetrating that I think they could see through the earth.

Through his work as a UFO field investigator, Vallee had come across nearly identical descriptions of "spacemen" offering similar accounts of their prowess. When he took a closer look at the fairy-faith, Vallee encountered "documented stories of babies kidnapped by the elves and of the terrestrial animals they hunt and take away," themes echoed respectively in modern abduction narratives and in accounts of cattle mutilated by outer space predators (described in chapter eleven).

In his impressive 1982 doctoral dissertation on correlations among UFOs and similar phenomena in folklore, both contemporary and past, folklorist Thomas Bullard pursued leads similar to those that intrigued

---

*The idea of an unambiguous dividing line between modern UFO reports and ancient accounts with similar themes eventually encounters serious logical difficulties. For instance, Budd Hopkins, who holds that alien abductions are real, hard-edged events, fiercely challenges Jacques Vallee's view that UFO abductions are "nothing new." Hopkins dismisses as "dubious folklore" reports of abductions throughout human history. At the same time, he notes that he has come across the case of an abductee who is over ninety years old. This places the "alien abduction phenomenon" near the beginning of the twentieth century, close to the 1896–1897 airship wave, well before the modern age of flying saucers. When does "dubious folklore" end and "accurate history" begin?

Vallee, specifically comparing the activities of UFO occupants with activities of fairies, nineteenth-century airship crews, and dwarfs. Bullard discovered impressive likenesses between these different frames of reference:

In UFO landing sightings, a witness may see one or more strange beings, often near the craft. The beings may stand around, walk normally, waddle, limp, run, cavort, leap, float or fly, sometimes apparently making repairs on the craft, gathering samples (especially rocks), often using tools or implements in the process. When the beings see a human, they may respond peacefully with a show of friendly actions, or communicate in a language either incomprehensible or quite clear, usually concerning superficial matters. They may instead respond with hostility: warning or threatening, paralyzing the human witness with a light gun, causing physical injury (sometimes clawing or attempting to kidnap). Or they may simply flee to the UFO, enter, and take off.

In accounts of strange airships reported through the United States in 1896–1897, witnesses typically report seeing a remarkable airship landing or already on the ground. One or more men usually step out of the ship and stand around or mill about as they inspect or use tools to repair their ship. In the presence of humans, the crew may speak in a foreign language or accented English, or in perfectly clear English, typically telling all about the trip, how the ship operates, and who the inventor is. In less friendly cases, the airship operators tell only a little and keep witnesses away, or else return quickly to the ship, enter, and depart the ground.

In fairy encounters, the witness typically sees a light, hears music, voices, and notices one or more humanlike beings near a "fairy mound" or a circle in the earth. The fairies may stand or walk, run, limp, cavort and dance, float or fly, while engaging in funerals, celebrations, battles, hunts, and food gathering. These beings may steal, especially food, and use musical instruments, common tools, and weapons. Spying human witnesses, fairies may invite them to dance or join their feast, not infrequently speaking in a musical, incomprehensible chatter, or else — in clear speech — ask favors, enter bargains, and negotiate exchanges. Hostile fairies may warn or threaten, pinch, beat, paralyze, blind, and even kill witnesses. These strange creatures may place humans in trances, play pranks, and they then may flee, climb to a cloud, or simply vanish.

And then there are the dwarfs. A human witness typically sees one or more small humanlike beings, perhaps near a cave, crag, or hill. The beings may stand, walk, run curiously fast, cavort or dance, while participating in funerals, celebrations, food gathering, or skilled crafts. Dwarfs may steal, especially food, and use musical instruments as well as tools of their craft and common tools. Dwarfs who see nearby humans may allow them to join in. Traditionally speaking in a voice like a child learning to speak but usually comprehensible, dwarfs may ask favors, provide aid, enter bargains, or exchange services. If hostile, dwarfs may warn or threaten, cause blindness, beat or otherwise punish, kidnap, play pranks, or flee, go underground, or vanish.

Debunkers have no difficulty dismissing all of the above comparisons as *nothing but* folklore, meaning "fundamentally insubstantial." But among researchers who believe UFO phenomena are not intrinsically insignificant, the question about parallels vexes like no other. Are these phenomena essentially the same, with minor surface differences, as Vallee and others suggest? Or are these realms essentially different, with coincidental thematic parallels?

Whitley Strieber, author of the best-selling book *Communion*, concerning his own encounters with beings he termed "the visitors," insists that only when the phenomenon is redefined "as part of the fundamental mythology of human experience" does it even become possible "to begin to raise questions about it of sufficient depth and resonance to be meaningful." Researchers committed to the extraterrestrial visitation hypothesis, and to the idea that the UFO phenomenon is a unique, late-twentieth-century happening, emphatically disagree, insisting that *definite* limits must be placed on the phenomenon lest it become so broad as to be meaningless.

Extraterrestrial advocate and alien-abduction specialist Budd Hopkins cites the dangers of "stewpot thinking." This lazy intellectual habit, says Hopkins, consists of stressing reassuring similarities among various phenomena and ignoring their differences. The stewpot thinker "habitually tosses into the same pot all available information about superficially related situations, assuming that this process adds something to the world." Hopkins argues that the syndrome known as Legionnaires' disease came into view as a unique syndrome only when researchers began to examine ways in which the disease's symptoms differed from symptoms of pneumonia and other known illnesses.

Likewise, Hopkins insists, the 1961 Betty and Barney Hill encounter provided a *clear* line of demarcation between 1950s-style reports of contacts with kindly, long-haired space people and reports of encounters which resemble kidnappings. "Abductions are a decidedly recent, unique, discrete class of events, with no meaningful precursors," Hopkins states.

Look again, this time *closer*, says Vallee, noting that a fifteenth-century French calendar, the *Kalendrier des Bergiers*, depicts demons piercing their victims' abdomens with long needles. "Let us recall that while under hypnosis, Betty Hill reported that a long needle was inserted into her navel, causing great pain," Vallee observes. "To find alien abduction parallels in primitive magic, mythology, occultism, and the fairy-faith, all one has to do is remove one's blinders and look."

As part of his exhaustive dissertation on UFO parallels in folklore, Thomas Bullard placed modern UFO abduction accounts side by side with reports of visits with fairies. Let's see what he discovered, beginning with UFO abductions:

I. At night in a remote area or at home, a witness sees a UFO and tries to flee. II. He enters a zone of strangeness as surroundings lose normal appearance, machines misbehave, his volition is impaired and his memory blanks out. Strange humanoid beings appear and float or carry him inside the UFO. III. He enters a uniformly lighted operating room where one or more alien beings subject him to a medical examination, sometimes of a painful character. IV. Afterwards he may see long tunnels and other parts of the ship, or travel a great distance in a short time to a dark and desolate other planet, then to a light and airy realm, both of which have buildings. Among the aliens he may also see a human being, and receive messages. On returning to earth, he finds a memory gap and injuries, and may receive later visits and extranormal manifestations.

Here, then, are the typical stages of visits with fairies:

I. At night in a remote area or in the vicinity of a fairy mound the witness II. Finds his surroundings unfamiliar as he encounters mist or is "led astray," or loses his volition as he hears enchanting music. He encounters one or more unusual beings who invite or lure him away with them, and afoot or by some unusual conveyance, he passes through a dark tunnel, takes a ride in darkness or sails on a stormy voyage to an otherworld inside the mound or across the sea. III. He enters a dimly or indirectly lighted hall, room or otherworldly country, and joins a society of beings in feasts, dances, games or pleasures, or assists a woman in childbirth, which is often painful. While there he may see a captive human, and acquire extranormal powers of knowledge. V. He becomes a captive or returns after supernatural lapse of time, which causes him to turn to dust, or he receives later punishment for powers gained while in fairyland.

Once again, the question arises: Is this essentially the same experience viewed through different cultural filters, or are the common themes simply coincidental to two fundamentally different *kinds* of events? Recalling from chapter two Einstein's statement that "it is the theory which decides what we can observe," and G. Spencer Brown's observation along similar lines ("The concept of randomness bears meaning only in relation to the observer"), it must be said that *no absolute answer is possible.*

The philosopher Ernst von Glasersfeld, in a thought-provoking essay on the ideas of sameness and difference, makes the straightforward point that any two items of experience can be viewed as two mutually independent objects; but the same two items of experience can also be understood as two experiences of one and the same individually "existing" object. In any given case, the verdict of "sameness" means either that we have two objects that are equivalent in terms of properties compared, or else one object that has remained unchanged during the interval between the two experiences. If, instead, the verdict of "difference" emerges from the comparison, we have either two objects with different properties or one object that has changed since our prior experience of it. It is clear, then, that Budd Hopkins and others who consider UFOs *different from* mythic and folkloric parallels fall into the second category. Jacques Vallee and others who consider UFOs *equivalent to* such parallels fall into the first.

What is perhaps less clear is this important distinction introduced by von Glasersfeld: "The criteria by means of which sameness or difference is established are criteria which are created and chosen by the judging, experiencing subject and cannot be ascribed to an experiencer-independent world." This is not to say that UFO experiences or their thematic parallels in other realms are unreal, or "merely subjective." Von Glasersfeld's point is a different one, namely that in terms of the sameness/difference distinction "it does not matter what an object might be like in 'reality' or from an 'objective' point of view; what matters is exclusively whether or not it performs or behaves in the way that is expected of it, that is, whether or not it fits."

And it is the *observer* who determines what constitutes fit, "dependent on a particular point of view, namely, *what* is being considered, and with respect to *what* sameness is demanded."

In short, there are answers enough for everyone with a question about the true nature of UFO experiences. Said another way: in the final analysis, discovery is invention. "Reality" is what we say it is. In a very real sense, *the universe changes each time our theories change.*

Allegory, as Angus Fletcher mentioned earlier, "seems to aim at both clarity and obscurity together, each effect depending on the other. Enigma, and not always decipherable enigma, seems to be allegory's most cherished function." We can imagine Fletcher deliberately missing a beat before adding: "And who will doubt that confusion in the symbolism will aid this function?"

Chalk up yet another win for Proteus, Hermes, Trickster, and Dionysus — and one more defeat for the age-old fantasy that humans can ever finally be certain that we know what we believe we know, about not only UFOs but also the world at large.

ELEVEN

————— ✕ —————

IN THE social and cultural universe of the UFO phenomenon, there seems to be an invisible threshold that a particular theme must cross in order to become significant enough to "stick," or to become assimilated into the UFO mythos. In the late 1960s, the unlikely idea that outer space aliens were systematically mutilating cattle in the American West and Midwest had not even approached this threshold. It was considered ludicrous, even by the standards of much that flies under the UFO banner. But by the mid-1970s, the notion of aliens as grisly high-tech predators of cattle, horses, and other animals had found a lively and controversial career in the larger UFO epic, whose trench warfare over the definition of evidence the mutilations fracas mimicked enthusiastically.

Americans got their first hint that the methodical murder of range animals had edged into UFO mythology when news bureaus around the world conveyed to their readers this October 5, 1967, wire service dispatch:

> ALAMOSA, Colo. (AP) — Snippy, a 3-year-old Appaloosa horse didn't return to the Harry King ranch from her usual evening drink Sept. 7 and her owner is blaming a flying saucer or at least a radioactive surgeon.

The article revealed that the horse, missing for about a month, had been founded completely skinned, with no tracks nearby. The cut around the neck was completely smooth, not a jagged edge. No blood remained in the horse's body, and there was none on the ground. A search of the immediate area had turned up fifteen circular exhaust marks covering an area about 100 by 500 yards. Just north of the carcass was found a three-foot bush that had been squashed to within ten inches of the ground. The area within a ten-foot radius of the bush was said to have been flattened to within ten inches of the ground. A closer inspection revealed still more compressed brush, along with six indentations forming a circle three feet in diameter. Each indentation was two inches across and four inches deep. The report indicated that a check of the area by a forestry official with a civil defense geiger counter found the radiation count to be high. "The exhaust marks were radioactive as were the areas where the brush had been flattened," said the Associated Press.

Subsequent investigation challenged the basic facts of this story. Skeptics revealed that only the horse's head and neck, not its entire body, had been skinned. The rumor that a Denver pathologist had found the brain, spinal, and abdominal cavities of the horse "unexplainably" empty could not be confirmed. The "exhaust marks" appeared to be a fungus known as black alkali; photographs showed no crushed grass; and the indentations were explained as weathered hoofprints. A forest ranger had checked the site but found no evidence of radioactivity. Dr. O. R. Adams, a physician from Colorado State University, did find suggestions of a severe infection in the hindlimb, which could have incapacitated the horse. He speculated that the knife incision may have been caused by someone attempting to put the suffering horse to sleep, or by "a curious boy wondering what his knife would do to a dead horse."

Further investigation revealed that, unable to clarify the rumors in advance, reporters went to press on the strength of interviews with the horse's owner, flying saucer enthusiast Mrs. Nellie Lewis, whose eighty-seven-year-old mother had seen an object in the sky around the time Snippy disappeared. There was one additional detail that Philip Klass would have loved to be the one to reveal: the mother wasn't sure what the object was because, at the time, she wasn't wearing her glasses.

The rumor that Snippy had been butchered by extraterrestrials, although now "officially" discredited, was speeded in its travels one month later thanks to a nationally syndicated newspaper story, SNIPPY'S DEATH JUST CHAPTER IN STELLAR RUSTLING, by UFO researcher

John Keel, who linked the horse's death with other gruesome incidents involving flying saucers and animals. Hundreds of such mutilation cases had been investigated by UFO researchers, Keel wrote, but as yet there was no concrete proof to make the UFO rumors fact. This he followed with two highly suggestive sentences:

> Indeed, millions are still awaiting some kind of tangible proof that the UFOs, themselves, are real. If, however, flying saucers are really only "swamp gas," then what is butchering and stealing animals around the world?

As with other corners of UFO mythology, the mutilation phenomenon blends mundane and fantastic themes in such a way that observers are typically moved to conclude that either every claim must be factual or else not a single claim merits credibility. Surely the truth rests somewhere in between — but where is the line?

There is no doubt that in the mid to late 1970s, something of an epidemic of animal mutilations in states including Minnesota, South Dakota, Iowa, Kansas, Nebraska, Colorado, Idaho, Wyoming, and Texas took place. By May 1974, more than 100 cattle had been found dead and gruesomely mutilated in Iowa, Kansas, and Nebraska alone. In case after case, ranchers and farmers reported that an unknown person had killed the animals, and removed with surgical precision body parts including sex organs, tongues, ears, eyes, or anuses. "I've yet to see a coyote who can chew a straight edge," said the organizer of a patrol to protect the animals. The killers were elusive, leaving no footprints or other evidence of their presence. Often the mutilations were committed in what should have been plain sight or within hearing distance — close proximity to a farmhouse, for instance — but no sights or sounds were reported.

In the September 30, 1974, issue of *Newsweek*, an article entitled "The Midnight Marauder" described the reaction of ranchers and farmers to the growing mystery:

> Each day, just before dusk, ranchers and farmhands pile into pickup trucks and fan out across the rolling prairie of northeastern Nebraska. They park mostly on ridges or hilltops, where they can scan the pastures and the narrow roads that wind through them. With rifles and shotguns leaning against their trucks, the men watch nervously, smoking cigarettes and talking with each other over a network of citizen's-band radios. Some

of the men will stand guard all night, yet none of them knows what he is looking for. "I've never seen anything like this," says State Sen. Jules Burbach, who has represented Knox County for eighteen years. "Folks are almost hysterical."

Daniel Kegan and Ian Summers, authors of *Mute Evidence*, a 1984 book examining the epidemic, argued that all of the allegedly mysterious aspects of cattle mutilations could be explained in mundane terms. Like skeptics of other UFO-related claims, Kegan and Summers zeroed in on the investigators, claiming their research was second-rate at best. None of the "mutologists," the authors insisted,

> had access to any experts in veterinary medicine, livestock or any other fields that bear on the cattle mutilation question, and it was obvious that there was not one seriously qualified investigator in their underground. . . . Not one of their testimonies would be acceptable as expert or even informed in a court of law.

Kegan and Summers insisted that only veterinary pathologists are truly qualified to make judgments about the cause of an animal's demise. By the time that the real experts got involved in the cases, the Legend of Unexplainable Mutilations had developed a life of its own. Confronted with evidence that the truth behind the uproar might be rather mundane, the legend's disciples refused to abandon their "make-believe mystery," preferring instead to call the veterinary pathologists incompetent or guided by sinister motives. Kegan and Summers further argued that, apart from animal deaths caused by predators, the mutilations were of two kinds: ritualistic killings by cult members (perhaps satanists), and "copycat" incidents in which pranksters carved up the bodies of already dead animals (including victims of predators, injuries, and disease).

The authors of *Mute Evidence* succeeded in explaining a good many mutilations in prosaic terms, yet many people found their account of the matter unsatisfactory. Why no footprints — nor predator tracks? What about the strange lights and unmarked helicopters? What about the "unearthly" high-tech surgical methods of the killers? What about eyewitness accounts of alien cattle rustlers? Thomas Adams, of the Mutual UFO Network office in Paris, Texas, is one researcher who points to elements in the mutilation mystery that are reported too consistently to be ignored or considered mere coincidence. He insists that any complete reckoning with the mutilation mystery will have to take into account:

- The "clean, bloodless, sometimes incredibly accomplished removal of parts and sections from the bodies of livestock."
- Absence of "evidential residues such as tracks or ground markings, even where such markings should exist."
- Reports of "bloodless incisions and, sometimes, bloodless carcasses; of mutilated animals found in trackless mud or snow, or in pastures other than their own; of power outages and engine failures with UFOs overhead; of mutilated carcasses decomposing at an abnormally slow rate or an abnormally fast rate; of farmers chased and shot at by occupants of helicopters; of searchlight beams and soft glows and lights of unforgettable brilliance; of near-panic in ranch country, with ranchers red-eyed and bleary from sleepless nights on watch, ready to open fire on any airborne or ground intruders; of livestock people who have shared their land with predatory animals all their lives, and who maintain without hesitation that classic mutilations are not attributed to natural predators."
- Reports of scavenging and predatory animals refusing to feed on the mutilated carcasses, "and the odd reactions of farm dogs upon confronting (or refusing to confront) a mutilated carcass."

It is the reports of strange lights, unmarked helicopters, and saucer-shaped craft near the time and physical location of some mutilations that disturb many mutologists. In September 1980, one witness watched what seemed to be a helicopter silhouetted against the western sky near his home, although he could not see its rotor blades. Soon the craft had become a silver, ball-shaped object dangling a long "fluttering" appendage from its side. Eventually the object shot straight up until it disappeared. Such reports prompted Thomas Adams to ask: "Is it possible that we are being confronted with UFOs disguised as helicopters? A sufficiently advanced non-terrestrial technology should have no problem constructing 'helicopters' to allow them to operate surreptitiously."

Adams's speculation begins to seem modest when measured against the conclusions reached by mutilation expert Linda Moulton Howe, an investigative journalist, documentary film producer, and author of a coffee table–sized tome featuring full-color photographs of grotesquely mutilated animals (a book that comedian David Letterman might say anyone would be proud to display in their living room). Howe reports that she was taken into the confidence of a government intelligence agent who displayed allegedly top-secret documents that convinced her that

> at least one non-human intelligence is manipulating and harvesting earth life, that the alien life forms are controlling and using human ignorance to accomplish the [one-way] harvest, and that the purpose of the harvest is for sustenance and genetic experimentation.

Many UFO researchers insist that Howe was the credulous victim of a disinformation plot designed to pull ufology further into ridiculous blind alleys and thus retard investigation of true UFO phenomena. Perhaps so. But, as always, the question remains: which UFO data are "true," and by whose criteria? Speaking of Howe's attempt to find a meaningful single pattern with which to connect reports of human abductions and animal mutilation, Jacques Vallee said:

> The story told by Linda Howe is as intriguing and absorbing as a good spy novel. But, as a good spy novel, it also raises new questions: In this hall of mirrors, are there alternative scenarios that may explain some or all of the fleeting images we see?

Perhaps such alternatives exist. But will they be as exciting as the more fantastic theories? Recently a physician came forward to say what fear for his career would not allow him to say twenty years earlier: that he had conducted an autopsy on Snippy and found evidence of laserlike surgical methods that simply did not exist in 1967. Thus the legend that Snippy was "taken" by extraterrestrials continues to thrive in the animal mutilations corner of the UFO epic.

DURING the same period, a different kind of epidemic was making itself known in other parts of the world: a display of UFO sightings impressive in their vividness of detail and their "high strangeness," in Allen Hynek's phrase.

Tarragona, Spain. Two married couples and the three children of one couple, all from Almosa, underwent an unnerving experience in a field. The event was described for a Madrid news outlet by one of the adults:

> We heard a very loud noise, like that of a train travelling at a great speed, and we were very surprised because the railroad is a long way off. Then

we saw something heading directly for us and travelling at very high speed; it stopped in its tracks, so to speak, but continued to spin. It was very near us. Then immediately afterwards it turned and went away. I thought it was going to land on top of us all. I pushed the children and yelled to everyone to hit the ground. It neither gave off sparks, nor smoke, nor any light at all. But it did give off a tremendous noise, a whistling sound, just like the jet planes when flying low. The olive trees bowed under the blast, as when there is a strong wind, lifting leaves and branches from the ground like a whirlwind. It was an earthy color, about 70 or 80 centimeters in diameter, round like a plate with another plate on top of it but upside down.

Xztum, Poland. At about 9 P.M., Miroslaw Goralski and Krzysztof Kobus were cleaning their tools after working in Goralski's garden, when a UFO descended abruptly into the enclosure. One of the men described the object as a "ring," the other from a different angle as "two silver deltas connected by a cross." Both men experienced an extremely high frequency sound in their heads. They were engulfed by a dense white fog and illuminated by a bright white light as they approached to investigate; they also felt as if they were ascending at high speed. Kobus felt himself resting against an unknown "cushion" that suddenly vanished as he experienced a kaleidoscope of colors and sensations that gave him the feeling that ideas were flowing into his mind from an external source.

Goralski perceived unseen entities of whom he felt moved to ask fundamental questions ("What is matter?"), to which he received answers ("The most important attribute of matter is its ability to pervade through other matter"). Then he experienced a visual display like a time warp, including people in costumes of ages past. Suddenly they "fell" and found themselves back in the garden. Both were greatly shocked and confused by the experience, although subsequent testing showed no signs of psychopathy.

Milford Haven, Wales. On a midsummer morning, Mr. D. J. Harris, a Welsh insurance agent, was walking along the street when he suddenly heard the kind of whispering sound associated with a low-flying glider, simultaneous with seeing an enormous (150 feet in diameter) object of metallic gray, resembling weathered aluminum. The object appeared as a flattened ellipse rotating slowly before disappearing sharply behind nearby Tabernacle Tower. Harris ran toward the object, assuming it must have crashed into the waters of the Haven River, but nothing whatever was in sight. Nor was anything ever reported.

Matles-Barbosa, Brazil. Brazilian newspapers carried the report of an automobile encounter involving brilliant illumination, levitation, strange creatures, abduction, and physical examination. Herminio and Bianca Reis, a couple in their thirties, had pulled off the highway at about 11:30 P.M. to rest before continuing on their journey. Herminio wakened to the sound of his wife screaming and an intense bluish light illuminating the area. "As if through a chimney" their Volkswagen was suddenly "absorbed" and they found themselves in a brightly lit circular area. Two small beings approached and gestured for them to leave the car, speaking in an unintelligible language while escorting them up a staircase into a large room full of "instruments." Given headsets plugged into an apparent computer, Herminio and Bianca heard a voice say in Portuguese, "My name is Karen, calm down. . . ."

Bianca was later examined and then placed in a strange compartment where she received something like an electric shock that caused her to lose consciousness for a period. Later she and her husband were given a green liquid that tasted like a mixture of sugar and iodine. A dark-haired woman appeared and announced that she and her associates were performing medical research, and that there was no death in their world. Herminio and Bianca both felt they remained in contact with "Karen" after the experience.

THESE four cases, taken as a whole, give a clear sense of the decidedly mixed nature of events associated with the acronym *UFO*. A hard-core debunker could easily dismiss all as lacking independent witnesses and physical evidence. Slightly less strident skeptics might mention "honest misidentification" for the Spanish and Welsh cases, and cite the Brazilian and Polish cases as "hallucinations."

As for open-minded researchers, there is plenty in all four cases to enliven the ongoing debate about whether abductions are the handiwork of three-dimensional, mass-bearing space aliens, or whether they instead express the workings of a complex *paraphysical domain* parallel to, yet somehow enmeshed with, "ordinary" reality. Or perhaps both theories are in some sense correct — maybe different *kinds* of "UFOs" emerge from different realms.

The important point, in terms of effects on collective consciousness, is that all four sightings — like others of similar tenor — were *compelling* enough to be reported and published; yet also sufficiently *absurd* to be formally "unbelievable" and "inadmissible." As Jacques Vallee predicted, events structured in this way cannot avoid touching religious depths while keeping rationalists at a distance.

Nowhere would these dynamics become more clear than in a controversial mid-1970s sighting case involving an obscure Swiss villager named Eduard Meier.

ON JANUARY 28, 1975, Eduard Meier, known to his neighbors, friends, and admirers as Billy, felt an odd compulsion to set off on his motorbike with his camera in tow. He said he did not know where he was going. At 2:12 P.M., beyond the edge of town, Meier said he saw a silver, disk-shaped craft circling overhead, which he began to photograph in rapid succession.

The craft landed. Meier ran toward it. A being departed the saucer and walked toward him. This was to be the first of many such contacts, which, according to Meier, continued over a period of weeks, months, and years. He would go where telepathic voices told him to go, and the ships would arrive. There are, roughly, two opinions among UFO researchers about the Billy Meier case. Either it is (1) the single best-documented case of a UFO landing yet, proof positive of one of the greatest events in human history, or (2) the most elaborate and skilled (some would add *notorious*, others *laughable*) hoax in UFO history.

Meier and his followers (there are many throughout the world) say we should believe him because he has produced hundreds of high-quality color photographs, color films, and sound recordings of UFOs that he calls "beamships." His detractors say Meier should not be believed precisely because he "produced" this evidence, falsely. His supporters point to records of landing traces and physical samples, and to other eyewitnesses who have even filmed some of the events themselves. They cite that Meier has compiled over 3,000 pages of notes and dissertation well beyond his personal intellectual capacities, said to have been dictated to him by beings from the star cluster Pleiades. Even so, Meier's detractors are amazed only at how he pulled it off.

There's the fact of the photographs themselves: clear, detailed black-and-white and color shots of a large silvery ship hovering above a valley near Meier's hometown of Hinwil, Switzerland. Then there are the several "landing tracks": counterclockwise swirls in crushed grass that never turned brown and died yet never rose again. There are the audio recordings of the flying saucers: "an eerie and grating noise, like a high-pitched cross between a jet airplane and a chain saw," writes Gary Kinder in *Light Years*, a book about the Meier controversy. And there are the secondary witnesses, some of whom even got to film a "light show" put on by the Pleiadeans at Meier's request.

How could Meier, a one-armed pensioner with a sixth-grade education who kept chickens in order to sell eggs to neighbors, *alone* pull off a hoax of such complexity — if indeed it is the hoax that most American ufologists believe it to be? And who would help him do it, in a small remote Swiss village, most of whose residents were outraged at the publicity Meier's photographs and accompanying claims brought their peaceful hamlet? Writes Gary Kinder:

> Although little known in the United States before 1979, the case of Eduard Meier would emerge as one of the most controversial in the history of UFO phenomena. No case had ever offered so much evidence; in fact, Meier seemed to possess more evidence than nearly all previous UFO cases combined. But the evidence would be seen by few and studied by even fewer, because Meier's preposterous and sometimes misunderstood stories of traveling back in time to see Jesus and photographing the eye of God would be laughed at and dismissed as nonsense. . . . Meier's stories couldn't be true, but neither could the witnesses and the evidence be dismissed easily.

The evidence included various crystals that Meier said came from planets in other star systems, and four "states" of metal of which the Pleiadean beamships were said by Meier to be made. In 1979, Wendelle C. Stevens, an Arizona publisher and UFO enthusiast, arranged for these materials to be analyzed by Marcel Vogel, a distinguished IBM research chemist and holder of thirty-two patents. On studying the objects, Vogel was largely unimpressed. The crystal, although beautiful, was an ordinary terrestrial amethyst. The two metal specimens contained minerals plentiful on Earth: aluminum, sulphur, silver, copper, and lead.

But the metal surprised Vogel in one respect. "When I touched the oxide with a stainless steel probe, red streaks appeared and the oxide coating disappeared. I just touched the metal like that, and it started to deoxidize and become pure metal. I've never seen a phenomenon like that before. It's just something that was unusual."

Vogel was curious, but he offered nothing by way of supporting Meier's claims. Of Meier's photos, Bob Post of NASA's Jet Propulsion Laboratory in Pasadena said: "The pictures look good. . . . Under further scrutiny you might find out, 'Yeah, they're fake.' [But] from a photography standpoint you couldn't see anything that was fake about them." As for the audio recordings of alleged beamships, U.S. Navy sound engineer Rob Shellman immediately eliminated one possibility of hoax: Meier could not have used an electrical AC source to produce those particular sounds.

Steve Ambrose, sound engineer for the singer Stevie Wonder, said he was intrigued to hear "a single sound source recording that had an amazing frequency response," with no evidence of mixing or layering of sound, as with a synchronizer. "If it is a hoax," Ambrose said, "I'd like to meet the guy who did it, because he could probably make a lot of money in special effects."

Up to this point, the Meier case had all the right elements necessary to survive as an untarnished legend: much suggestive, if ambiguous, evidence in Meier's favor, with no *particular* evidence of fakery. That was before the negatives were more closely examined, and also before the rumors of models.

A set of transparencies made available for analysis proved to be several generations away from the originals, and thus useless to unbiased photo investigators. Meier said that the original negatives had been stolen, that only copies — and copies of copies — remained. Given the cultlike atmosphere that had grown up around Meier in Switzerland, it was conceivable that some of his disciples had spirited away one or more of the originals. But it was also possible that Billy Meier was an extremely talented con man. Increasing numbers of people suspected the latter.

An even greater blow to Billy Meier's credibility came from Martin Sorge, an early admirer of Meier and his mission who had soured on the drama. Sorge told of turning up several partially burned slides taken of a model bearing a striking resemblance to the beamships. Meier's wife, Popi, had run from the house in tears one evening after fighting with her husband. Later she secretly gave Sorge several color slides that had been burned by fire: slides of a model beamship either suspended in the setting or somehow superimposed.

Without telling anyone, Sorge set up an experiment in which he built a ten-inch model and tried to photograph it at several angles. His own photos were of considerably lesser quality than Meier's, but he became convinced that Meier (perhaps with confederates) could and probably did fabricate the photographic part of the overall evidence. Meier would later say he had carved a model of the beamships that appeared in the sky and then tried to photograph it. Sorge found this unconvincing, but he was not ready to dismiss Meier entirely.

> I am certain [Meier] has these contacts . . . but not in the way he's telling us. He may receive them in the form of visions, the way mediums receive things. He may not even know himself if these visions are real. But for him it is reality, and to prove it he has to go out and build these things. . . . He has experiences in this parallel world. He fakes the evidence to make people understand his experiences.

Even among those who strongly suspect Sorge is correct about Meier's fakery, the hoax hypothesis does not entirely satisfy. Dr. Robert Nathan of NASA's Jet Propulsion Laboratory is not a UFO buff, and is not inclined to give the benefit of the doubt to Billy Meier or his claims. But as he viewed the films of the apparent beamships seemingly moving through the sky, he was impressed by how Meier "could very steadily move the object from one side of the scene to the other and have it come to an abrupt stop without it appearing to swing." Nathan added, "If this is a hoax, and it looks like it is to me but I have no proof, this is very carefully done. Tremendous amount of effort. An awful lot of work for one guy." Especially a guy with one arm.

Gary Kinder, author of *Light Years*, ended with his own doubts — in both directions. After probing the Meier story in great depth, he couldn't understand how Meier could have created such sophisticated special effects in his photography, along with the audio recording, metal sample, landing tracks, films, and explanation of the beamship propulsion system. Yet Kinder also knew Meier had once contrived photos of the San Francisco earthquake. And Meier's contactee claims were outlandish.

"He may simply be one of the finest illusionists the world has ever known, possessing not the power but the skill to persuade others to see things that did not happen and do not exist," Kinder suggests. Or maybe Meier was selected, controlled, and used by "beings on a much higher plane" for their own reasons well beyond human comprehension. "I do know this: Trying to make sense of it all has been the most difficult thing I will ever do. Finally I realized . . . that the truth of the Meier contacts will never be known."

By contrast, for thousands of people around the world who have marveled at Billy Meier's full-color photographs, who know in their heart what the photos *show*, who have read Meier's account of his conversations with a female space being named Semjase, who know that the Pleiadeans have their own goals and ways of achieving them, the truth will never be in doubt. Myths die or they deepen. The myth of Eduard "Billy" Meier shows no signs of dying.

TWELVE

GREGORY Bateson stood before a class of college students with a phrase repeating itself in his mind: *The pattern which connects.* Behind this phrase lay several questions: *What pattern connects the crab to the lobster and the orchid and the primrose and all the four of them to me? And me to you? And all six of us to the amoeba in one direction and to the back-ward schizophrenic in another?*

The reach of this inquiry was not out of the ordinary for Bateson, a scientist-philosopher whose lifelong search for unity between mind and nature led him to become fluent in the languages of anthropology, biology, psychology, philosophy, art, literature, communication, and information theories, and in analyzing the logic of systems. On this day, Bateson would ask his class these questions, but not directly. Instead he produced a paper bag containing a freshly cooked crab, which he promptly placed on the table in front of him. Then he offered his students a challenge.

> I want you to produce arguments which will convince me that this object is the remains of a living thing. You may imagine, if you will, that you are Martians and that on Mars you are familiar with living things, being indeed yourselves alive. But, of course, you have never seen crabs or lobsters. A number of objects like this, many of them fragmentary, have arrived, perhaps by meteor. You are to inspect them and arrive at the

conclusion that they are the remains of living things. How would you arrive at that conclusion?

Bateson deliberately placed his students on another planet, Mars, in order to strip them of habitual associations with life as they knew it — "lobsters, amoebas, cabbages, and so on" — and to force them into identification with what Bateson referred to as "the living self." He told them that they carried all the benchmarks, all the criteria, they needed to look at the crab and find that it, too, carries the same marks.

Only later did Bateson realize he was presenting his students with an aesthetic question, involving recognition and empathy. *How are you related to this creature?* he was asking. *What pattern connects you to it?*

The students looked at the crab and came up with the observation that its right side resembled its left; the crab was *symmetrical.*

"Very good. You mean it's *composed*, like a painting?" Bateson asked. The class remained silent. Where was their wily professor leading them? Soon someone observed that since one claw was bigger than the other, the crab was not symmetrical after all.

Bateson responded by suggesting that if a number of these clawed specimens had come by meteor, it would be discovered that in nearly every case the same side (left or right) would carry the bigger claw. More silence as the students weighed this new information.

The idea of symmetry returned when a student said, "Yes, one claw is bigger than the other, but both claws are made of the same parts."

Bateson felt a surge of delight that a student had dismissed "the idea that size could be of primary or profound importance and went after the pattern which connects." The student intuitively "discarded an asymmetry in size in favor of a deeper symmetry in formal relations," Bateson noted. This was precisely the point he had hoped to make: the two crab claws embodied *similar relations between parts.* The important point was not quantity, but shapes, forms, and relations; these are what characterized the crab as part of the living world.

For Gregory Bateson, the "living" world is that vast, inclusive domain in which *differences* and *distinctions* (and their patterns) can be causes. Ideas are made up of differences that make a difference, Bateson frequently said. By contrast, the nonliving world of billiard balls and galaxies is that realm where *forces* and *impacts* are taken as what makes things happen. As a scientist and philosopher, Bateson devoted his career to examining the living world in search of differences in patterns and patterns in differences.

Those who knew him best say his eye was always tuned to the poetry, the aesthetics, the rhythms and repetitions, the often circular flows, of everyday life. Whether studying the structure of crabs, human and nonhuman communication, problems of beauty, or problems of problem solving, Gregory Bateson never tired of looking for what he termed "the pattern which connects." Toward this end, he was especially interested in mapping corresponding sets of relations between corresponding parts of objects and ideas.

For instance, Bateson found that each of the crab's claws embodied similar relations between parts, and more, that these relations extended down the series of the walking legs. "We could recognize in every leg pieces that correspond to the pieces in the claw," Bateson said. The same is true of the human body: "Humerus in the upper arm corresponds to femur in the thigh, and radius-ulna corresponds to the tibia-fibula; the carpals in the wrist correspond to tarsals in the foot; fingers correspond to toes."

The term *homology* is used by biologists and other scientists to describe formal resemblances in structure, position, proportion, value, origin, and so on. The human's limb bones are homologous — similar in pattern — to those of a horse, as the appendages of a crab are homologous to those of a lobster. Note that this is not the same as saying these structures are identical in substance; clearly they are not. *Homologos* is the Greek word for sameness of relation, correspondence in form.

Bateson extended this idea to define various *orders* of resemblance. Patterns within the individual crab (such as bilateral symmetry) constitute first-order homologies. The patterns that connect corresponding parts between crab and lobster (or between horses and humans) constitute second-order homologies. When the comparison between lobsters and crabs is then compared with the comparison between horses and humans, the result is third-order homology.

"My central thesis can now be approached in words," Bateson said. "*The pattern which connects is a metapattern*. It is a pattern of patterns. It is that metapattern which defines the vast generalization that, indeed, *it is patterns which connect*."

Notice the singular word: *metapattern*. Notice the plural word: *patterns*. These were not mutually exclusive for Bateson, nor for someone else we have gotten to know in the pages of this book: the god Proteus. Over and over again, this shape-shifter has been telling us: *Look for resemblances, larger patterns which connect smaller ones.* When Bateson notes that "any A is relevant to any B if both A and B are parts or components of the same 'story'," he is speaking as a protean.

By the same token, if "A" is taken to stand for those events specific to the flying saucer frame of reference, and "B" is taken to stand for *structural parallels* to these events in mythology, religion, the fairy-faith, and other related domains, then, according to Proteus, A and B are indeed connected parts of a common story, parts of a larger context, a *pattern of patterns moving through time.*

Gregory Bateson's perspective allows us to proceed in search of homologous patterns of various orders — that is, similar relations between parts. Like a crab, the "UFO encounter experience" can be considered a single bilateral entity: *contactee* encounters on one side, *abduction* encounters on the other. When their respective *structures* are compared for structural correspondences, we would expect to arrive at first-order homologies.

These could then be compared with corresponding "limbs" within, say, the angelic frame of reference. Likewise, the shaman's journeys to other worlds could be compared to the near-death experience. Through such comparisons (UFO encounters to angelic encounters; shamanic journeys to near-death experiences), we would arrive at second-order homologies.

Third-order connections, if we chose to pursue them, would then emerge when the comparison between flying saucer experiences and angelic encounters is compared with the comparison between shamanic journeys and near-death experiences. If Bateson is correct, comparisons between these ostensibly different species of phenomena and bodies of experience should bring into view a larger context revealing similar relations between parts.

In short, we should expect to find a pattern of patterns — a metapattern of parallels in the *anatomy* of different *bodies* of extraordinary experience.

But what would the boundaries of this larger pattern of patterns be? Using Bateson's model, our search can begin with first-order comparisons inside the "flying saucer frame of reference."

• • •

IN 1972, J. Allen Hynek introduced the following categories for classifying varieties of UFO encounters:

Close Encounters of the First Kind (CE-I): A UFO is seen at close range without interaction between the UFO and the environment (apart from the evoked psychological reaction of the observer).

Close Encounters of the Second Kind (CE-II): A UFO is observed at close range and physical effects on the environment (disabled vehicles, frightened animals, ground indentations, broken or crushed plants, burned or scorched ground) are reported.

Close Encounters of the Third Kind (CE-III): "Intelligent beings" are reported in or around the UFO, sometimes apparently collecting rock samples or "repairing" their craft. Interactions between human "contactees" and UFO occupants fall into this category.

Investigators later added a fourth category:

Close Encounters of the Fourth Kind (CE-IV): The contactee is abducted by the UFO occupants, taken aboard the landed craft, and subjected to a variety of "tests" and "experiments." Some investigators claim to have recovered physical evidence of these interactions in the form of scars from alien surgical incisions. Some abductees report memories of devices being implanted within their bodies, typically through the nose.

In the first years of the UFO phenomenon, those who saw unidentified flying objects, either up close or at a distance, were typically known simply as "witnesses." By the mid-1950s, a new kind of witness known as a "contactee" emerged claiming prolonged meetings and continued contacts with aliens from other planets. Immediately the mainstream of UFO researchers moved to distance themselves from these individuals, justifiably fearing that contactees' claims of personal, ongoing, often telepathic interactions with beings they termed "Space Brothers" could only damage the overall fortunes of the struggling discipline of ufology.

While there are of course many variations, the contactee experience typically takes the form of a savior story. The contactee is cast as a modern prophet, an intermediary between recalcitrant mortals and extraterrestrial helpers intervening to save humankind from its reckless ways. Many contactees report early life experiences with strange aerial phenomena and meetings with strange beings who offer advice, esoteric teachings, and overall life guidance at key points in their lives. Some contactees seek contact with superior beings; others have premonitions of impending contact; still others say they are chosen.

Contacts with the Space Brothers typically (although not always) happen in a remote spot, perhaps a wooded area, where the contactee has been "directed" to go. Like biblical prophets before them, the most famous contactees of the 1950s — George Adamski, Truman Betherum, Daniel Fry, and George Van Tassel — literally went into the desert for their contacts. Some contactees report face-to-face meetings while a saucer hovers nearby; for others, telepathic "channeling" constitutes the primary form of contact.

Frequently the aliens are quite attractive and humanlike, often with flowing hair and piercingly beautiful eyes, and are able to speak the native tongue of the contactee. Thus they can slip in and out of the general human population without much difficulty. Through conversations and/or visions, sometimes involving travel with the aliens to other worlds, many contactees learn of their own extraterrestrial origins and are charged with a mission that is uniquely theirs to carry forth.

The aliens may present a message high in ethical and prophetic content — typically concerning the need for human beings to change their ways before the coming apocalypse — along with detailed answers about their universe of origin, how their saucer works, and why they have decided to come to Earth. Many contactees emerge with heightened psychic abilities and spiritual awareness, only to face harassment, ridicule, and scorn from "nonbelievers." Some of the more famous 1950s contactees ended up feeling betrayed by their spacefaring hosts when their prophecies failed to be fulfilled.

Before moving on to the abduction experience, we should note certain additional parallels between the lives of contactees and the lives of prophets. The Old Testament prophet Moses had unusual birth and childhood experiences, and later journeyed to a remote area where he received a supernatural calling. Saul of Tarsas, through a profound epiphany on the road to Damascus, converted to the very Christian faith that he had persecuted. Joseph Smith founded the Mormon faith on the strength of an illuminating vision of the angel Moroni.

All three experienced their transformative visions in solitude, and suffered persecution — as did the most famous contactees of the 1950s — when they sought to bring their heretical messages to "the masses."

A very different tone emerges in the abduction accounts, where contactees — if we may use this word by way of extending its reach — are forcibly removed from the mundane world into a zone of high strangeness by short, bug-eyed, large-skulled reptoid creatures who emerge from landed flying saucers. As familiar sights lose their familiarity and everyday causality breaks down, abductees typically lose control of their fate, even their own body and mind. Loss of consciousness and later of memory accompany this pervasive "theft" of free will.

The classic abduction culminates in a quasi-medical examination during which, while in a state of dreamlike paralysis, the abductee undergoes the taking of bodily samples (blood, sperm or ova, tissue biopsies) via procedures that travel a thin line between the technological and supernatural.

Clearly there are differences between the reports of contactees and abductees, yet in these very differences reside significant symmetries as well. Both classes of experience open onto larger archetypal universes. Just as contactee encounters are rich with prophetic undertones and images of ascent to worlds in space, abductee encounters feature striking echoes of mythological journeys to the world below, the underworld, the realm of the dead and the dispossessed, the infernal regions of the collective soul.

Prior to Christianity, when the underworld became demonized and renamed *hell* to suit the ideological necessities of church fathers, Hades was the Greek god responsible for a dominion known simultaneously as the source of all treasures and wealth of the Earth, and as a dark realm inhabited by the invisible shades of the dead. Modern depth psychology, with its emphasis on descent into tormenting masses of confusion in search of buried riches of soul, understands this double legacy well.

The experience of the underworld is typically described in mythologies throughout the world as gloomy, confined, dark, doleful, and humid. Abductees speak of being confined in quarters usually termed dank, oppressive, humid, and dimly lit. Many report that a spaceship of relatively small dimensions seemed curiously spacious inside, with dark mazelike corridors apparently leading to the proverbial light at the end of the tunnel, reminiscent of Alice's adventures in Wonderland. The landed saucer becomes a scene of traditional underworld torments, a prison of suffering inflicted by primeval demons. According to folklorist Thomas Bullard,

The piercing instruments used by aliens in their examination bear a similarity, albeit genteel, to the piercing tortures which devils inflict on sinners in Christian art and fundamentalist belief. In accounts of the afterlife we find not the scientific examination of curious aliens but the close parallel of highly formalized, sometimes mechanistic and potentially unpleasant moral inquisition.

Given the protean thematic richness of the UFO epic, we should not be surprised to find that the continuum of alien encounters runs from uplifting contactee accounts, at one end, to terrifying abduction chronicles, at the other. Nor should it seem too amazing that between the "classic" positions at either end lies a middle realm of shared motifs. For instance, the aliens reported by contactees and abductees seem equally to have mastered the arts of telepathic communication and of materializing and dematerializing on the spot.

Likewise, the motif of repeat encounters throughout a witness's life — once exclusive to contactee reports — is now shared by contactee and abductee narratives alike. (Abduction specialist Budd Hopkins contends that many of his subjects are kidnapped by aliens repeatedly, like "tagged elk" being studied as if by extraterrestrial game wardens.)

The idea that all contactee reports are based on religious experiences rather than real events, while abductions are real events having no religious dimensions, continues to be popular among ufologists, even though available evidence favors a middle hypothesis. For instance, many self-styled contactees who describe being taken against their will ("abducted") report that they do not identify with the "ufologically correct" victim status promoted by some abduction researchers. Such witnesses report finding their encounter experience transformative, along the lines of a cosmic rite of passage.

And, rather than being free of "religious" implications, abductions are frequently described in terms of terror before the awe-inspiring mystery (*mysterium tremendum*) of a presence that stands as "wholly other" (*ganz andere*). Such imagery touches the very core of religious experience as expressed in cultures throughout the world. Many abduction accounts, with their emphasis on confrontation with numinous or godlike beings emanating supernormal presence, read like passages from *The Dark Night of the Soul* by the great mystic Saint John of the Cross.

Returning to the question of formal resemblances in structure and proportion, it bears repeating that contactee and abductee accounts —

as *classes* of experience — shade into *different yet parallel* thematic realms: contactee narratives resounding with motifs from the prophetic tradition, abduction details echoing primal encounters with underworld darkness as depicted in worldwide myth. The most striking symmetry between the two classes of experience manifests as polarity: two apparently disparate realms held together by a common motif of *encounter with an unknown Other.*

W H A T is an angel? This is the question that must be asked now, before we can probe the pattern that may connect angelic and alien encounters in search of second-order comparisons. The term *angel* derives from a Greek translation of the original Hebrew *mal'akh*, later *malaika*, which originally meant the "shadow side of God," but later came to mean messenger or herald. Both terms, interestingly enough, refer to a function or status rather than an essence. Yet questions of angelic substance have been debated for centuries.

The ancient Greeks thought of angels as resembling humans but also possessing the nature of a "geometric point-soul," or "pure thought." The biblical view held that angels were "from above" yet were essentially humanlike and not, as a rule, invisible. According to Saint Thomas Aquinas, angels were "pure soul," beings lacking the bodies of humans. Lactantius, a Christian apologist writing in the third and fourth centuries A.D., argued for a principle of relativity: compared to humans, angels are immaterial, but in relation to God, angels appeared embodied. Thus they might be said to possess "subtle bodies."

In the ancient city of Ur in the Euphrates Valley, settled around 4000 B.C., a stone pillar was unearthed depicting a winged figure descending from one of several Sumerian heavens to pour the water of life into the cup of a king. A vision of an angel? Perhaps; certainly an echo of the Greek messenger god Hermes, a messenger who wore wings on both his cap and his feet. The idea of angels as gods, sons of gods, servants, ministers, watchers, holy men, appears throughout the ancient civilized world.

Although we might expect the Christian Bible to be the definitive source for the names, attributes, and functions of angels, the Old Testament mentions only three angels by name. Most of the detailed information that has come to us about the angelic order derives from esoteric texts that were later declared heretical, such as the three great Chronicles of Enoch, compiled around the second century B.C. from still earlier sources. This text spills over with angelic vitality: names, duties, characteristics, and personalities of the host of angels. It is known that much of Enoch's apocryphal (from the Greek word for "hidden away") material covertly made its way into the New Testament.

A certain Hermes-like ambiguity existed from the start concerning angels — and their close relatives, the demons. The Old Testament makes no mention of fallen angels, and offers no evidence that Satan was evil. The Hebrew word *ha-Satan*, the "Adversary," stood for an office, a position, and by no means a diabolical one. Yet by the time of the New Testament, one-third of the angelic choir, led by a now decidedly evil Satan (decided by church fathers, that is) had fallen squarely into the abyss of eternal damnation. Even the fall is vague: a minimum of seven conflicting accounts describe this steep descent, which took nine days to reach bottom.

Prior to the third century A.D., angels themselves possessed a distinctly double nature, "appearing as Dukes of Hell one moment and singing Hallelujahs around the Celestial Throne the next, without a trace of tarnish to their celestial haloes," writes Malcolm Godwin in his fine book *Angels: An Endangered Species*. Godwin notes that angelic lore presents not "a static and consistent mosaic" but rather "a dynamic and constantly evolving panorama of the warring forces of Righteousness and Malevolence." Thus when the astronomical findings of the sixteenth century removed Earth from the center of the universe, a good many theologians were only too pleased to dismiss the very notion of angelic and demonic hierarchies as hopelessly antiquated.

Yet ambiguities remained. Speaking for embryonic Protestantism, Martin Luther repudiated the entire angelic superstructure with one broad sweep of his hand. But he did not throw out Satan and his evil hordes; they remained necessary to secure meaning for Christ's role as redeemer. At the Vatican, the current pope, John Paul II, has made clear his faith in an actual demonic spirit called the Devil. Even so, skeptical Catholics insist that the choice inherent in our exercise of free will locates sin within the individual. Catholic bishops remain split on the reality of angelic and demonic beings.

It is almost impossible to imagine angels apart from the winged gossamer-gowned, halo-crowned figures created by Renaissance painters. Yet throughout history angels have most often been described either as radiant beings surrounded by brilliant light or as very ordinary-looking humans. The German poet Rainer Maria Rilke's words conjure the former: "But if the archangel, now, perilous from behind the stars took even one step down toward us: our own heart, beating higher and higher, would beat us to death." The latter, more mundane image of the angel is conveyed in this biblical passage (Hebrews 13:2): "Be not afraid to have strangers in your house, for some thereby have entertained angels unawares."

The image of angels as intermediaries between God and humanity has its roots in pre-Christian ideas about *daemons* and the *daemonic world*. Plutarch, in his essay "On the Cessation of Oracles," speaks of a "family of Daemons, intermediate between gods and men, and after a certain fashion bringing thought together and uniting in one of the society of both." In Plato's *Symposium*, Diotima describes Eros as "a great spirit [daemon], and like all spirits he is intermediate between the divine and the mortal." Eros "interprets between gods and men . . . he is the mediator who spans the chasm which divides them, and therefore in him all is bound together, and through him the arts of the prophet and the priest, their sacrifices and charms, and all prophecy and incantation, find their way." Diotima concluded: "These spirits or intermediate powers are many and diverse. . . ."

It is crucial to note that prior to Christianity's *demonization* of the daemonic world, daemons did not have an exclusive evil coloring. Writes Angus Fletcher: "Very early in history the term demon had a religious and spiritual signification, and referred to the other-world." In pagan antiquity, *demon* (interchangeable with *daemon* and *daimon*) was used in a threefold sense: "for gods, for intermediaries, and for the souls of the dead without any direct connection with intermediaries," Fletcher notes.

Thus we begin to glimpse common ground between the modern imagination of aliens and the traditional imagination of angels and daemons.

Beings from these realms appear to be intermediate between mind and matter, able to change their forms at will in the sight of select witnesses in select locations.

Over forty years of UFO sightings have led to the creation of an alien hierarchy (tall, Nordic-looking "blonds" and short, repulsive "grays" being only two types) no less daunting than the multileveled choir of angels, a richness bound to be documented in vivid detail some-day by some enterprising folklorist.

Just as most information about angels comes from outside "approved" theological channels, and is based to a considerable extent on eyewitness testimony, likewise there is no room in the orthodox texts of Big Science for a class of phenomena that dares to originate outside the halls of orthodox institutes and academies, among "mere folk." In their own ways, angels and aliens are both heretical.

Angels and aliens alike can easily be seen as messengers, as both are more visible in their functions — their effects — than as any known essence. But of course questions about what aliens and their amazing vehicles *are made of* and *where they are from* continue to haunt much ufological discourse, no less so than Thomas Aquinas's speculations about precisely how many angels could dance on the head of a pin.

For example, if angels can be said to have "subtle bodies," what should we say about aliens who pass through walls, float inches above the ground, and withstand (inside their vehicles) extraordinary accelerations in velocity and shifts in trajectory?

Today's alien abductors continue to show more than passing interest in human sexuality and reproduction, a tradition that extends to Antonio Villas-Boas's seduction by a gorgeous female "angel" with cherry-red pubic hair. Abduction researcher Budd Hopkins's well-elaborated posi-tion that aliens are "harvesting" a population of hybrid babies, using human women as breeders, echoes the ancient phenomenon of the otherworldly lover: the "incubus/succubus" tradition. *Incubus*, a male demon who copulates with sleeping mortal women, derives from the Latin *incubard*, meaning "to lie down on." *Succubus* (from *succubare*, "to lie under"), is a female demon that copulates with men in their sleep. Angel scholar Malcolm Godwin offers this additional point of reference:

> All the evidence points to the incontroversial fact that Angels really are extremely vulnerable to corruption when in the company of human beings. It is difficult to make out whether it is the wanton nature of the manifest, material world which corrodes their armor of righteousness, or whether there is some magnetic field within the flesh that plays havoc with their virtuous compasses. Whatever the cause, Angels are unques-tionably susceptible to "a friendship of the thighs. . . ."

It is widely suspected that the pagan hierarchy of demons eventually found its way into the Christian hierarchy of angels. Have the same agents made their way into the modern UFO mythos? The beings who visited George Adamski in the California desert appeared in pleasing human form (angels of light?), whereas the Men in Black portend distinctly sinister overtones (angels of darkness?).

Without making the conceptual blunder of reducing complex realms to one another ("Aliens are simply today's angels"), it seems safe to posit that aliens and angels both manifest as *daemonic agents*, following Rudolph Otto's definition in his classic book *The Idea of the Holy*:

> ... the daemonic, a character ascribed to certain definite operations of force, be they strong or weak, extraordinary or quite trivial, the work of a soul or a "non-soul." The quality can be only suggested through that unique element of feeling, the feeling of "uncanniness" ... whose positive content cannot be defined conceptually, and can only be indicated by that mental response to it which we call "shuddering."

Bearing in mind our interest in formal resemblances across different domains, *patterns which connect*, Rudolph Otto's link between the daemonic, uncanniness, and "shuddering" offers grounds for considering the legendary 1917 "Miracle at Fatima" in a discussion of parallels between angels and aliens. A review of what is known of this remarkable episode in the history of celestial marvels seems very much in order.

On May 13, 1917, three illiterate shepherd children, at work tending sheep outside Fatima, Portugal, were surprised by a bright flash in a nearby pasture called Cova de Ira, widely known as an old sacred place. Approaching the pasture, they were caught in a luminosity that nearly blinded them. In the center of the blaze of light, they perceived a little woman who told them she was "from Heaven" and warned that worldwide suffering could be averted only if people did not stop "offending God." The illuminated figure — who quickly became known as Our Lady — asked them to return to the same spot every month.

On June 13, the children returned. This time fifty witnesses watched as the three knelt in prayer and the oldest, ten-year-old Lucia, addressed an unseen entity whose answers were unheard by anyone other than Lucia and her two young companions. One witness reported hearing a faint voice or beelike buzzing. At the end of the dialogue, witnesses heard an explosion and saw a small cloud rise near a tree.

Forty-five hundred witnesses joined the three children near the same tree in the same pasture on July 13. This day several witnesses reported "a buzzing or humming sound, a decrease in the sun's glow and heat, a small whitish cloud about the tree of the apparitions, and a loud noise at the Lady's departure," writes Joseph Pelletier in his book *The Sun Danced at Fatima*.

On August 13, the crowd grew to 18,000, but the three children were not among them. They had been jailed by local officials eager to "put an end to this nonsense." Even so, those present in the field reported a clap of thunder followed by a bright flash and a cloud surrounding the same "magical" tree. One month later, a crowd of 30,000 watched in astonishment as a globe of light appeared in plain view, advancing through the valley floor from east to west, coming to rest on the same tree.

Two deeply skeptical priests — who arrived expecting to find evidence only of contagious hysteria — reported that a white cloud formed around the tree as "falling flowers" descended from the sky and disappeared as witnesses reached to touch them.

The most amazing display occurred in Fatima on October 13, when 70,000 gathered in the pouring rain. Many came to keep faith with the prophecy of Our Lady, others to taunt what they saw as a display of vile medieval supernaturalism. Shortly after noon, thick gray clouds suddenly parted and rolled back like curtains of a stage, as a strange sweet fragrance filled the air. The sun appeared against the clear blue sky as a flat silver disk revolving on its own axis and sent forth shafts of red, violet, yellow, and blue light in all directions. Suddenly the disk plunged erratically downward in zigzag fashion, causing thousands of witnesses — believers and disbelievers alike — to fall to their knees in public confession of their sins before the world ended.

The disk stopped short and began slowly rising into the sky in the same irregular way, disappearing into the sun, which stood once again fixed in its natural brilliance. The entire display lasted less than fifteen minutes. No less amazing was this fact, confirmed by the managing editor of Lisbon's largest daily newspaper: the streets and clothes of thousands of witnesses were no longer wet, even though heavy rains had fallen within the hour. Throughout the countryside, strange healings were reported.

After thirteen years of painstaking investigation, the Catholic church offered its report: "This phenomenon, which no astronomical observatory registered and which therefore was not natural, was witnessed by persons of all categories and of all social classes, believers and unbelievers, journalists of the principal Portuguese newspapers and even by persons some miles away. Facts which annul any explanation of collective illusion." Jacques Vallee offers this estimation:

> The final "miracle" had come at the culmination of a precise series of apparitions combined with contacts and messages that place it very clearly, in my opinion, in the perspective of the UFO phenomenon. Not only was a flying disk or globe consistently involved, but its motion, its falling-leaf trajectory, its light effects, the thunderclaps, the buzzing sounds, the strange fragrance, the fall of "angel hair" [the flowerlike petals] that dissolves upon reaching the ground, the heat wave associated with the close approach of the disk — all of these are frequent parameters of UFO sightings everywhere. And so are the paralysis, the amnesia, the conversions, and the healings.

Regardless of whether encounters with "aliens" and "angels" can ultimately be traced to a shared source, Rudolph Otto's description of demonic "operations of force" speaks to a *category of experience* shared by the thousands who witnessed the brilliantly streaming pulsations of a celestial disk at Fatima in 1917, by people throughout the world who speak of angelic apparitions at the time of a loved one's death, by air traffic controllers perplexed by strange pips on radar screens, by Kenneth Arnold on a fateful summer day in 1947, and by those who — without knowingly offering permission — have been led across the threshold between mundane and fantastic in the compelling interaction known as "alien abduction."

Slowly, a pattern of patterns is beginning to build, as Gregory Bateson predicted. Now let's consider yet another realm of comparison: this time between the traditional journeys of shamans and the near-death experience.

SHAMANISM is the oldest visionary tradition known to humanity, a practice of entering altered states of consciousness for the purpose of traveling to other realms at will and there contacting gods and spirits of the natural world, in order to learn, gain knowledge, help, and heal. "In the sense that the shaman acts as an intermediary between the sacred and profane worlds, between mankind and the realm of gods and spirits, he has special access to a defined cosmos," writes Nevil Drury in his book *The Shaman and the Magician*.

The vocation of shaman may come naturally to a psychically gifted or sensitive person, such as the young Karagasy shaman from Siberia who recalled how "the little one, the little spirit used to come to me. He had flown into my mouth and then I used to recite shaman songs. When I had no more strength left to suffer, finally I agreed to become a shaman. And when I became a shaman, I changed entirely." As a child another shaman, Eduardo, from Peru, learned to keep his unusual experiences to himself, afraid people would think him crazy if he confided in them:

> I have seen things as if someone opens a door and the door is closed.
> I have had nightmares, but not ordinary ones. I have seen myself intro-
> duced through a hole in the air, and I went through an immense, im-
> mense void. I have felt numbness in all my body as if my hands were
> huge but I could not grasp; I could not hold up my hand.

The vocation of a shaman may come through a lifetime of introverted tendencies and mysterious "possessive" illnesses, through life-threatening accidents culminating in a profound vision, or through a self-selected or imposed rigorous training program involving ordeals of psychic death and rebirth. Sacred mysteries are disclosed to the future shaman as he learns to enter into otherworldly realms and acquires his own "power animals," sacred songs, secret language, and so on. Writes psychologist Kenneth Ring:

> After his initiation is complete, he returns to his community as a healer,
> a psychopomp, a master of ecstasy, a mystic and a visionary — as a man
> (or woman), in short, who now knows how to live in two worlds: the
> world of the soul as well as that of the body. And though indispensable
> to the welfare of his community, he often remains somewhat apart from
> it precisely because of his special knowledge and his unusual and some-
> times disturbing presence.

In modern culture, shamanic themes arise unexpectedly in a seemingly different yet parallel domain: among reports of people who appear to return from the threshold of immediate biological death as a result of "deciding" to return to life. The "near-death experience" (NDE) first came to widespread public attention in 1975, with the publication of Raymond Moody's best-selling book *Life After Life*. Researchers estimate that as many as 40 percent of people who are declared clinically dead have had an NDE, even though most remember nothing as a result of a near-death crisis. Still, a consistently high percentage of those who claim to have some conscious recall offer reports that conform, at least in part, to a standard NDE pattern.

Basically there are two types of NDEs, the first consisting of deathbed visions. A person, usually ill, typically bedridden, suddenly has a vision at the hour of death. The vision seems compellingly real and altogether objective: *more real than life itself*, most subjects report. Organic brain dysfunction does not appear to play a significant role in these experiences; in fact, the clearer and less impaired the subject's consciousness, the greater the likelihood of an NDE occurring and being registered.

A second type of NDE arises through any of a wide variety of near-death conditions, including cardiac arrest, combat situations, attempted rape and murder, near-fatal falls, vehicular collisions, sporting accidents, suicide attempts, near drownings, electrocutions, freezings, hangings, and a great range of strictly medical and surgical conditions. This wide variation seems to have a negligible effect on how the experience unfolds. Similarly, demographic variables such as race, social class, gender, or education have not been shown to be connected with NDE incidence or form. (The NDEs of atheists and agnostics, for instance, do not appear to differ from NDEs of those with strong religious beliefs or faith in postmortem existence.)

Based on the many reports that he studied, Kenneth Ring, author of *Life at Death* and widely respected authority on near-death experiences, describes five "stages" of near-death experience: peace, body separation, entering the darkness, seeing the light, and entering the light. Here, in summary, is Ring's model NDE:

Through a feeling of easeful peace that culminates in overwhelming joy and happiness, you realize that you are in the process of dying or have already died. You feel no pain, nor any other bodily sensations. All is quiet. You may hear a transitory buzzing or a windlike sound, and then find yourself looking down on your physical body as if from an external vantage point. You take in sounds and sights in the room with heightened clarity, and may even see and hear your own death pronounced by medical personnel. You might wonder what all the fuss is about "down there."

Next you may find yourself aware of two levels at once: your attention oscillating between the physical scene around you and "another reality" that draws you increasingly closer. You may drift or be ushered into a dark void or tunnel and feel as if you are floating through it, perhaps feeling periodically lonely yet possessed of great serenity and peace. Suddenly you become sensitive to a presence which, through words or thoughts, induces you to review your life toward determining whether you wish to remain here or go back.

Then you find yourself seeing, "as though in a million simultaneous yet precise and sharp images, everything that has ever happened to you in your life," according to Ring, and all without a sense of judgment and free of the weight of time and space. "You grasp the essential meaning of your life and in the moment of that realization, you see with absolute clarity that you must go back, that your family, especially your children, need you." The next thing you realize is that you are in excruciating pain, perhaps in a hospital bed or at the scene of a horrible accident or injury.

You know without a shade of doubt that it was no dream or hallucination, nor something you simply imagined. "You wish you could talk about it, but who could understand, even if you found words adequate to describe it?" writes Kenneth Ring. "All you know is that this is the most profound thing that has ever happened to you and that your life — and your understanding of life — will never again be the same."

When he compared the journey of the shaman with contemporary accounts of journeys to the edge of death and back, Dr. Ring discovered interesting structural similarities. The shaman's training often begins with an experience of imminent biological death, an experience amplified by later enactments of psychic death and rebirth in the refinement of shamanic practices. In the modern near-death experience, subjects encounter a guide — a cosmic shaman, says Ring — who facilitates answers to all kinds of life questions; and then they are returned to the world to take up their commitments to family and community. Similarly, the shaman's journey is not considered complete until he or she breaks off the encounter with beings in "upper and lower worlds" and returns with knowledge of value to the community as a whole.

WE HAVE traveled a great distance from the moment when Gregory Bateson reached into a bag, pulled out a freshly cooked crab, and asked his students a provocative question: *What pattern connects the crab to the lobster and the orchid and the primrose and all the four of them to me? And me to you? And all six of us to the amoeba in one direction and to the back-ward schizophrenic in another?*

Our own questions are similarly broad: *What pattern connects contactees and abductees and angels, shamanic encounters and near-death experiences? And all of these to the tenuous dimension known as ordinary reality?* These are questions to which we will return in pages to come. Now it is time to turn back to center stage, where the pursuit of clear, definitive answers to the UFO mystery has continued without hint of pause.

THIRTEEN

—————— ✕ ——————

$\mathbf{T}$WO books published at the out-
set of the UFO phenomenon's fourth decade defined the themes that
would animate, impel, and finally possess UFO researchers — proponents and debunkers alike — throughout the 1980s and into the 1990s.
The Roswell Incident, co-authored by William Moore, revived the longstanding rumor that a flying saucer had crashed in July 1947 in the
desert of New Mexico, a fact that he said had been obscured by a pervasive *governmental* conspiracy. *Missing Time*, by Budd Hopkins, con-
tended that alien abductions of innocent human beings had reached
epidemic levels, a fact that he said had been obscured by a pervasive
alien conspiracy. At a time when the UFO debate seemed close to terminal exhaustion, these two books, focusing on different aspects of
the UFO puzzle, paraphrased specific versions of essentially the same
idea: *Our persistence, diligence, and keen insight in pursuit of the truth
have finally paid off. After decades of deception, the cover-up is collapsing.
Because we dared to press our case against the forces of darkness, at last
we find ourselves closing in on the core secrets of the phenomenon. It is
only a matter of time before we prevail.*
    Others saw things differently, of course.

$\mathbf{R}$UMORS of crashed saucers were nothing new — they were present
from the start, a core motif in ufology's creation mythology. *Variety*

columnist Frank Skully's best-selling 1950 book, *Behind the Flying Saucers*, spoke of crashed Venusian spacecraft in Aztec, New Mexico, and Arizona. Forty-eight dead aliens were supposedly recovered, all about four feet in height, each with "perfect teeth." Although Skully's claims were debunked two years later, and several times more in succeeding years, the crashed saucer legend continued to thrive.

A woman who for many years held a high-security clearance at Wright-Patterson Air Force Base told in a deathbed confession of witnessing two chemically preserved alien bodies, which, but for their strangely sloped eyes and larger-than-normal heads, otherwise resembled humans. At a 1978 UFO conference, a tape was played of an anonymous speaker describing being inside a top-secret hangar when a forklift unloaded crates of alien corpses. Leonard Stringfield, a UFO researcher specializing in collecting uncorroborated conspiracy accounts, revealed that the witness — forbidden by superiors to tell any more secrets — later moved with his family without leaving a forwarding address. Stringfield's clear implication, according to skeptic George W. Early, was that the entire family was sequestered to prevent future leaks, or perhaps (for simplicity's sake) killed and "buried under a section of superhighway along with Jimmy Hoffa."

UFO historian Jerome Clark found that most of the crashed saucer rumors followed a predictable storyline:

> In the late 1940s and maybe even later, several flying saucers crashed in the Southwest. The remains, including the bodies of gray-skinned humanoid beings, were retrieved by government and military agencies. The material was taken for study to Wright-Patterson Air Force Base in Dayton, Ohio, and subsequently some of it was sent elsewhere. The entire matter is highly classified and only a small number of individuals within the government know the whole story. The secrecy has been maintained both to prevent panic and to keep the Russians from knowing we have access to extraterrestrial technology. At the appropriate time the government will release the information.

In July 1947, newspapers around the nation carried the first government admission that a crashed saucer had been recovered, examined, and shipped on to higher headquarters. The event, alleged to have taken place near Roswell, New Mexico, made headlines like these: RAAF CAPTURES FLYING SAUCER IN ROSWELL REGION. NO DETAILS OF

FLYING SAUCERS ARE REVEALED. Soon thereafter it was revealed that through a comedy of errors a huge weather balloon had crashed on a rancher's land and been reported as a flying saucer. This clarification ensured that for thirty years the matter would remain little more than a curious footnote in UFO history.

Yet the rumor that something extraordinary had happened near Roswell lived on. In January 1978, Stanton T. Friedman, a UFO enthusiast known best for an entertaining lecture — called "Flying Saucers ARE Real" — that he delivered regularly at college campuses was introduced to the manager of a television station who casually mentioned that Friedman should make a point to talk to Major Jesse Marcel, who "way back" had actually handled a UFO. Friedman, an outspoken advocate of the extraterrestrial hypothesis and a declared foe of all UFO debunkers, couldn't resist calling Marcel, who confirmed that while in the the army air force in New Mexico he was involved in processing a great quantity of debris from a crashed flying saucer near Roswell.

Friedman was impressed with Marcel's sincerity but dubious that he had heard anything more than another unverifiable yarn about the much-whispered "Ultimate Secret." Not long thereafter, Friedman got together with William Moore, a schoolteacher, aspiring writer, and UFO buff from Minnesota, to swap Roswell stories. Moore had heard an anecdote or two of his own, and both men concluded there was reason to check out whether there might be a basis for the rumors. The case that has come to be known to ufologists simply as "Roswell" consumed their energies over the next few years, during which they located (*enrolled*, said debunkers) 100 or so informants — some of them supposedly firsthand witnesses, others family members of eyewitnesses, still others possessed of background information.

In 1980, with Bermuda Triangle popularizer Charles Berlitz, Moore coauthored *The Roswell Incident* — like most UFO books, a mixture of documented facts, rumors, speculations, and theories — intended to convince readers that an alien spacecraft had indeed gone down near Roswell. *Fate* magazine dismissed the book, which was filled with factual errors, as "about as bad a book as could be written on a subject of such potential importance." But Moore was not to be deterred from what had become a personal mission. With Friedman he continued to hunt for additional witnesses to build their case that a UFO crash had been covered up by a high-level conspiracy involving both civilian and military government officials. The narrative they pieced together quickly became a legend in UFO circles:

It was the evening of July 2, 1947, little more than one week after Kenneth Arnold's famous Washington state sighting of nine strange craft whose undulating motion reminded him of "a saucer skipping over water." During an intense electrical storm over Roswell, a sheep ranch manager named W. W. "Mac" Brazel heard an enormous explosion that seemed too loud for thunder. When he went out to check on the sheep the next morning, Brazel discovered the remnants of what appeared to be some sort of aircraft scattered over an area several hundred feet wide and a quarter mile long. Later, showing the debris to his brother-in-law and a few friends, Brazel learned for the first time of the flying saucer reports of a week earlier.

Brazel's neighbor, Floyd Proctor, remembered that on the day he found the material, Brazel "was in a talkative mood,"

> which was rare for him, and just wouldn't shut up about it. He described the stuff as very odd. He said whatever the junk was, it had designs on it that reminded him of Chinese and Japanese designs. It wasn't paper because he couldn't cut it with his knife, and the metal was different from anything he had ever seen. He said the designs looked like . . . some sort of figures all done up in pastels, but not like writing we would do.

Brazel gathered up some of the material and took it to the sheriff's office in Roswell. The sheriff then notified nearby Roswell field, home of the 509th Bombardment Group. Ranking intelligence officer Major Jesse Marcel interviewed Brazel and accompanied him to the sight where they found, in Marcel's recollection over twenty years later,

> small beams about 3/8ths or a half-inch square with some sort of hiero-glyphics on them that nobody could decipher. These looked something like balsa wood and were of about the same weight, although flexible, and would not burn. There was a great deal of an unusual parchmentlike substance which was brown in color and extremely strong, and a great number of small pieces of a metal like tinfoil, except that it wasn't tinfoil.

Things moved quickly. Lieutenant Walter Haut, Roswell public information officer, sent a dispatch to the Associated Press that began: "The many rumors regarding the flying disc became a reality yesterday when the . . . Roswell Air Field was fortunate enough to gain possession of a disc through the co-operation of one of the local ranchers and the sheriff's office of Chaves County. . . ." This release earned what the *Washington Post* called a "blistering rebuke" from Brigadier General Roger M. Ramey and deputy air force chief Lieutenant General Hoyt S. Vanenberg, who instructed the Roswell Base commander in no uncertain terms to pack up all the crash debris and send it to Eighth Air Force Headquarters in Fort Worth, Texas. Roswell Base staff were also told to keep their mouths shut.

When Marcel arrived with the debris aboard a Texas B-29, General Ramey ordered him to stay away from reporters. Ramey appeared on local radio to inform the public that a weather balloon, not a flying saucer, had been recovered at Roswell. Soon a reporter was called in to photograph the debris, which UFO investigators would contend was not the original debris at all but the remnants of a weather balloon that had been substituted for public relations purposes. "The cover story about the balloon [was] just to get the press off [Ramey's] back," Marcel said many years later. "The press was told it was just a balloon and that the flight to Wright was cancelled; but all that really happened was that I was removed from the flight and someone else took it to Wright." Years later, Ramey's then-personal assistant declared that the order to create a phony cover story came directly from the Pentagon.

Back in Roswell, Mac Brazel was held incommunicado for a week by Roswell Base officers, appearing only to make brief statements to the media confirming the cover story. When the Roswell incident attracted UFO researchers' interest years after Brazel's death, his daughter claimed that their whole family had been warned never to discuss the incident. "Back in those days, when the military told you not to talk about something, it wasn't discussed," said Bessie Brazel, who was twelve when the crash occurred. The Brazel family expressed great bitterness at the way Mac had been treated by the military. Their deepest regret is that he went to his grave without telling all he knew.

While Mac Brazel was being held, air force investigators scoured the crash site in an apparent attempt to gather every shred of material they could find. Bill Brazel, Mac's son, continued to find bits and pieces of the crash debris after investigators left the site: "Seems like every time after a good rain I would manage to find a piece or two that they had overlooked. After a year and a half or two years I had managed to accumulate quite a small collection — about enough that if you were to lay it out on this tabletop it would take up about as much area as

[a] briefcase." In 1949, after a few drinks at a local bar, Brazel regaled listeners with accounts of his flying saucer artifacts. The next morning his home was visited by military officials who demanded to see Brazel's collection. You'll have to surrender this material, they told him, along with any additional pieces he happened to find later. "Naturally I said I would but I never did because after that I never found any more," Brazel said.

Assuming everything up to this point of the story is factual, there is as much reason to believe the air force was using the balloon story to cover up the crash of a top-secret experimental military craft, or a weapons test gone awry, as there is to suspect a downed extraterrestrial craft. But this argument shatters into as many pieces as the debris found on the ranch *if* the following rumor is true:

During aerial photographic reconnaissance flights over the area, the bodies of four humanoid beings, who apparently ejected from the craft prior to its explosion, were discovered. Allegedly, one of the creatures was badly mauled by predators, but the others were found intact. In the years that followed, Moore and Friedman — and a second investigatory team operating independently — located some 300 witnesses to various aspects of the Roswell case, 50 claiming to know that alien bodies were indeed recovered. One military witness, O. W. Henderson, said he personally flew the alien corpses in crates from the Roswell Base.

Debunkers say they eagerly await evidence corroborating anything other than pro-UFO researchers' curious religious need to transform an ambiguous desert scenario into firm evidence of joyriding outer space aliens running one too many celestial traffic signs on a rainy night. Here, in summary, are the unapologetically contemptuous questions to which debunkers return again and again:

Are we really to believe that so many witnesses to such an indisputably world-shaking event would simply remain silent until, three decades after the fact, pro-UFO researchers arrived on the scene pressing questions based on thinly veiled assumptions authorizing folks to join their friends and neighbors in confirming a breathtaking new story of enormous historical significance? Who *wouldn't* want to substitute their vague anonymous memories of a long-ago set of events with a new plot that places them and their friends at the very edge of history? Even if witnesses' stories sound convincing when woven into the delusional tapestries conjured by UFO zealots, are we really to believe that proof positive of extraterrestrial life could be successfully hidden in an age when two presidents of the United States, Nixon and Reagan, tried to but could not thwart investigations of the Watergate and Iran-contra scandals?

And if there were *truly* an important story to be told, wouldn't we expect to find respected investigative journalists like Bob Woodward and Carl Bernstein taking up residence in Roswell, rather than those we do find: the same crowd of conspiracymongers who perennially — and conveniently — go searching for proof of something for which *only* anecdotal evidence exists? What better way to secure for themselves the minimal sense of personal significance they've not been able to achieve by distinguishing themselves in legitimate social pursuits!

Wait until we present our complete case, which is *not* entirely based on anecdotes, respond Roswell advocates. (They add: *Then* we'll see who's deluded.)

BUDD Hopkins is an award-winning painter and sculptor whose art appears in the Guggenheim and the Whitney Museum of American Art. Much of his work falls in the tradition of abstract expressionism: the modern movement in art and literature committed to giving objective expression to special emotions and passions. Perhaps as a corollary to his artistic orientation, Hopkins labored throughout the 1980s to bring the subterranean complexities of the alien abduction phenomenon into view as real, hard-edged, unquestionably objective and literal events enacted on anguished human beings by uncaring extraterrestrial entities.

Hopkins's introduction to UFOs came in the summer of 1964 while on vacation at Cape Cod, where, with several friends, he watched a dark, elliptical object the length of two cars hang in the sky motionless for about a minute before slowly disappearing into a bank of northeast clouds. It could not have been a balloon, he reasoned, because it appeared to move in a direction different from that of nearby clouds. His curiosity about what he had seen led him to UFO literature, including books about two famous abduction cases: the Pascagoula, Mississippi, case of Charlie Hickson and Calvin Parker and the New Hampshire case of Betty and Barney Hill.

Before long, Hopkins found himself taking notes when his friends mentioned their own UFO sightings, which in turn led him to check into reports of strange lights in the Cape Cod area. He didn't realize it at the time, but he was "hooked" — the UFO phenomenon intrigued him and he wanted to understand it. He got his first full-scale chance to try in 1975 after returning to New York from his annual Cape Cod summer respite.

One night, Hopkins stopped into the liquor store across the street from his apartment and noticed, as he had on many recent occasions, that co-owner George O'Barski seemed troubled by something. Hopkins and O'Barski weren't close friends, but they had known each other for fifteen years — long enough to know something about one another's rhythms. This night O'Barski was complaining about a "cold in the knee" as one of many things bothering him, along with "this thing that came down out of the sky," leaving him "goddamn scared."

Hopkins immediately perked up. He asked O'Barski, who knew nothing of Hopkins's interest in UFOs, to say more. As O'Barski proceeded to tell about a gigantic, brilliant UFO that came down next to his car as he drove through North Hudson Park, Hopkins interrupted him, ran across the street to get his tape recorder, and returned to capture O'Barski's vivid details. Realizing he had a serious case on his hands, Hopkins immediately consulted Ted Bloecher, a New York UFO investigator with twenty-five years of experience listening to such stories and following leads.

Together they located additional witnesses, including a night watchman at a high-rise apartment building; they concluded that a UFO had landed across from Manhattan at 3 A.M. on January 6, 1975. Five nights later, the craft returned to North Hudson Park where its humanoid occupants appeared to dig up soil samples and fired a projectile of some sort against a plate-glass window of the apartment building as the night watchman tried to place a telephone call to a tenant.

Hopkins later wrote a long article for the *Village Voice* about the adventure of pursuing traces of a flying saucer that, by all accounts, had landed within four miles of the *New York Times*. Not long thereafter, Hopkins's new colleague Ted Bloecher introduced him to a young man, Steven Kilburn, who sat in on a few informal discussions concerning the use of hypnosis to recover abduction memories. One night Kilburn told Hopkins: "There's probably nothing to it, but something may have happened to me when I was in college. I can't remember anything specific, but something has always bothered me about a certain stretch of road I used to pass through whenever I left my girlfriend's house." When Hopkins asked whether he had seen a UFO, Kilburn said, no, he simply felt something had happened to him one night as he drove home, and he wanted to try hypnosis.

A hypnosis session was arranged with a psychologist characterized by Hopkins as "very skeptical" about UFOs. During the session, Kilburn recalled (1) a stretch of road that frightened him for no apparent reason, (2) pulling his car to the side of the road, (3) having his shoulder placed in a painful "clamp" or "wrench," and (4) seeing creatures "all dressed in black . . . can't see their faces." During a second session, a full seven months later, Kilburn realized his car had been *pulled* off the road as if by a strong magnetic force. "Oh, God! I know why I pulled over. Oh no! I see two lights in the sky when I'm driving!" During a third session, Kilburn found himself in the presence of alien beings but unable to recall the intervening events.

Hopkins was perplexed that Kilburn next remembered being back in his car driving to Baltimore, and by Kilburn's remark: "I don't want to remember. I'm not supposed to remember." Kilburn's experience seemed to parallel other abduction reports, such as the Hill encounter, which Hopkins had adopted as his general model for abduction encounters. Yet Hopkins found there was "one basic and striking deviation from the [classical] model. Other abductees remembered seeing a UFO, but Steven could only recall, vaguely, seeing two undistinguished lights ahead of him."

These were not (as Kilburn first assumed) headlights from an approaching vehicle, Hopkins determined. A combination of factors — Kilburn's curious general interest in UFOs, his anxiety about a strange stretch of road, his memory of two lights followed by fleeting images of aliens followed by finding himself inexplicably driving much farther down the same road — led Hopkins to hypothesize that Kilburn had, indeed, been abducted. *The key was the missing time.*

Budd Hopkins was now a bona fide UFO investigator, specializing in abductions, which he suspected to be the key to the whole UFO mystery. The *Village Voice* article prompted people to contact him with questions about their strange experiences and unanswered questions. (Critics would later insist that, unknowingly, Hopkins helped "create" abductees by publicizing a set of symptoms sufficiently ambiguous to plant the idea of alien abduction as a probable prognosis. Philip Klass argued that by modeling his research after the "notoriously flawed"

Betty and Barney Hill abduction case, all of Hopkins's subsequent "findings" were worthless from an evidential standpoint. Hopkins challenged these assertions with increasing indignation.)

Many of those who contacted Hopkins offered, others agreed, to explore their memories, some using hypnosis, others not. In case after case, Hopkins reported, a disturbing profile emerged:

An eerie light on a lonely stretch of road . . . the car going dead . . . an unaccountable memory lapse of an hour or more . . . images of interaction with strange humanoid creatures . . . quasi-medical examinations . . . biopsylike operation on a particular part of the body, typically the calf or thigh . . . later noticing a strange scar corresponding to this operation . . . confusion about where the scar comes from . . . images of implanted devices: transmitters? . . . aliens saying "for your own good you will remember none of this" . . . abductees later drawing pictures of terrifying alien faces resembling pictures drawn by other such subjects, none of whom had delved into UFO literature prior to the abductions . . . images of recurring encounters at various intervals in the subject's life . . .

In his book *Missing Time*, Hopkins asserted that his abduction research supports the findings of other UFO investigators, prompting him to speculate:

> Memory blocks may . . . have to do with the abductee's role as a "human specimen" unwittingly being studied over a period of years. If people are being picked up as children, implanted with monitoring devices, and abducted a second time after puberty, at the very least the first abduction would have to be concealed. If the study is truly long range, the subjects would have to be kept in the dark about their role for many years, and a strongly effective block would have to be imposed . . . There lurks the disturbing possibility that these enforced memory blocks may be extremely effective; the few hundred cases in which the amnesia has been pierced may ultimately represent only a tiny percentage of the actual number of abductees. The epidemic, I believe, may be almost entirely invisible.

Hopkins's willingness to speculate so boldly made him at once a popular and controversial figure in UFO circles. The absence of ambiguity and ambivalence in Hopkins's portrayal earned him a loyal following among close encounter witnesses weary of having their experiences dismissed as fantasy, hoax, or delusion. At the same time, Hopkins became something of a role model for mainstream UFO investigators, many embracing his "master narrative" (Hopkins believes aliens have come in search of human genetic material to restore their dying race) as a vivid framework for their own abduction research.

Yet precisely in demonstrating so little doubt about his theories, Hopkins also earned an equally loyal contingent of intellectual adversaries. Some challenged his refusal to entertain parallels among UFO abduction narratives and anecdotal reports from other domains, especially mythology and folklore, the psychology of altered states of consciousness, and the entire continuum of human encounters with spiritual entities. Dennis Stillings, a longtime investigator of extraordinary experiences, argued that Hopkins's preexisting bias against such parallels, besides being contrary to the spirit of scientific discovery, "unjustifiably homogenizes the diversity, reduces the complexity, and flattens the depths" of abduction phenomena, in the service of fostering a new popular mythology.

Stillings, along with Jacques Vallee and many others not wedded to the "ET hypothesis," disputed the logic of Hopkins's insistence that any acceptable account of the alien abduction experience must begin by taking abduction reports at *face value*, exclusively within the UFO frame of reference. And they questioned Hopkins's bold conclusions about alien genetic tampering, which seemed to them a huge imaginative leap based on a comparatively limited number of cases having mixed evidential value. Philosopher and religious scholar Michael Grosso argued that, even if abductees are reporting contact with real intelligences, "spiritual traditions throughout the world warn against putting much trust in the actions and claims of invisible 'deities' who delight in playing mischievous tricks on human naivete."

And then there are the critics who view "alien abductions" as completely trivial and lacking in substance, a contingent led by ufology's premier party-spoiler-in-residence. After retiring in 1986 from a distinguished career as an award-winning journalist for the magazine *Aviation Week*, Philip Klass devoted many hours to debunking Hopkins's claims, with unrestrained relish. Klass continues to insist that the only question about UFO abductions worth asking is this one: are needless fears being foisted on the public by a cult of UFO fanatics? Each time he answers his own query with a resounding *yes*, no one doubts he has Budd Hopkins in mind.

Klass made it clear that he took the Steven Kilburn case and others like it as irredeemable evidence of Hopkins's a priori faith in the truth of alien abductions. Kilburn had attended discussions in Hopkins's own studio about the use of hypnosis to recover abduction memories, Klass noted, only after which he had, in Hopkins's words, a "vague feeling that something he could not remember happened to him one night on a particular stretch of road." Hopkins responded that it *often* happens that way: in case after case, abductees either develop an intellectual interest in UFOs to compensate for the hidden alien injunction against remembering the abduction — or else their memories get sparked by hearing others talk about UFOs.

That's a convenient myth for supporting UFO researchers' fantasies about alien visitors, and nothing more, Klass retorted, noting that it was Budd Hopkins who *concluded* that Kilburn had been abducted, although Kilburn never even saw a UFO. But he saw *lights*, just as many abductees do, Hopkins countered, insisting that his sessions with many people from many walks of life, most of whom held little prior interest in UFOs, offer ample evidence for his theory that "an unknown mind control technology — for which 'alien' is an appropriate description — ensures that the events immediately prior to abductions are seamlessly joined to events after the abduction, with missing time in between."

Klass noted that seven months passed between Kilburn's first and second hypnosis sessions, during which "it would be surprising if Kilburn's curiosity did not prompt him to read about the claimed experiences" of other, more famous abductees. Furthermore, the fact that UFO researcher Ted Bloecher, whose biases were well known to Kilburn, had participated in asking Kilburn questions during his hypnosis session, violated one of the most fundamental safeguards established precisely to prevent the creation of false memories.

Hopkins responded by citing the testimony of an independent, skeptical psychologist, Aphrodite Clamar, Ph.D., who had read nothing about UFO abductions prior to her own hypnosis sessions with clients brought to her by Hopkins. Dr. Clamar stated: "The events recounted by a variety of people from scattered places are strikingly similar, suggesting that there might be more to the whole business than mere coincidence. In different years, different people from different parts of the country all report nearly identical experiences."

And why shouldn't they? Klass asked, noting that a prime-time television movie about the Betty and Barney Hill abduction had been broadcast two weeks prior to the famous 1975 abduction of Travis Walton. Klass urged Hopkins to pay closer attention to what else Dr. Clamar had noted, specifically her statement following two years of joint research with Hopkins: "I cannot say whether the experience [recounted by the subject] was 'real' or not. I do not know — nor could hypnosis claim to establish — whether the UFO experience actually 'happened.' "

The battle between Hopkins and Klass would grow considerably more bitter in coming years, serving as a focus for an apparently deepening split in the public psyche. On one hand, something surpassing strange seemed to be going on, something not reducible merely to cultural sources (the "people who read about abductions report abductions" theory), nor to some new category of psychopathology. Many thoughtful researchers — some with no interest in or clear position toward UFOs — found the abduction phenomenon a genuine mystery, especially in light of the remarkable constancy of abduction narratives among so many different kinds of people.

On the other hand, the very idea of alien abductions — especially their manner — stretched credulity. Gray reptilian dwarfs technologically advanced enough to get here largely without detection, spending their time digging holes in the ground? How many rocks samples do they really need? If they can paralyze individuals to extract blood, sperm and ova, one supposed they could also enter a university medical center late some night and get all the blood samples and genetic material they need to clone a whole race of androids. In short, how could these events be happening the way witnesses describe?

For every such argument against the apparent absurdity of the abductors' actions, proponents could — and usually did —respond with curiously circular logic: "Ah, yes, but do we really *know* what their true motivations might be? You see, they could have a very *complex* agenda." Skeptics could — and usually did — answer back: "So it's a fallacy for *us* to question the nonsensical character of UFO events, but *you* are allowed to interpret this same absurdity as evidence of their exquisitely subtle master strategy? That's the mentality of a cult!"

Hopkins's overall case was not helped by the lurid milieu surrounding abduction claims, fostered not only by supermarket tabloids, but, ironically, by the sensationalistic passage that appeared on the paperback cover of his own book, *Missing Time*: "DOCUMENTED STORIES OF PEOPLE KIDNAPPED BY UFOS AND THEN RETURNED WITH THEIR MEMORIES ERASED . . . IT MAY HAVE HAPPENED TO YOU!"

Even so, Hopkins showed no sign of modifying his claims. To the contrary: At the 1981 conference of the Mutual UFO Network in Cambridge, Massachusetts, Hopkins concluded his presentation with these words: "If one wants to be truly jarred, consider this proposition: There may be as many abductions as there are UFO reports." (By this recursive logic, Hopkins — a witness to a silvery disk in the sky in 1964 — himself might be a closet abductee, as might anyone who feels an emotional reaction of any kind when reading abduction accounts. But he insisted that he shows "none of the warning signs" — anxiety attacks, flashbacks, and so on — of harboring a hidden abduction experience.)

No matter what was "really" happening in the experience called alien abduction, the continuing elaboration of unconfirmable speculation about its origins and prevalence was like a high-dose vitamin shot to the emerging abduction *mythology*. This development had two effects. Debunkers (and honest skeptics) continued to have a field day by simply noting the logical leaps required for taking abductions at face value, as Hopkins insisted they must be. At the same time, a third group of observers — an emerging middle ground — began to investigate abductions apart from the all-or-nothing mentality that seemed to have "abducted" the reports themselves.

For instance, Jacques Vallee, pressing parallels between modern alien abductions and thefts of children in fairy lore and folkloric accounts of visits from the "Sky People," continued to urge that abductions be seen as real manifestations of a larger intelligence enacting its latest mythic drama for the purpose of sustaining human belief. "Abductions practically *beg* to be read symbolically," Vallee argued, even as he admitted that the popular extraterrestrial visitation hypothesis had become an article of religious faith for many, if not most, mainstream UFO researchers.

Thus the plot thickened on this most controversial aspect of UFO research. With each new rendition, the "abduction sonata," as it might be called, like a piece of contrapuntal music in which a basic "plainsong" is accompanied by other melodies set over or against the original theme, was becoming more complex, and ever more interesting.

IN 1982, a Los Angeles television producer, Jaime Shandera, joined forces with William Moore in the continuing effort to crack the Roswell case. (Fellow crashed-saucer tracker Stanton Friedman remained involved — although less so, temporarily — from his new home in Canada.) In December 1984, Shandera received a package in the mail, wrapped in plain brown paper, taped with brown tape along all seams, with a neatly typed address label and no return address. Inside the envelope was a second package, similarly sealed, containing yet another envelope, this one white, enclosing a canister that held a roll of unprocessed 35 mm film.

Shandera knew immediately, even before the film was developed, that what he held in his hands would be of interest to his colleague Bill Moore. When the film was processed, Moore and Shandera found themselves in possession of prints of a nine-page document stamped TOP/SECRET/MAJIC/EYES ONLY and titled as follows: BRIEFING DOCUMENT: OPERATION MAJESTIC 12/PREPARED FOR PRESIDENT-ELECT DWIGHT D. EISENHOWER: (EYES ONLY) / 18 NOVEMBER, 1952. The briefing officer was identified as "Adm. Roscoe H. Hillenkoetter (MJ-1)." Hillenkoetter had served as the first director of the Central Intelligence Agency between 1947 and 1950. Page two of the document stated:

> OPERATION MAJESTIC-12 is a TOP SECRET Research and Development/Intelligence operation responsible directly and only to the President of the United States. Operations of the project are carried out under control of the Majestic-12 (Majic-12) Group which was established by special classified executive order of President Truman on 24 September, 1947, upon recommendation by Dr. Vannebar Bush and Secretary [of Defense] James Forrestal.

The twelve members of MJ-12 were listed as including the secretary of defense, the air force chief of staff and vice chief of staff, the head of MIT's aeronautics department, the director of Central Intelligence (precursor to the CIA), and several other distinguished military and civilian luminaries, including Donald Menzel, the famous Harvard astronomer who wrote or cowrote three books debunking UFOs.

The document made explicit reference to the saucer crash at Roswell:

On 07 July, 1947, a secret operation was begun to assure recovery of the wreckage.... During the course of this operation, aerial reconnaissance discovered that four small humanoid-like beings had apparently ejected from the crash at some point before it exploded. These had fallen to earth about two miles east of the wreckage site. All four were dead and badly decomposed due to action by predators and exposure to the elements during the approximately one week time period which had elapsed before their recovery.

A preliminary "covert analytical report" authorized by President Truman concluded that the crashed saucer was most likely a "short range reconnaissance craft." Dr. Detlov Bronk, a specialist in aviation physiology, arranged autopsies on the alien remains. Consequently Bronk surmised that "the biological and evolutionary processes responsible for their development has [sic] apparently been quite different from those observed or postulated for homo-sapiens." Bronk's team suggested that the term " 'Extraterrestrial Biological Entities,' or 'EBEs', be adopted as the standard term of reference for these creatures...."

Admiral Hillenkoetter informed President-elect Eisenhower that efforts to decipher a form of writing found in the wreckage, and to determine the craft's method of propulsion or power transmission dynamics, had remained largely unsuccessful. Another TOP SECRET EYES ONLY document on White House letterhead ("Attachment A"), purported to be written and signed by President Harry Truman, authorized Admiral Hillenkoetter "to proceed with all due speed and caution upon your undertaking," understood to be the maintenance of a tight embargo on all facts pertaining to the Roswell incident.

Were these documents authentic, or part of a well-orchestrated hoax? Moore says he and Shandera set out to answer this question first, rather than rushing to release the document. The two received unexpected help when two postcards, mailed from New Zealand, arrived bearing cryptic messages directing them to the National Archives at Washington, D.C. Moore had already been informed by his colleague Stan Friedman that more than 100 boxes of once top-secret United States Air Force intelligence documents, dating from 1946 to 1952, were being considered for declassification. Look closely through these documents, the postcards said.

So they did. In July 1985, Moore and Shandera reported finding, amid hundreds of boxes of declassified documents, a memo from President Eisenhower's assistant, General Robert Cutler, referring to an "MJ-12 SSP [Special Studies Project] briefing" to "take place during the already scheduled White House meeting of July 16. . . ." The exact nature of MJ-12 was not disclosed, but this memo was the first *apparently* legitimate document to mention independently the existence of a project by the name MJ-12.

The obvious next question: was this document real or might it, too, be a fake planted in the National Archives? Perhaps tricksters in the American intelligence community, eager for sport, had placed bets with one another about whether they could entice a couple of credulous UFO zealots to leap through a series of hoops. In previous years, Jacques Vallee had speculated that there might be a covert group somewhere in the world interested for political reasons in fostering and maintaining faith in "the plurality of inhabited worlds." Were Moore, Shandera, and Friedman caught in a disinformation loop vaster than they imagined — vaster than they even *could* imagine? Or were some or all members of this ufological trio themselves running a scam on the rest of ufology?

Moore and Shandera said they hoped to keep what came to be known as the Cutler memo secret while they questioned its authenticity, but then they got word that a British ufologist, Timothy Good, author of *Above Top Secret: The Worldwide UFO Coverup*, had received his own copy of the MJ-12 briefing papers and was on the verge of making it public. Not wanting to be scooped in what might be the greatest story of the millennium — and perhaps robbed of a place in history books next to Darwin and Galileo — Moore quickly mailed copies to reporters and ufologists, but not before taking a fateful step that would seriously diminish his credibility on the MJ-12 matter from that point on.

Moore blacked out classification designations and even some of the text, an act that convinced many open-minded observers that, far from being interested in disclosing all relevant facts, William Moore was a man with a covert agenda of his own. Chief among the skeptics was longtime debunker Philip Klass, who, as a professional journalist specializing in matters relating to aviation, space, and military technology, had been busily training his sights on a target with Bill Moore's claims as the bull's-eye. Now Klass was ready to begin shooting.

Like Moore and Shandera, Klass was skeptical about the authenticity of the MJ-12 briefing papers. But it was the claims of these two researchers that raised his gravest doubts. Why, for instance, had the undeveloped film been sent to Shandera, who was not known as a UFO researcher, as opposed to Moore, coauthor of a well-known book about Roswell, or his sidekick Friedman, a popular UFO lecturer sometimes billed as "The Flying Saucer Physicist"? How would the sender of the film even know that Moore and Shandera were friends, or that the film would find its way to Moore?

And why, Klass continued, would Shandera automatically assume — as he said he did — that his receipt of an undeveloped roll of film sent in an unmarked wrapper would obviously be of interest to Moore — so much so that Moore chose to be present as the film was developed? Moore was on record as saying that the sender of the film must have photocopied the entire set of MJ-12 documents in two duplicate sequences to ensure at least one clear copy of each page. Klass wondered why the sender would not have simply developed the film and sent prints, removing any doubt about their legibility?

It was curious, Klass thought, that Admiral Hillenkoetter, the briefing officer named in the documents, would be entrusted to manage a cover-up of unprecedented complexity and sophistication, when he was on active duty as a naval commander outside the United States during the year prior to the alleged briefing. And why, Klass continued, would President-elect Eisenhower not have been briefed by the chairman of MJ-12, who surely would have remained closest to the committee's activities? (Since Dr. Vannebar Bush, president of the Carnegie Foundation, was listed as "MJ-1," Klass logically assumed he was the chairman.)

But it was certain anomalies in the document's format that most raised Klass's eyebrows. "Whoever typed the Hillenkoetter briefing document used a peculiar style for writing dates — an erroneous mixture of civil and military format," Klass noted. The standard military format, he said, was as follows: 18 November 1952. But the Hillenkoetter document used a highly unusual (for a military format) extra comma: "18 November, 1952." This was no one-time error, but constant all through the document: each date uses the "erroneous extra comma." Listen to what Klass said next: "By a curious coincidence, this is precisely the same style used by William L. Moore in *all* of his letters to me since 1982, when our correspondence began."

Equally strange, to Klass's way of thinking, is the Hillenkoetter document's use of a "zero" preceding a single-digit date, a practice that came into limited use *long after* 1952, when the briefing document was allegedly written. This, Klass said, was the standard format for CIA documents from the 1950s through the 1970s: "1 August 1950." By contrast, the Hillenkoetter document contains "01 August, 1950" and "07 July, 1947," and "06 December, 1950." Then Klass made another pointed reference to William Moore's own writing format: "My files of correspondence from Moore show that he used a single digit *without* a zero until the fall of 1983 — roughly a year before the Hillenkoetter document film was reportedly was sent to Shandera —when he then switched to the same style used in the Hillenkoetter briefing document."

As for Truman's signature, there is no question of its authenticity, Klass admitted. "But thanks to the invention of the Xerox machine, it is easy to substitute bogus text on a photocopy of an authentic original, obtained, for example, from the Truman Library, in Independence, Missouri, which both Moore and Freidman visited prior to late 1984." Klass found many other instances of what struck him as highly unlikely discrepancies — including the fact that the keys of the typewriter used for the MJ-12 documents appeared not to have been recently cleaned, and the ribbon seemed oddly worn, both "in contrast to the more elegant typeface, fresh-ribbon appearance of authentic Truman memoranda written at about the same time."

Klass then looked to Moore's own statements about Roswell with suspicion, noting that two years prior to learning of Vannebar Bush's involvement in MJ-12, Moore told a Canadian UFO conference that Bush would be "the logical choice for an assignment to set up a Top Secret project dealing with a crashed UFO." Klass praised Moore's "remarkable psychic abilities" in predicting the MJ-12 document's content so far in advance. Quoting Moore's statement that "if I was going to pick a panel at that time, capable of dealing with a crashed UFO, I would certainly want to consider [those on] that list," Klass took this to mean that "the members of MJ-12 were persons whom Moore himself would probably have selected for such a committee."

Turning his attentions to the Cutler memo reportedly found in the National Archives, Klass noted, with characteristic sarcasm, that "Lady Luck smiled, allowing Moore and Shandera to discover a sorely needed sheet of paper that could authenticate the MJ-12 documents on the

35 mm film." No doubt aware of libel law, Klass never went so far as to accuse Moore or his associates of forging the MJ-12 papers or of planting the Cutler memo in the National Archives. Instead he noted that, by Moore's own admission, he and his team were the first researchers to be granted access to the newly declassified papers. And then Klass gave the blade one final twist:

> More significantly, Robert Cutler could not possibly have written the memo on July 14, 1954, telling of last-minute changes in the president's schedule, because Cutler had left Washington 11 days earlier (July 3) to visit major military facilities in North Africa and Europe and did not return to Washington until July 15. This is shown by his subsequent report to the president, date July 20, housed in the Eisenhower library.

If Klass did not call Moore a con man, directly, neither did Moore respond by calling Klass a pathological liar, exactly. Instead he went to work trying to debunk the debunker's own claims. First: Moore said it was well known to his own contacts within the intelligence community that Shandera was working closely with him on the Roswell project. These same contacts, according to Moore, had told them to expect something important soon by mail; thus Shandera was not surprised when an unmarked package arrived bearing undeveloped film.

Contrary to Klass's allegations about "standard" document format, the styles used in the MJ-12 document, although unusual, are found in *some* other documents of the same period, said Moore. All of Klass's suggestions that Moore had anything to do with creating either the MJ-12 documents or the Cutler memo constitute the lowest form of character assassination, Moore insisted. *And, yes, Philip,* Cutler was indeed out of town during the period the memo was dated, but surely Cutler's assistant, acting on his boss's previous instruction, could have had a secretary prepare the memo over Cutler's name and have it passed through appropriate channels, Moore reasoned.

And so it went. For those given over to labyrinthine intrigue, this high-velocity exchange of charges and countercharges about *secrets* — set against a continuing failure to reach a definitive resolution — made for spellbinding dramatics. *Spellbinding* seems precisely the word, as both sides appeared increasingly possessed by their allure of their own rhetoric: Moore and his adherents claiming a compelling case against the hoax hypothesis, Klass and the debunkers declaring precisely the opposite. Sideline observers, seeking to make up their own minds, complained that each faction's case, standing alone, free from external challenge, seemed convincing — until the other camp's argument was considered in its own equally isolated rhetorical vacuum.

"So far, the clearest winner is runaway monolithic thinking," noted a weary observer at a recent California UFO conference. He added: "This whole thing is not exhausted yet."

Exactly: *not exhausted yet.* So long as the primary facts about the Roswell incident, the genesis of the MJ-12 documents, and the alien abduction phenomenon remained officially unconfirmed, each side could continue to render its arguments consistent, plausible, largely irrefutable, and even apparently inevitable. As of the mid-1980s, the jury remained out on Moore's claims of massive government conspiracy, Hopkins's claims of massive alien conspiracy, and Klass's massive dismissal of both.

Forty years earlier, according to Project Blue Book director Edward Ruppelt, the first investigators at the Air Technical Intelligence Center "were confident that within a few months or a year they would have the answer to the question, 'What are UFO's?' " Thus the mid-1980s assumption that the jury was soon to return with a definitive final verdict, revealing at last the phenomenon's long-hidden core facts, was a time-honored assumption, a reiteration of a cherished ufological theme: "*Any day now . . .*" By embracing this faith literally, reflexively, all sides could avoid the decidedly less upbeat question of whether a verdict would — or even *could* — ever be returned in terms satisfying to either side, let alone both.

Yet a growing number of observers now saw this question as unavoidable. Many had begun to join the line of speculation opened years earlier by Jacques Vallee's heretical suggestion that perhaps the very expectation of a final decree existed primarily to perpetuate itself, and with it human faith in the overall UFO mythos. From this perspective, the ever-recurring motifs of conspiracy and cover-up had some abysmal necessity all their own — some hidden, circular, inexhaustible compulsion whose ritualized enactment, decade by decade, required actors (pro and con) who knew their lines by heart, and who would *stick to the script.*

Not surprisingly, the ufological mainstream had little interest in engaging such speculation, correctly discerning that it could prove subversive to the important, straight-ahead work yet to be accomplished. For instance, the Mutual UFO Network was full of steam to implement its "major goal" to have a "State Section Director assigned to every county or parish in the U.S.A." Presumably this would put in place ufology's equivalent of "ghostbusters," ready to go on-site, anywhere, anytime. Thus deputized, ufologists could fill dead time doing what they did best between landings: taking on battles against debunkers, public apathy, hostile news media, scientific ridicule, and UFO sightings that didn't fit the official ET myth; in short, "all the usual suspects."

Philip Klass eagerly affirmed the idea that pro-UFO researchers were enmeshed in self-fulfilling rituals, but insisted that this did not apply to his own small company of debunkers. Theirs was rather a necessary — and largely unpleasant — task of exposing ufology as a space-age religion masquerading as science. "I would be desperately happy to leave this field for good tomorrow morning," Klass said. Most observers continued to be impressed by the zeal and apparent delight with which Klass consistently approached his noxious chore.

A few scientifically oriented researchers, shunning the term *ufologist* for its dismal public connotations, continued (mostly outside the limelight of established UFO groups) investigating sighting reports and compiling interesting patterns. But as a collective, ufologists mostly seemed drawn — like moths to a flame — to ritualized warfare among themselves about the future of their field and the nature of the phenomenon it was committed to "resolving." This was what ufologists continued to do best as the 1990s approached.

FOURTEEN

———— ✕ ————

OF ALL the difficult questions asked by people who have had UFO experiences, perhaps the most perplexing, and the most common, is "Why me?" It is the sense of having been selected for some unknown reason to carry out some unknown purpose or mission that I want to discuss in this chapter. Through many long conversations with dozens of individuals who have chosen — quite bravely, I feel — to come to terms with their experiences, I have found that the "Why me?" question usually manifests itself as "Have I been inducted or initiated? If so, by what or whom? Toward what end?"

That the metaphor of initiation comes up again and again for so many witnesses seems appropriate, for there are significant parallels among the stages, structures, and dynamics of traditional initiation ceremonies and experiences with the unknown Other called UFOs. Here I am concerned with what people report about their experience, not about what is ultimately, "objectively" true. As we have seen, the latter domain is a vast unknown, whereas it is possible to take as primary data the body of UFO encounter *reports*.

The intensity of the existential and spiritual crisis that may be precipitated by a UFO experience (UFOE) does not appear to depend on whether a percipient feels he or she has interacted with a traditional flying saucer or other "unidentified flying object," or instead feels he or she has had a powerful "psychic," "imaginal," "archetypal," "mythological," "near-death," "shamanic," "out of body," or "angelic" experience. The experiential authenticity of a UFOE seems largely to depend on the extent to which the percipient experiences interaction with otherworldly beings, presences, entities, or objects as significantly substantial and fundamentally real, even as "more real than real."

If these conditions are met, neither does the profundity of a UFO-related crisis seem to depend on whether the percipient hypothesizes the "UFO beings" to be denizens from "outer space," "parallel universes," "the collective unconscious," "heaven," "hell," or other numinous locales. It is the patterns that appear common to these accounts that I take as a starting point in exploring UFO experiences as modern initiations and rites of passage.

Professor Arnold van Gennep has defined rites of passage as "rites which accompany every change of place, state, social position, and age." The passage from womb to tomb is punctuated by a number of critical transitions marked by appropriate rituals meant to make clear the significance of the individual and the group alike to all members of the community. Such ritualized passages include birth, puberty, marriage, and religious confirmation, including induction into mystery schools of various kinds — to which I add a new category of experience: the human/UFO encounter.

Looking at what seems the central paradox of human-alien interaction — namely, the continuing unsolvability of the UFO phenomenon by conventional means and models, coupled with the continuing manifestation of the phenomenon in increasingly bizarre forms — it is difficult to avoid the impression that the very tension of this paradox has had an initiatory impact. While the debate between true believers on both sides of the UFO question presses on with predictable banality, personal and collective belief systems have been changing in ways that have been at once imperceptible and momentous.

Without our notice, the human mythological structure has been undergoing a fundamental shift. Public opinion surveys and other measures of the collective pulse reveal that more people than ever now take for granted that we are not alone in the universe — "inner" as well as "outer" universes, if such a division is finally possible. The very unwillingness of the UFO phenomenon either to go away or to come considerably closer to us in a single step has been conditioning us — initiating us, if you will — to entertain extraordinary possibilities about who we are at our depths, and what the defining conditions of the game we call Reality might be.

Van Gennep showed that all rites of transition are marked by three faces: separation, marginality, and aggregation or consummation (return). Phase one, separation, involves the detachment of individuals and groups from an earlier fixed social position or set of cultural conditions, a detachment or departure from a previous state. For example, the young male who proceeds into a male initiatory ceremony in a traditional culture is forced to leave his self-identification as "boy" at the door of the initiation lodge.

Phase two, marginality, involves entering a state of living in the margins, betwixt and between, not quite here and not quite there. Marginality (also called liminality, from the Latin *limen*, meaning "threshold") is characterized by a profound sense of ambiguity about who one really is. The young male is no longer a boy but has not yet become, through specifically designated ritual, a man.

Aggregation, then, is a time of coming back together but in a new way, moving out of the margins into a new state of being. This is the time of consummation or culmination of the process. Now the male has earned the right to be called, and to consider himself, a man.

Joseph Campbell, easily the late twentieth century's most creative and insightful mapper of mythic realms, wrote a great deal about the many forms the separation phase might take. In his classic work on the universal myth of the hero's journey, *The Hero with a Thousand Faces*, Campbell writes: "A hero ventures forth from the world of common day into a region of supernatural wonder." What a magnificently succinct description of the first moments of a UFO encounter — even though, of course, UFOs are not mentioned once in Campbell's book. He speaks further of this first phase of the journey as the Call to Adventure, signifying

> that destiny has summoned the hero and transferred his spiritual center of gravity from within the pale of his society to a zone unknown. This fateful region of both treasure and danger may be variously represented: as a distant land, a forest, a kingdom underground, beneath the waves, or above the sky, a secret island, lofty mountaintop, or profound dream state; but it is always a place of strangely fluid and polymorphous beings, unimaginable torments, superhuman deeds, and impossible delights. The hero can go forth of his own volition to accomplish the adventure, as

did Theseus when he arrived in his father's city, Athens, and heard the horrible story of the Minotaur; or he may be sent abroad by some benign or malignant agent, as was Odysseus, driven about the Mediterranean by the winds of the angered god Poseidon. The adventure may begin as a mere blunder, as did that of the princess in the fairy tale "The Frog Prince"; or still again, one may be only casually strolling, when some passing phenomenon catches the wandering eye and lures one from the frequented paths of man. Examples might be multiplied, ad infinitum, from every corner of the world.

I have quoted this passage at length because of the many parallels between the hero's call to adventure in mythology and the numerous examples from UFO lore of individuals summoned "from within the pale of society to a zone unknown . . . a place of strangely fluid and polymorphous beings, unimaginable torments, superhuman deeds, and impossible delights." Popular legend has of course familiarized us with the way UFOs seemingly disappear "above the sky," but there are a good many impressive reports of luminous disks retiring "beneath the waves."

Many contactees open with curiosity, even excitement, to the encounter with aliens, just as Theseus went forth voluntarily. Most abductees report being taken away against their will, like Odysseus buffeted by the winds of angry Poseidon. And, of course, we have learned in the preceding pages of a far more common motif: the UFO encounter entered into through some kind of "blunder," or in consequence of witnesses simply going about their lives, minding their own business.

In any case, the hero (or contactee or abductee; for present purposes the terms are interchangeable) is separated or detached from the collective, the mainstream, in a powerful and life-changing way. This brings us to the quite frequent response to the Call to Adventure: the refusal of the call. Because separation from the collective is fearsome, the hero often simply says, "Hell, no, I won't go," or later, "I *didn't* go." The contactee or abductee concludes (often as a way to preserve his or her sanity) that "it couldn't have been real . . . It didn't happen to me . . . It was only a dream . . . If I just keep the memory to myself, maybe it will go away . . ."

Refusing the call, writes Campbell, represents the hero's hope that his or her present system of ideals, virtues, goals, and advantages might be fixed and made secure through the act of denial. The world's great religious and philosophic traditions speak in different ways about the crucial aftermath of declining the call, which may be described, based on Jacob's experience in the Old Testament, as wrestling with the angel. "One is harassed, both night and day, by the labyrinth of one's own disordered psyche. The ways to the gates have all been locked: there is no exit."*

The numinous Other in any of its guises — as alien, angel, or archetype — frequently demands something that seems to the initiate unacceptable; yet refusal seems impossible in this new and unfamiliar zone. The terror is often overwhelming, as Whitley Strieber writes in *Communion*:

> "Whitley" ceased to exist. What was left was a body in a state of fear so great that it swept about me like a thick, suffocating curtain, turning paralysis into a condition that seemed close to death. I do not think that my ordinary humanity survived the transition. . . .

How graphic this depiction of being forcibly separated from one's deepest sense of oneself by an utterly alien agency, and left hanging in the ambiguous margins of being. We recall Antonio Villas-Boas's unsuccessful attempt to flee on a disabled tractor, Hickson and Parker being grabbed by "claw-men" from the dusky banks of the Pascagoula River, and Barney Hill's incredulous response to the creatures who peered back at him from inside a landed saucer: "I don't believe it! I don't believe it! This is ridiculous!"

Are we justified in supposing that what is at stake in human-alien encounters is a certain concept of humanity? Professor Carl Raschke, of the Department of Religious Studies at the University of Denver, suggests the answer to this question is yes. The correct problem "is *not* whether [UFOs] exist, or in what sense they exist, but what ultimate aim they serve," says Raschke. "Our interest in them should center on how the spreading and deepening convictions about them subtly, yet

---

*At collective levels of the UFO rite of passage, it is the debunker's job to refuse the call posed by the shape-shifting phenomenon whose aliases include Proteus, Hermes, Trickster, and Dionysus. In an archetypal sense, the debunker serves to shore up the collective psyche's sense that "yep, everything's fine here, just another meteor . . . just another misidentification of Venus . . . just another psychotic fiction writer claiming abduction by aliens . . . just another instance of ball lightning . . . ," and so forth, like a repeating tape on a telephone answering machine intended to provide reassurance at all times. Here and there, the debunker succeeds, but the Call to Adventure is larger than any single case.

irreversibly, remolds [sic] not just peripheral religious or metaphysical ideas, but entire constellations of culture and social knowledge." Raschke maintains that UFOs serve as "agents of cultural deconstruction," referring to

> a process whereby long-standing and pivotal "structures" of thought and action are dismantled so that new, more fluid, and semantically fruitful modes of reflection can take place. . . . The work of deconstruction is not sudden, but slow and inexorable. It is more akin to a sculptor chipping away at stone so that he can craft a figure. . . . So far as UFOs are concerned, the deconstructive movement works upon human culture as a whole, although it may also have devastating effects at times on individual lives.

From the perspective offered by Dr. Raschke, it seems likely that our culturewide ambivalence toward accepting the UFO phenomenon as real reflects a collective sense that the stakes of the game are high indeed. Meeting the gaze of the Other requires embracing the poet Rilke's painful recognition: "There is no place at all that is not looking at you: You must change your life."

As a culture — perhaps as a species — we seem fatally drawn to, beckoned by, this mysterious unknown; and yet abductee Whitley Strieber's fear is not his alone.* Acknowledging the long-term existence of what Strieber calls the "visitor phenomenon" invites us to accept, in his words, "that we very well may be something different from what we believe ourselves to be, on this earth for reasons that may not yet be known to us, the understanding of which will be an immense challenge."

The ancients knew the importance of maintaining an intimate conversation with one's double or daemon, called "genius" in Latin, "guardian angels" by Christianity, "reflex man" by Scots, "vardogr" by Norwegians, "doppelganger" by Germans. The idea was that by taking care to develop one's "genius," this spiritual being would provide help throughout the mortal human's life and into the next. Humans who

---

*One variation of the fear associated with the UFO phenomenon finds expression in a book entitled *UFOs, Satan and Evolution*. Author Sidney J. Jansma offers that "UFOs are neither flying nor normal objects. They are IDENTIFIABLE as SATANIC paranormal APPARITIONS by their violation of the laws of nature in speed and motion and to dematerialize at will. The coldness of UFOnauts, their sulfuric stench, and their lying also testify to their Hellish origin. They are ISAs, not UFOs."

did not attend to their personal Other became an evil and menacing entity called a "larva," given to hovering over terrified sleepers in their beds at night and driving people to madness.

The hero, then, moves beyond refusing to accept the call because, finally, it is impossible not to accept it — which brings us to the second, and in some ways even more difficult, initiatory phase: living in the ambiguous not-quite-here-and-not-quite-there. In his classic essay "Betwixt and Between: The Liminal Period in Rites of Passage," the anthropologist Victor Turner writes that the major function of the transition between states is to render the subject *invisible*. For ceremonial purposes, the neophyte — the one undergoing initiation — is considered structurally "dead." That is, classifiable neither in the old nor in a new way. Invisible — not seen.

In his book examining the details of several alleged UFO abductions, *Intruders*, Budd Hopkins includes an extensive section of a letter he received from a young Minnesota woman who reported having been abducted by UFO aliens as a child and then again as an adult. Because this woman is so articulate in describing the existential crisis faced by abductees, I quote at length from her correspondence:

> For most of us it began with the memories. Though some of us recalled parts or all of our experiences, it was more common for us to have to seek out where they were — buried in a form of amnesia. Often we did this through hypnosis, which was, for many of us, a new experience. And what mixed feelings we had as we faced those memories! Almost without exception we felt terrified as we relived these traumatic events, a sense of being overwhelmed by their impact. But there was also disbelief. This can't be real. I must be dreaming. This isn't happening. Thus began the vacillation and self-doubt, the alternating periods of skepticism and belief as we tried to incorporate our memories into our sense of who we are and what we know. We often felt crazy; we continued our search for the "real" explanation. We tried to figure out what was wrong with us that these images were surfacing. Why is my mind doing this to me?

This woman shows that she understands quite well the feelings associated with being rendered "invisible" by virtue of reporting an experience at variance with the possibilities allowed by "consensus reality":

And then there was the problem of talking about our experiences with others. Many of our friends were skeptics, of course, and though it still hurt us not to be believed, what could we expect? We were still skeptics ourselves at times, or probably had been in the past. The responses we got from others mirrored our own. The people we talked to believed us and doubted us, they were confused and looked for other explanations, as we had. Many were rigid in their denial of even the slightest possibility of abductions, and whatever words they used, the underlying message was clear. I know better than you what is real and what isn't. We felt caught in a vicious circle that seemed to be imposed on us as abductees by a skeptical society:

Why do you believe you were abducted?
You believe it because you're crazy.
How do we know you're crazy?
Because you believe you were abducted.

To summarize: many UFO abductees and contactees, along with those who have had other forms of "spiritual emergency," know what it feels like to be invisible to those who have not been similarly called — or who may be refusing their own "call" to move beyond a way of life devoid of vitality and meaning. This ambiguity is no less pronounced for those who have returned from the edge of death. Having been declared clinically dead and having floated toward a tunnel peopled by beckoning beings of light, only to return to the living with an inexplicably radiant sense of being and purpose, many near-death initiates report no longer feeling human in exactly the same way.

Likewise, the traditional shaman — skilled at traveling between worlds and interacting with nonordinary beings — often remains critically apart from his community because of what Kenneth Ring terms "his special knowledge and his unusual and sometimes disturbing presence."

Here we begin to get a sense of the metapattern that our comparisons in chapter twelve brought to view. Without doubt, there are significant *surface* differences between UFO encounters, angelic visitations, shamanic journeys, and near-death experiences. Yet in all of these realms we find archetypal images of initiation involving otherworldly journeys amid extraordinary — *and apparently autonomous* — beings. Many ufologists, seeking to keep their precious field of study unique and discrete, question such parallels because, they say, there is no evidence that the beings described in non-UFO reports are "from the same place" as UFO beings. What they seldom point out is that there is no evidence, either, of where "UFO beings" are from!

Even if the passengers of flying saucers originate from zip codes in outer space (a proposition for which verifiable evidence has yet to be produced), it requires an act of will *not* to notice thematic parallels between ceremonies of dismemberment undergone by shamanic initiates inside traditional round initiation huts, on one hand, and the invasive "medical" procedures experienced by UFO initiates inside rounded operating theaters inside disk- or oval-shaped craft, on the other hand.

In the process of conducting research for this book, I spoke with many UFO contactees and abductees — including an insurance agent, an elementary school teacher, a cab driver, an architect, a journalist, and a senior vice president of one of America's largest banks — who instantly identified with the feelings of marginality. For some, the "UFO" appeared to be an actual craft. For others, an anomalous light triggered a profound experience. One spoke of "UFO entities" appearing without any vehicle in view.

These differences seem less important than the fact that it is as if the "UFO initiate" glimpses something so profound that certain facts of life prior to the experience are no longer exclusively true. Often he or she is frustrated that others do not see that the rules of the game no longer hold, or that the old rules were always only one of many ways of organizing perception rather than ironclad "laws of nature." A good many abductees identify themselves as "victims" during the period following their encounter, understandably mourning the loss of clear boundaries, of black and white, right and wrong, us and them.

Over time, many come to see that on the other side of the frustration of life in the margins lies a perception available to those willing to enter it: that not being able to classify oneself is also a freedom from having to cling to a single identity. Willingly embracing the marginal, liminal, twilight realms of being, the domain of uncertainty and not-knowing, can make possible new insights, new ways of "constructing reality." In this sense, the UFO encounter experience prods us to take apart easy ideas about the supposedly interminable gulf between mind and matter, spirit and body, masculine and feminine, nature and culture, and other familiar dichotomies.

While many UFO researchers continue their search for definitive, unambiguous answers, it is impressive to meet subjects of close encounters who move from an initial view of paradise lost to celebrating the freedom from having to keep a particular one-dimensional sense of paradise intact. They realize that they can choose to enter paradox and live there, as social psychologist Donald Michael puts it, "landing with both feet firmly planted in midair."

This is a place where fuzzy edges present not simply a challenge to reimpose lost order (the characteristic response of mainstream ufology, ever in search of the Single Correct Pattern), but an opportunity to play in the vast polymorphous perversity of the Creative Matrix. This is the space where Trickster resides, part Mother Teresa (the saintly angelic aliens of Adamski), part Darth Vader (the demonic Men in Black), part Pee-wee Herman (the absurd messages given Ed Walters and other witnesses by their alien-angel communicants, as we shall see in the next chapter).

There is also a collective dimension of marginality, as the continuing borderline awareness of UFOs since the late 1940s makes clear. Whether we like it or not, our culture, human culture, is also living in the margins, on the edge, in between. Heidegger has said that we are living in the time between the death of the old gods and the birth of the new, a theme that resonates with Jung's idea that UFOs are fundamental symbols of "changes in the constellation of psychic dominants, of the archetypes, or 'gods' as they used to be called, which bring about, or accompany, long-lasting transformations of the collective psyche."

But how are we to ground, to *real*-ize, such ideas? By starting where we are — here, spanning the "crack in the cosmic egg." By definition, transitions are fluid, not easily defined in static or structural terms; and so it is with UFO initiations. In 1904, America's first great psychologist, William James, wrote that "life is in the transitions as much as in the terms connected." James noted that events at these transitions — as between the visible and the obscure, the mundane and the marvelous — have a special vibrance, as if the slight hesitations we experience there significantly heighten and energize life.

As an experiment in experiencing the "blurred reality genre" that characterizes many kinds of UFO experiences, Professor Peter Rojcewicz, a folklorist and philosopher of anomalies, suggests standing in front of your bedroom mirror with an apple cupped in both hands. "As you look at the mirror, it appears as if you and apple fuse with the reflected image," Rojcewiz notes. "The area extending from the mirror's surface beyond to your reflected image is . . . an ambiguous reality, neither entirely real nor entirely unreal, but lying somewhere indeterminate between these two states."

Rojcewicz hypothesizes that "there exists a continuum of experiences where reality and imagination imperceptibly flow into each other" as through a "crack between worlds . . . where one realm passes through and blurs the boundary between two realities — for example, the mundane and the sacred, the material and the imaginative — that are simultaneously perceived by the same witness."

This description comes close to the idea of juxtaposition as put forward by the 1920s–1930s surrealist movement, which sought to blend the perceptions of the unconscious mind with the external realities of the phenomenal world. The surrealist poet Pierre Reverdy defined *juxtaposition* as "the bringing together of two realities which are more or less remote. The more distant and just the relationship of these realities, the stronger the image — the more emotive power and poetic reality it will have."

The UFO close encounter literature offers abundant testimony to the efforts of witnesses across lines of age, sex, race, and geography to reconcile fantastic events that seemed to emerge out of, and blend into, mundane reality. I have been deeply touched by my conversations with many such witnesses, people who through an unexpected encounter with strange beings alighting in equally strange luminous craft have been left with a gut sense of juxtaposition of two very different realities whose relation appeared both *distant* and *just*, profoundly different yet intimately connected.

Many UFO witnesses emerge from their sighting experience or close encounter with a surrealistic appreciation that the world is filled with enormous vistas and abysses. It is as if they have glimpsed the edge of reality so precisely defined by the surrealists, and now can never go back to the mechanistic Newtonian world absent of depth, beauty, significance, and soul. In contrast, both extremes of the UFO debate — proponents and debunkers — seem committed to forcing witness interpretations into narrow boxes that witnesses themselves tend to see as inadequate. This is surely one of the richer ironies of the unfolding UFO epic.

If the UFO phenomenon is a rite of passage, personal and collective, how will the initiation culminate? Joseph Campbell speaks of the one who moves from ordinary reality into contact with supernatural wonders — and then back to ordinary reality again — as the Master of Two Worlds. Free to pass back and forth across the divisions between realms, from time to timelessness, from surfaces to the causal deep and back again to surfaces, the Master knows both realities and settles exclusively for neither. Says Campbell:

> The disciple has been blessed with a vision transcending the scope of normal human destiny, and amounting to a glimpse of the essential nature of the cosmos. Not his personal fate, but the fate of mankind, of life as a whole, the atom and all the solar system, has been opened to him; and this in terms befitting his human understanding, that is to say, in terms of an anthropomorphic vision: the Cosmic Man.

Notice Campbell's insistence that the transformative vision is revealed "in terms befitting his human understanding." The witness is faced with the inevitable challenge of holding a transpersonal vision in personal terms. This is no simple task. Precisely because the UFO vision seems absurd to ordinary, "noninitiated" consciousness, the experience (and the one who had it) will be ridiculed by the collective. With feelings of rejection as insult added to the injury of the reality-shattering UFO experience, the UFO initiate is constantly tempted to relieve the feeling of being thus rendered less than ordinary by pretending to be *super*-ordinary, sometimes taking on the role of cosmic prophet who has glimpsed the new cosmic horizon.

More and more abductees seem to be taking a middle road between the 1950s-style contactee's pursuit of publicity, on the one hand, and complete isolation and invisibility, on the other. Many have concluded that being "invisible" to the culture at large can be as much a blessing as a curse, and that the burden of being disregarded by skeptics, scoffers, and debunkers is preferable to the burden of trying to convince doubters that they, as UFO witnesses, have had an experience that makes them "special."

"I'd rather spend my time comparing notes with others who have seen and experienced what I've seen," one abductee told me, "than trying to convince the Carl Sagans of the world that UFOs are real." A growing number of witnesses share this perspective. They seem genuinely pleased to be free from having to know what reality is ultimately all about, satisfied to have the opportunity to thrive outside accepted realms of classification, to ask questions about matters they once took for granted, to focus on what they see as an even larger transition than their personal one: the shift for a new way of being for humanity.

What about the *collective* UFO initiation?

Dr. Leo Sprinkle, a psychologist in private practice in Laramie, Wyoming, has interiewed many hundreds of UFO witnesses over a period of more than twenty years. Sprinkle is convinced that UFO activity — ranging from sightings to close encounters — is part of an "educational program for humankind on planet earth." He hypothesizes that aliens have placed an embargo on communications with Earth in order to minimize panic. "It is possible that we are being slowly introduced to ETs through movies and science fiction, until the evidence of ET visitation becomes more acceptable to the 'morality' of physical scientists," Sprinkle says. With a weary smile, he adds: "Of course, I can't prove this, and I have given up trying!"

Longtime UFO observer Jacques Vallee takes a different view of the collective significance of sightings and encounters, focusing not on stages leading to eventual "contact" but rather on what he calls the "recursive unsolvability" of the overall phenomenon. In mathematics a recursive function is one in which a solution can be reached not by predictable linear operations, but rather through continuous, partial tallies, each of which gradually redefines the problem itself. Vallee notes that the UFO phenomenon began with the expectation of an imminent, concise, and straightforward solution, but through successive, partial tallies has revealed an increasingly murky horizon.

"What we see emerging in the UFO phenomenon is not gradual contact but rather gradual control — of our beliefs, expectations, fears, hopes and dreams. . . . We know from behavioral psychology that the best schedule of reinforcement is one that combines periodicity with unpredictability," says Vallee, citing the ongoing pattern of intense UFO activity followed by quiet periods when it seems to have gone away entirely. "Learning is then slow but continuous," he adds. "It leads to the highest level of adaptation. And it is irreversible. It is interesting to observe that the pattern of UFO waves has the same structure as a schedule of reinforcement."

But who or what is behind the control system? What are its mechanisms?

"Those are the questions to which I most want answers," Vallee responded. "I have been led to conclude that there is a spiritual control system for human consciousness and that paranormal phenomena like UFOs are one of its manifestations. It is possible that this control is natural and spontaneous. It might be explainable in terms of genetics, or by the principles of social psychology, or as an unknown aspect of ordinary phenomena. It is possibly artificial in nature, under the power of some superhuman will. Perhaps the answer consists of a combination of these — no one can say for certain."

Vallee finds the metaphors of initiation and rites of passage helpful so long as they aren't taken in a literal or linear sense. "The very expectation of a 'culmination' may simply reflect the larger schedule of reinforcement," Vallee suggests. "Today's predictions of an imminent resolution continue to be put forth with no apparent recognition that each of the past four decades has featured similar prophesies which remained unfulfilled." He adds:

> What interests me is that with each new wave of sightings, the social impact becomes greater. Conventional science appears more and more perplexed, befuddled, at a loss to explain. Pro-ET ufologists become more dogmatic in their propositions. More people become fascinated with space and with new frontiers in consciousness. More books and articles appear, changing our culture in the direction of a new image of man. Meanwhile, the phenomenon offers occasional rational elements to entice credible researchers, while offering an equal number of ludicrous elements so as to effectively deny itself, annihilate evidence of itself. Ufologists, by and large, remain blissfully unaware of their role in the feedback loop.

As for the new generation of researchers who announce that they have finally "cracked the code" of the abductions phenomenon, Vallee is not impressed. "What kind of alien doctors are these, who need to produce such trauma in hundreds of patients to collect a little blood, a few embryos? The idea that aliens must travel many light-years to perform such experiments to enrich their race is merely another contribution to the absurd character of the entire phenomenon."

By *absurd*, Vallee means that, if the phenomenon is forcing us through a long-term learning curve, "then it has no choice but to mislead us." Like a rat in a maze pushing buttons for food, seeking to hit upon the right one, "man is hungry for knowledge and power, and if there is an intelligence behind the UFOs it must have taken this into account." Also like the rat, we have no real choice in the matter, given our hunger. "We must eventually study UFOs, and the study, unavoidably, will in turn contribute to the reinforcement itself."

To say that Jacques Vallee's words fell on deaf ears is not quite accurate. Budd Hopkins and other UFO researchers committed to taking abduction reports at face value attacked his views as "unsubstantiated conspiracy thinking." (Ironically, those who challenged Hopkins's ideas about abductions had leveled the same charge at him.) It is more accurate to say that Vallee's views were heard, but not really *heard*. In a sense this was inevitable, for Vallee's irritating (to mainstream ufology) habit of consistently and persistently directing attention to ufology's unconscious seemed to undercut the basic premises of the struggling discipline.

Most UFO researchers found such fundamental self-criticism a luxury they could ill afford, especially since there were *so many important sightings to resolve*. Vallee and many other new-school antiufology ufologists responded that the very impulse to "actively resolve" the phenomenon by pursuing the same kinds of cases in the same ways could only consolidate profoundly mistaken assumptions about the phenomenon's scope and depth. And so it went, into the decade of the 1990s: fresh variations on a well-established circular debate about the appropriate focus of UFO investigation.

Yet the confusion in communication indicated much more than that two basic schools of UFO researchers had come to speak very different languages. The deeper issue was the ambiguous "grammar" of UFOs themselves. In any communication, writes philosopher-psychologist Paul Watzlawick, "when one of the messages is garbled, leaving the recipient in a state of uncertainty, the result is confusion, which produces emotions ranging all the way from mild bewilderment to acute anxiety, depending upon the circumstances."

The Greek god Hermes might object to his messages being called "garbled." This guardian of thresholds, passageways, and *margins* simply prefers not to be pinned down to one set of meanings — just like his spiritual brother Proteus. After all, how very *boring* compared with the more boisterous alternative presented in Genesis 11:7:

Let us go down and there confound their language, that they may not understand one another's speech.

FIFTEEN

———— ✕ ————

SAUCER *Smear* is a semiregular newsletter of UFO-related gossip, innuendo, personality conflict, and opinion — usually pointed, often scathing — whose pages are potentially open to anyone who cares to write a letter to its editor and publisher, James W. Moseley, a wealthy Florida antiques dealer who has observed and commented on nearly every UFO case since Kenneth Arnold's 1947 sighting. Offering itself as "dedicated to the highest principles of ufological journalism," *Saucer Smear* opens a unique window onto the tangled soul of ufology, revealing the strangely magnificent preoccupations of a small cadre of observers who, year after year, continue trying to make sense of the wretchedly excessive events defined by the acronym *UFO*.

The February 1985 issue of the publication features a confession by Moseley of his rapidly dwindling faith: "It seems that whenever a supposedly excellent UFO report is pursued objectively & in depth, it tends to fall apart — or, at the very least, strong weaknesses show up — so that it becomes a no-longer-excellent report. The result is that after nearly forty years of Saucerdom, we have hundreds of first-rate mysterious cases but *no* totally proven ones!" Woefully, Moseley admits that ufology has been slow to come to terms with three "sickening conclusions":

(1) Human perception is not as good as is generally thought.... Which of us has the nerve to tell Muhammed Ali that his sighting while training in Central Park a few years ago was really a street light? ... (2) Background checks on UFO sighters *are* important.... (3) The Will to Believe is an overwhelming force for many people [who too often] discard or ignore elements of a case that don't "fit," and Emphasize the Positive in a "hurrah for our side" attitude which is far, far removed from even the loosest interpretation of Scientific Method.

Yet all is not lost, Moseley assures. "There *is* some sort of mystery going on, even if it eventually turns out to be merely psychological." The question is: "*What* is the true nature of this mystery?" If UFOs are only delusions or mass hysteria, Moseley wonders, "why do so many people claim to have had very close sightings, contacts, and even abductions?" If UFOs are only some kind of strange psychological manifestation, "we'll *still* need an explanation as to *why* so many people suffered such bizarre and similar hallucinations!"

By the end of his agonizing admission of doubt, Moseley — like the sinner who returns to church, or the alcoholic who hops back on the wagon — reembraces one of the central tenets of UFO mythology: "With enough time, *MONEY*, and research by trained scientists, the *real* truth can be learned eventually." His faith now restored — not for the first time, not for the last — Jim Moseley assures his readers that he won't let them down.

In the following issue, a writer affirms Moseley's confirmation: "Just as what appears to be complete despair sets in," new cases and information emerge, "and thus the carrot is once again there to keep me alert and ever hoping for some breakthrough." The beat continues.

STAR WARS DEFENSE SYSTEM NOT FOR PROTECTION AGAINST RUSSIANS, BUT SPACE ALIENS! An article with this headline, appearing in the November 1, 1985, issue of the supermarket tabloid *The Globe and Mail*, reveals that President Reagan's Strategic Defense Initiative missile defense system is actually aimed at protecting America from attack by extraterrestrials, not the Soviets.

Saucer Smear editor Jim Moseley attributes the report to a "usually reliable source in Washington," but admits he has no way to prove the allegation. "If true," Moseley adds, it is "surely the Big Story of the Decade!"

Philip Klass fires off a letter to Moseley saying he and his colleagues at *Aviation Week* magazine would surely have heard whether this rumor is true. Thus another evocative legend — complete with the necessary skeptical rejoinder — appears at the ever-shifting interface of fact and fantasy in the ufological cosmos. If sustaining and reinvigorating the UFO mythos is the unspoken name of the game, such rumors do their part simply by *appearing*.

THE 1985 conference of the Mutual UFO Network, the largest civilian investigation group in the United States, meets in St. Louis to serve up helpings of the two kinds of messages for which its annual gatherings are legendary: case study reports focused on the UFO's physical reality, and quasi-religious exhortations aimed at reminding the faithful of the importance of prevailing over ufology's premiere enemies: debunkers and public apathy.

Among the former, Budd Hopkins gives an update on his abduction research, reporting on nine cases in which abductees described physical examinations inside UFOs resulting in permanent scars still visible on their bodies. Most of the scars, he reports, were inflicted when the abductees were children, usually around age six or seven. In one case, a woman who was abducted at five, then at sixteen, then again at nineteen, received a circular scar when a three-pronged device was used to take flesh from her leg. Hopkins reports encountering two types of scars: a thin, straight, hairline cut, about one-third inch long, and a circular, scooplike depression about one-eighth to three-quarter inches in diameter.

Why is this happening? Hopkins says samples of some kind — blood, flesh, skin, sometimes blood or ova — are almost always taken, and abductees' bodies are usually invaded by probes or scanning devices of some kind: transmission implants. Based on thirty-four "solid" cases and forty-three in need of further study, Hopkins concludes we are being observed and monitored, subtly conditioned, used in some sort of genetic experimentation. "Are there motives we have not yet the technology to imagine?" He suspects the answer is yes; details to be announced when discovered.

Among the exhorters, Stanton T. Friedman begins his talk by reminding his audience that he has delivered his "Flying Saucers *ARE* Real" lecture at "more than 500 colleges and to dozens of professional groups in 48 states and 8 provinces as well as in the District of Columbia and Puerto Rico." Then he engages in the time-tested ufological practice of condemning "noisy negativists" — the late Harvard astronomer Donald Menzel and NASA consultant James Oberg among them — for challenging the logic of the idea that we are being visited by interplanetary spacecraft. Friedman singles out science popularizer Carl Sagan for insisting that UFO researchers must produce hard evidence, even though Sagan has yet to offer hard evidence for his own claim that there must be other civilizations far older and more advanced than our own.

Friedman concludes his remarks with this succinct advice: "Beware noisy negativists." The applause that follows signals a satisfied congregation. In a similar accentuate-the-positive vein, Mutual UFO Network publicity director Marge Christensen takes to the rostrum to call on all good ufologists to support the rapidly approaching National UFO Information Week, designated to "arouse the public from its state of oblivion and ignorance of the UFO phenomenon." It would, she feels, be a good idea to have more posters, press releases on campuses, and photo exhibits at libraries and shopping malls.

J. ALLEN Hynek's death on April 27, 1986, comes as no surprise to those who knew him best. Even so, it is not easy to accept. After learning of the brain tumor that would eventually take his life, Hynek had quietly withdrawn from the field that he, more than any other person, shaped toward a serious discipline of scientific study. For twenty years he was the chief consultant to the air force's UFO research project, an endeavor he abandoned when he realized it was little more than a public relations operation. His true UFO research began when he founded his own center, in 1973.

Steady and cautious by nature, Hynek invariably displeased players on both teams. Debunkers thought him insufficiently tough-minded toward UFO claims; proponents wondered what took him so long to bid farewell to the air force payroll. His longtime adversary — everyone's longtime adversary, it seems — Philip Klass never tired of characterizing Hynek as typical of the failed and aging scientist who has turned to flying saucers in a last, desperate effort to grab a little glory. His longtime friend and colleague Jacques Vallee naturally remembered Hynek quite differently: as a man who "never forgot that beyond the modern scientist's efforts to come to grips with atoms, galaxies and computers there was another quest for an even more important truth: the identity of man and his cosmic consciousness."

Hynek "picked his way carefully through this minefield, always choosing his spots, qualifying his pronouncements, counseling against rash judgments and advocating a thoroughly scientific approach," recalled David Jacobs, author of *The UFO Controversy in America.* In a field garbled by untestable theories about the phenomenon's origins, extravagant speculations about its ultimate aims, byzantine fantasies about its pervasive cover-up by federal bureaucrats, and doctrinal feuding reminiscent of medieval Christiandom, this was no small achievement. Former UFO researcher Eugene Steinberg spoke for many with this remembrance:

> When Dr. J. Allen Hynek, over twenty years ago, became a born-again ufologist, there was a sense of the credible and the possible that had never existed before. Those fabulous and eerie disks from the skies would somehow become known to us eventually in all their alien glory.... The voice of authority of that gentle college professor gave a nearly discredited field of offbeat study a new (if brief) lifetime of knowledge and incredible possibility.... It is true that UFOs are still seen in scattered parts of the world. Perhaps such things will be seen till the end of time for reasons that we cannot know. But their reality has died for many, and the world will never be the same....

Hynek told friends he wanted to go out the way he came in — "with the comet." On May 5, 1910, at five years of age, young Allen had been taken up to the roof to see Halley's comet. Some of his first astronomy students recalled Hynek telling them the comet would be back, in 1985–1986. *Look for it,* he said. The man whose phrase Steven Spielberg borrowed for his film *Close Encounters of the Third Kind* had a proverbial last wish: he wanted to see the comet again before he died, like Mark Twain, who saw it at the beginning and the end of his life.

So at 4 A.M on March 26, 1986, Allen Hynek climbed into the Honda's reclining right-hand seat, a pillow beneath his head, the March issue of *Sky & Telescope* and a pair of binoculars in his lap, his wife Mimi at the steering wheel, his longtime friend and fellow researcher Jennie Zeidman in the back. All were filled with Allen's great expectancy as they passed observer-filled cars parked off to the side and continued into the desert where they found a quiet place to park on a dirt road.

"The three of us got out of the car. Gravel crunched underfoot, traffic hummed in the distance and there were the low whisperings of other observers nearby," Zeidman remembers. "We could have been in an art museum or at some religious place, where there is great respect for the privacy and emotion of others."

They spotted Saturn and Mars easily enough. Then they thought they saw the comet, but were mistaken. They turned their flashlights to the charts so they could try again. Hynek leaned against the car. Suddenly, there it was! "No wonder we hadn't seen it before," Zeidman says. "It was just now rising, the tail streaming like a feather in its cap." Hynek stood in silence as *his* mythic comet rose and the Earth turned. Soon they knew it was time to leave, and they did. It was all over so quickly. Hynek had gotten his wish.

Zeidman recalls fifteen years earlier, 1971: Allen Hynek had taken refuge as a guest in Zeidman's home, to write his book *The UFO Experience*. Zeidman was worried about the chapter headings: "Close Encounters of the First Kind," "Close Encounters of the Second Kind," and so forth. "It's all too choppy," she told him.

"Well," he said, "I kind of like them. I think they'll stay."

And stay they will, I think, forever, Zeidman writes after her friend and mentor is gone.

IN THE wake of Hynek's death, many wonder who — if anyone — will take his place as the Father of UFO Researchers. "A cohesive force has gone, and we will see changes," writes British ufologist Pete Tate in *Saucer Smear.* "If ufology continues on its present course, as an organized interest it will founder in the relatively near future." American UFO researcher David Jacobs disagrees, saying the prognosis for UFO research is bright, indeed, due to "the sheer magnitude of the phenomenon, its persistence, its extraordinary relationship to society and individual people, its intrinsic interest, and its inherent importance."

Surveying the same terrain, *Saucer Smear* correspondent Tom Hackney of New York City finds a very different post-Hynek ufology, characterized by "a lackluster bunch of 'experts,' dilettante ragmen, blowhards, demi-gods, publicity seekers, fortune hunters, anal retentives, practical jokers, wishful thinkers, hard-boiled new agers, deluded soulmongers, dimwits, wide-eyed psychos, religious fanatics and various other assorted monkeys." Philosopher Dennis Stillings, critical of what he sees as the endlessly circular wishful thinking of ufology's pro-ET mainstream, pronounces the field a "playground for the bungled and the botched."

If UFO research is vast enough to cover this much ground, then the surreal events of the next few years — and the equally fantastic debates they will foster — should seem incredible only to someone who has not been paying attention to the UFO's adventures during the previous forty. Soon it becomes unmistakably clear: there will be no new Father, only new factions — and many old ones, too.

ENTER Whitley Strieber. In early 1986, he appeared at the doorstep of a leading UFO researcher, desperate for help in coming to terms with the terrible aftermath of his abduction by nonhuman "visitors," as he called them. Within a matter of months he found himself accused of callously betraying this researcher for personal and professional advancement. By the time he exited the UFO universe a few years later, this author of two best-selling memoirs detailing bizarre encounters with aliens stood condemned by orthodox ufology as a man deluded by the frenzy of his overdriven imagination — yet also celebrated by thousands of readers as a sort of prophet, a modern seer beyond the edges of the known.

Who is Whitley Strieber — and who are his "visitors"?

He had become known in the 1970s as a writer of horror fiction, including *The Wolfen*, a commercially successful and critically acclaimed novel featuring gray creatures who, in Strieber's description, "hid in the cracks of life, and used their immense intelligence to hunt down beings as their natural and proper prey." A professional writer, Strieber had more recently coauthored two nonfiction books that hadn't sold well. His career at a crossroads, Strieber decided to return to fiction. By 1985, he was well at work on a historical novel set in Russia.

Then, by all accounts, his life began to fall apart.

In the days following Christmas of 1985, Strieber entered a depression so severe that he couldn't continue writing or even reread his writing in progress. While staying with his wife, Anne, and young son Andrew at their family cabin in upstate New York, Strieber began lashing out at his family and friends, becoming confused by simple events, and fearing that "strange people" were hiding in their house at night. He developed the habit of secretly checking closets and under beds before going to sleep at night, and always kept a shotgun nearby. All this, even though he had already equipped the cabin, located in a peaceful rural area, with an expensive burglar alarm system.

These psychological symptoms were accompanied by an unexplainable infection in the forefinger of his right hand and by rectal pain that made it difficult for him to sit for any length of time. Bouts of extreme fatigue alternated with flulike chills. He was convinced he was being watched at all times and felt on guard against some vaguely pervasive threat. Things got so bad that he became convinced he and his family must sell their rural cabin and their Greenwich Village apartment and move to Austin, Texas, Strieber's hometown. While looking for property in Texas, Strieber became convinced they should stay in New York after all. Outraged by her husband's manic behavior, and feeling increasingly threatened by his paranoia and verbal abusiveness, Anne contemplated filing for divorce.

Strieber pinpoints January 3, 1986, as the day he understood what was happening to him: "The confused swirl resolved into a specific series of recollections, and when I saw what they were, I just about exploded with terror and utter disbelief." Strieber remembered being abducted from his bedroom in the middle of the night, taken into an enclosed area, and subjected to a gruesome series of operations by four kinds of nonhuman creatures: small, robotlike beings; short, stocky ones in dark-blue coveralls with wide faces, deep-set eyes, and pug noses; taller, slender beings with "prominent and mesmerizing black eyes"; and a group of "huddled" beings with round, black, buttonlike eyes.

Perhaps his memories were not real at all. *"You may be going mad, or you may have a brain tumor,"* he said to himself. In any event, life had taken a disastrous turn for Whitley Strieber. Here, summarized from his book *Communion*, is the experience he recalled:

On the evening of December 26, after enjoying a meal of Christmas leftovers with his wife and child, Strieber conducted his covert tour of the house for possible intruders and turned on the burglar alarm before retiring for the night. Several hours later he wakened to "a peculiar whooshing, swirling noise coming from the living room downstairs," as if a larger number of people were moving rapidly around the room. Alarmed and frightened, Strieber checked the burglar alarm panel next to the bed and found it still set.

He admits that his next action — settling back into bed — makes no sense, in light of his fear. "If something is strange enough, the reaction is very different from what one would think. The mind seems to tune it out as if by some sort of instinct." Then Strieber noticed the double doors to his bedroom opening. He says he checked his state of mind and found himself completely lucid. His heart began to beat very fast. What could be moving the door? Then he found out. A "compact figure" wearing a smooth, rounded hat with a sharp rim — a figure with "two dark holes for eyes and a black down-turning line of a mouth that later became an O" — rushed into the room and approached the bed where Strieber now sat next to his sleeping wife.

Next Strieber recalls being paralyzed, devoid of all sensation, and being whisked out of the room in a state of utter panic. After blacking out, he woke to find himself in a depression in the woods, yet surprised to find no snow on the gray earth. Still unable to move, he peeked out of the corner of his eye and saw some of the creatures named above. To his right, a being in dark-blue coveralls was "working busily at something that seemed to have to do with the right side of my head." Then Strieber got the impression of branches moving across his face and of being suddenly "above the trees."

Now he found himself in a tight, dry, cramped, "messy round room" where he was filled with a dread "so powerful that it seemed to make my personality completely evaporate." There were tiny beings rushing all around him in a way he found "disturbing" and "ugly." One of the creatures showed him a tiny gray box with a sliding latch, inside of which lay "an extremely shiny, hair-thin needle mounted on a black surface." Instantly Strieber understood that they intended to insert this needle into his brain.

Stop, he implored; "You'll ruin a beautiful mind." But his bargaining was to no avail. "The next thing I knew, there was a bang and a flash." The operation had been performed; Strieber recalled "sinking down into a cradle of tiny arms." But the worst was yet to come. After being taken to what seemed a small operating theater, he was shown "an enormous and extremely ugly object, gray and scaly, with a sort of network of wires on the end." When this foot-long, narrow, triangle-shaped object was rammed into his rectum, for the first time his fear turned to fury. He felt raped.

Strieber then recalled his captors making a painless incision in his right forefinger. "Abruptly, my memories end. There isn't even blackness, just morning." He found himself in his bed "grappling with a distinct sense of unease and a very improbable but intense memory of seeing a barn owl staring at me through the window sometime during the night."

This brings us back to the days of malaise following Christmas, when Strieber began undergoing a distinctly ominous shift in personality that culminated in the flood of memories just described. Unable to write, and increasingly frightened by what was happening to him, Strieber tried to read a book given him by his brother. The book's title: *Science and the UFOs*. Strieber insists he had never before read a book about flying saucers nor expressed any interest in the subject. But here was a book from his brother, so he read it. When he came upon the section concerning the "archetypal abduction experience," describing encounters frighteningly like his own, he fell into shocked silence. Then he slammed the book shut "as if it contained a coiled snake."

No one must ever know about this, Strieber thought to himself, *not even Anne*. He decided to lock the memories away in his mind and go on with his life. This proved impossible. He remembered the book mentioning that a man named Budd Hopkins, a New York artist, was an expert on alien abductions. Returning to Manhattan from the country cabin, Strieber found Hopkins's name in the phone book. "But how could I call him? What a stupid thing to have to admit. Little men. Flying saucers. How idiotic." Strieber decided it was either call Budd Hopkins or walk out of an upper-story window. He called him.

On hearing only a bit of Strieber's story over the telephone, Hopkins invited him to come to his apartment, a mere ten-minute walk from Strieber's. "Hopkins was a large, intense man with one of the kindest faces I have ever seen," he later wrote. At this first of many meetings, Strieber learned that he was not alone in his suffering, that many others had been through similar ordeals. "I went from wanting to hide it all to wanting to understand it," he said, feeling the ground underneath his feet for the first time in weeks.

But the meeting was fateful for another reason. It marked the opening chapter of a relationship that began with a shared commitment to restoring Strieber's shattered sense of self, grew to include considerable ideological differences between two complex individuals, and eventually collapsed amid bitter accusations of opportunism, mental disturbance, and betrayal.

Hopkins says what he remembers most of all about his first meeting with Strieber was his extraordinary state of fear. "Of the more than two hundred abductees I've dealt with for over a decade and a half, Strieber was, when I met him, the most profoundly frightened and clearly disoriented," Hopkins says. "He was the only abductee who described himself as having been suicidal and the only one I absolutely insisted see a psychiatrist before any regressive hypnosis could be undertaken for investigative purposes."

At Hopkins's suggestion, Strieber began seeing Dr. Donald Klein of the New York State Psychiatric Institute. During the first session together, attended by Hopkins, Strieber recalled more details of his abduction. The creature that approached his bed had touched his head with a silver-tipped wand, enabling Strieber to see pictures of the world being destroyed in a massive apocalypse. In future sessions, Strieber remembered becoming sexually aroused by an apparently female being he described as old, bald, big-headed, with bulging eyes that reminded him of a "bug."

According to Hopkins, a curiously animated Strieber phoned daily, "describing what he believed to be frequent new encounters and putting forth new theories as to the nature and purposes of his 'visitors.' His calls were frequently filled with emotional desperation, and often maze-like in their mystical complexity." It was during the first months of his therapy that Strieber began working on a book about his experience, a decision that Hopkins urged him to reconsider until he gained greater perspective on his experience. Strieber declined Hopkins's suggestion, saying he wanted to write while his experience was still fresh in his mind.

The question of the reliability of Strieber's memory took center stage in the first of two incidents that drove a sharp wedge between him and Hopkins. Kathy Davis, a young abductee who is the central character in Hopkins's book *Intruders*, came to New York to continue hypnosis sessions with Hopkins. Strieber wanted to meet her, so Hopkins arranged for them to have lunch. According to Davis, during their meeting Strieber fixed his eye on her and said there was something he should tell her . . . but then again, no, he shouldn't, because it would just upset her. Yet perhaps he should tell her, but no, it was probably best not to. This went on until Davis was quite nervous, at which point Strieber decided to tell her.

"I think I've seen you before, Kathy, inside a UFO, but it wasn't all of you. It was just your head, and it was alive, and it was on a shelf." Davis, who had been telling Strieber how vulnerable, confused, and frightened she had been since her abduction experience, felt devastated by this remark — and suddenly deeply frightened by the man who was sitting across from her. When Davis returned to Hopkins's apartment, Strieber called to apologize. But it was too late, said Hopkins, for whom the incident corroborated his growing belief that Strieber's personality was becoming less, not more, well organized during the course of his psychotherapy with Klein.

During an interview with Strieber, I asked him if indeed he told Kathy Davis he saw her severed head on the shelf of a UFO. "Of course I didn't," he responded indignantly. I mentioned that Kathy Davis had made a sworn statement to the contrary, and that she and Hopkins's wife, April, both attest to overhearing Davis and Hopkins receive Strieber's subsequent phone call of apology. "Listen, I used to telephone Budd frequently about many things, but I repeat, I made no such statement to Kathy Davis." After pausing, Strieber began speaking in a hushed tone. "But what I find absolutely interesting is that Kathy Davis truly believes I made that remark . . . *and so does Budd.*" Then he said he had nothing more to add on the matter.

But it was over a matter of great professional concern to both men that the relationship between Whitley Strieber and Budd Hopkins collapsed beyond repair. In early 1987, just over a year after their first meeting, Strieber's book *Communion* and Hopkins's book *Intruders* were ready to go to press at approximately the same time. Unknown to Hopkins, Strieber wrote to Hopkins's publisher, Random House, urging that the publication of *Intruders* be delayed so it would not be overwhelmed by the likely impending best-seller status of *Communion*. The premise of Strieber's letter was that he was doing his friend a great favor.

When Hopkins received word of this move from his publisher, he felt both outraged and betrayed. Strieber had expressed no such intention when Hopkins and his wife dined with the Striebers three days earlier, yet surely he had already decided to write the letter. Hopkins began to see a pattern in Strieber's actions. Months before, Hopkins recalled, Strieber had told him that he installed the burglar alarm in his cabin and kept his houses stocked with guns because right-wing terrorists had threatened to kidnap his son. Strieber later admitted he made the story up because he was "frightened," Hopkins said. On another occasion, a tearfully hysterical Strieber told Hopkins (according to the latter) that the CIA was conspiring to keep *Communion* from being published. *This is a disturbed man whose words I simply cannot trust*, Hopkins concluded. Immediately he wrote Strieber a letter breaking off relations:

> I don't know anyone outside the Strieber family who agrees with you that your plea to my publisher was for my benefit.... Did you assume that I would be pleased, or even indifferent, if you went behind my back that way by writing to my publisher? ... Whitley, if you truly believed that Random House would alter all its plans in response to your letter, and that I — the man you said actually saved your life — would not be furious at your meddling, you are simply out of touch with reality.

During my interview with him, Strieber asserted that his honorable intentions had been misunderstood by Hopkins, who, according to Strieber, "was not able to accept the fact that I believe the so-called abduction phenomenon *ultimately* to be a positive experience — for myself, and for many others. Budd is so deeply committed to his 'intruders/invaders' hypothesis that he can't accept any other perspective. In my books I convey how truly bizarre and strange the visitor experience really is, and I didn't hesitate to explore its deep religious implications. This is why my books have received so tremendous a popular response. In contrast, *Intruders* was by and large a failure."

Actually *Intruders* made it onto the *New York Times* best-seller list, although the book never captured the number-one spot held by Strieber for many months in 1987, unprecedented for a UFO title. In *Communion* as well and its sequel, *Transformation*, Strieber stepped well beyond the flying saucer frame of reference to entertain visionary speculations consistent with his eclectic spiritual journeying over many years:

> It may be that the human species is the womb of the angels.... What we may be witness to is what the process of evolution looks like when it is applied to the conscious mind.... It is necessary to think in a new way to understand this material — to abandon determinism once and for all. It is possible to conceive of real, physical beings emerging out of nonphysical experiences, and to relate to those beings as if they were entirely valid — and then to throw it all into question.... We are at last, some of us, learning how to become conscious companions of God ... those of us who are in this process of demythologizing the emergence of sacred consciousness into the physical world. The visitor experience is part of this effort, in my opinion.

A reviewer for *Nation* magazine implied that Strieber, a professional writer of fiction, had simply made up his story in light of what he had read about alien abductions, and sold it as fact.* The engineering-oriented mainstream of ufology, suspicious of Strieber's freely admitted longtime interest in mysticism, shamanism, and witchcraft, made up its collective mind that Strieber probably had really been abducted, but had allowed his metaphysical imagination to run away with him in the aftermath. Psychoanalytic observers wondered about the symbolic implications of the "rectal probe" in his abduction account. Budd Hopkins, as we have seen, came to view Strieber with unmediated suspicion — and received the same from Strieber.

No definitive evidence emerged to invalidate any of these theories or responses — as usual in the universe of ufology. But quite apart from how ufology's designated *enfant terrible* would fare on a battery of psychological tests measuring integrity of character, ego coherence, and proneness to fantasy, clearly the ideas in Whitley Strieber's well-crafted books touched a nerve among many for whom the very structure of his narrative spoke to something unabashedly primordial — as had the epic tale of another traveler, named Dante, centuries earlier:

> *When I had journeyed half of our life's way,*
> *I found myself within a shadowed forest,*
> *for I had lost the path that does not stray.*
> *Ah, it is hard to speak of what it was,*
> *that savage forest, dense and difficult,*
> *which even in recall renews my fear:*

---

*Strieber's works of fiction recurrently depict people suffering mental disintegration and feature the theme of impending apocalypse. A wand wreaks mental havoc on the principal character in Strieber's novel, *The Night Church*. In *Communion* (subtitled *A True Story*) aliens invade Strieber's skull with a needle and tap his head with a wand, precipitating a frightening vision of global destruction. The author/protagonist insisted that these themes are present in his early fiction only as "screen memories," as motifs disguising a not yet conscious lifetime of encounters with his "visitors." Others came to different conclusions. Martin Kottmeyer, in an essay entitled "Dying Worlds, Dying Selves," wrote that Strieber's "early life, it is known, conforms perfectly with the recipe for creating a paranoid: a trauma-filled childhood, a proud and ambitious family, a fall from grace into financial ruins and social slights, rejections, and a subsequent withdrawal into himself."

so bitter — death is hardly more severe!
But to retell the good discovered there,
I'll also tell of other things I saw.

WEBSTER'S *New World Dictionary* defines a labyrinth as "a structure containing winding passages hard to follow without losing one's way." Welcome to the Gulf Breeze sightings, a complex set of encounters that, like the Billy Meier affair to which it was quickly compared, stood as either the long-awaited breakthrough that ufologists had waited for or a heavyweight competitor for the title of most notorious fraud in UFO history. As usual in the cosmos of ufology, it had to be one or the other.

The story begins on November 11, 1987, when Ed Walters, a builder-developer in the city of Gulf Breeze, Florida (population 6,000), saw an unusual glow behind a tall pine in the front yard of his suburban home. Filled with curiosity, he got up from the desk in his study and stepped outside to get a clearer view of the light's source: a top-shaped aerial craft bearing a row of dark squares and smaller openings ("portholes") between them across the midsection, sporting a luminous ring around the bottom.

Walters ran back inside to grab his old Polaroid camera and returned to the yard in time to snap a photo as the object moved out from behind a tree. He got three more shots of the craft as it drifted slowly toward the northeast. As Walters ran in the same direction to get more photos, the UFO — now above him — shot out a blue beam that first paralyzed and then lifted him several feet above the ground. A piercing odor, like ammonia laced with cinnamon, scorched and burned the back of his throat and caused him to feel suffocated.

As Walters began screaming, a voice inside his head groaned, "We will not hurt you." Walters kept yelling. The same computerlike voice in his head responded, "Calm down." Walters shouted back, "Put me down!" The voice in his head became more insistent: "S-t-o-p i-t." Finally, Walters got to the point: "Screw you!" Then to his further amazement his head was filled with "flashing dog pictures" rapidly turning over like pages in a book to the sound of a strange female voice. As precipitously as he had been lifted up, Walters was unceremoniously dropped to the pavement, the blue beam now gone. When he looked to the sky, the UFO was gone, too.

Walters discovered that his son had fallen asleep with the television volume turned up, thus missing the whole episode. When his wife, Frances, returned, she immediately noticed her husband's fear and the ammonia-cinnamon odor of which he reeked. "What's going on?" she asked. Ed told her. Later they told their children what had happened.

The Gulf Breeze UFO Adventure had begun.

Several days later, Walters went to visit Duane Cook, editor of the *Gulf Breeze Sentinel*, claiming that the UFO photos had been given him — along with a letter — by a Mr. X, who wished to remain anonymous. Cook ran the photos and letter in the paper along with a plea for information from anyone who knew what was going on. Several local residents came forward claiming they, too, had seen the object portrayed by the photographs. Over the next six months, Ed Walters continued to hear voices in his head, sometimes in Spanish: "They won't hurt you. Just a few tests. That's all." The voice insisted that Walters not take any more photos. *Just leave me alone*, Walters answered back.

No such luck was to be his — or his wife's. On December 2, Frances Walters saw the UFO for the first time, as Ed, standing next to her, heard voices speaking in Spanish about babies being fed bananas by "abductors." Ed got more photos of this sighting. Late that night, awakened by their dog barking, Ed encountered a four-foot-tall humanoid creature with big black eyes, standing outside their screened-in porch. The creature held a silver rod in its right hand. According to Ed, the being "stared at me with eyes that showed no fear. Eyes that were calm. Eyes that were almost sad. Eyes that seemed somehow curious."

Ed bolted toward the creature, giving the best chase he could. Suddenly a blue beam took hold of his leg and, as Frances watched in horror, began lifting it upward toward a hovering UFO some fifty feet in the sky. On two later occasions, the same or a similar UFO was seen by the two Walters children as well as by a family friend, while Ed videotaped it passing behind a tree.

On January 12, 1988, while driving on a deserted country road, Walters was momentarily blinded by a bright white flash of light that filled his arms and hands with the feeling of "pinpricks." Five hundred feet ahead of his truck a UFO hovered. Walters got out of his truck and climbed underneath it for protection. When he took a picture of the UFO, these words filled his head: "You are in danger. We will not harm you. Come forward." Knowing a double message when he heard one, Walters stayed under the truck. Then the forty-foot craft shot five separate beams to the road, each beam depositing a bizarre creature that began moving toward him in lockstep, each carrying silver rods. Walters began shouting obscenities. When the determined contingent of grotesques refused to retreat, Ed jumped back into his truck and sped away.

After what turned out to be Ed's final encounter on May 1, 1988, the cycle that has become familiar in previous cases — Betty and Barney Hill, Charlie Hickson and Calvin Parker, Father Gill, Lonnie Zamora — moved to its next phase. Like a circus that rolls into town and sets up its tents, the investigation of Ed and Frances Walters's remarkable claims began.

Ed made it over the first hurdle easily enough — the obligatory lie detector tests and psychopathology tests, none of which per se indicated evidence of deceit. To no one's surprise, Philip Klass — on the scene and ready to debunk every pro-Walters claim he heard — pronounced such tests intrinsically inexact. (In previous cases where UFO witnesses refused to take polygraph exams, Klass placed much more emphasis on the importance of these controversial tests. "Diminish witness credibility, period," seemed to be his rule of thumb.)

From this point the debate centered around Ed's photos, most of which were quite clear, vivid shots of what looked to be an unconventional aerial craft resembling a Japanese lantern. The only other UFO case featuring such clear photos and extended contacts was that of Billy Meier. "The whole thing was almost too compelling to be true," wrote Budd Hopkins, in his introduction to Ed and Frances's later book, *The Gulf Breeze Sightings*. "I had always predicted that when we would finally get good closeup UFO photos, they would inevitably appear to be fake, and this is what seemed to be happening."

There was a difference, Hopkins noted, between the Meier and Walters cases. In the former, small models resembling the "beam ships" in Meier's photos were later found. In a statement that would come to haunt Hopkins and others who took the Walters case at face value, Hopkins insisted there was no evidence of such fakery on the part of Ed or Frances. At the time he made the statement, he was correct.

Opinion — expert and otherwise — about the photos was typically mixed. Optics specialist Dr. Bruce Maccabee, a longtime pro-UFO researcher, said he could find no evidence of hoax in the photos, whereas

Dr. Robert Nathan, a researcher at NASA's Jet Propulsion Laboratory, said he found the photos "suspicious" and refused to vouch for their authenticity. Philip Klass noted that most of Walters's photos were taken with an early-model Polaroid camera that could easily have been used to create double exposures if the operator chose to leave the film in the camera after taking the first shot. Walters insisted that he had not created double-exposed photos, and further, that he had no idea such a technology was even possible with a simple Polaroid camera.

Ed's credibility was dealt a serious blow when Zan Overall — regarded as a tough-minded yet generally pro-UFO investigator — uncovered evidence that Walters had used his old Polaroid to take trick double-exposure photos at parties well over a year before publicly stating that he knew nothing about how to perform such feats. Overall located a photo taken by Ed with his old Polaroid at a party for his children at which, according to several of the teenagers in attendance, Ed predicted that a "ghost-demon" would materialize over the shoulder of a particular girl when he took her picture. Sure enough, a "ghost" image appeared hovering over her shoulder.

Walters later insisted that the image was merely a chance reflection off of a glass door in the north wall of the room. No way, responded Dr. Willy Smith, like Overall a generally pro-UFO researcher who questioned Walters's truthfulness and motives. When Smith enhanced Walters's "ghost-photo," he found there were no glass doors in a position to provide any such reflection. Walters later conceded that he knew how to take trick photographs by defocusing the lens of his old Polaroid — but insisted he created not a single double exposure (deliberately or otherwise) with his camera during the nearly twenty years he had used it.

In the meantime, a combination of debunkers and usual UFO proponents continued to hammer away at Walters's credibility. When Walters acknowledged spending nearly three years in jail for "passing a bad check," Klass reminded him that he had been convicted of the more serious crime of *forgery*, not passing a bad check. When Walters and Klass appeared together on "Oprah" in September of 1990, Walters denied that he had ever claimed to have been abducted by his alien tormenters. When Klass urged Walters to reread his own book, Walters responded, "I have never, quote, read my lips, I've never said that I've been abducted." (On page 261 of *The Gulf Breeze Sightings*, Ed Walters writes: "When I was 41 years old, I photographed a UFO and was abducted.")

Despite many such contradictions in the Gulf Breeze case, Walt Andrus, international director of the Mutual UFO Network (MUFON), announced that the Walters encounter "ranks as one of the most important UFO cases in the past 40 years. . . ." Andrus shocked many of MUFON's more scientifically inclined members when he offered an analysis reminiscent of the more fantastic contactee claims:

> If one were to briefly speculate on the solution to the enigma occurring in Gulf Breeze, it might take the following scenario. On or before Nov. 11, 1987, the intelligences behind the UFOs implanted a tiny communication device within Ed's head whereby they could communicate by voice or a humming sound to alert him to the proximity of their craft. . . . Ed was conceivably programmed to take the photographs for public distribution as part of the entities' ultimate plan to make themselves gradually known to the public and world governments. . . . A successful businessman and civic citizen was probably selected . . . so that evidence would be . . . accepted by the scientific community as factual.

Andrus's unmodified sanction of Walters's claims, based on what many longtime UFO investigators felt was little more than a cursory appraisal of the facts, served to widen a growing rift in the UFO community about the sighting. But the most bizarre turn came when the *Pensacola News Journal* reported that a UFO model made from plastic foam plates and drafting paper had been found in the attic of the Walterses' former residence at 612 Silverthorn, in Gulf Breeze. Things grew hotter still for Ed Walters several days later when Tommy Smith, a twenty-two-year-old son of a prominent Gulf Breeze attorney, appeared at a press conference with his parents to allege that he had seen Ed Walters fake certain UFO photos.

Under the headline STUDENT EXPLAINS DOUBLE EXPOSURE, *News Journal* reporter Craig Myers wrote: "He [Tommy Smith] said Walters lighted the model by shining a flashlight into it through a PVC pipe painted black and taped to the model. Walters took a photograph of the lighted model in a darkened room, with a black background, he said. Next, Walters went outside and exposed the model for a second time by making it appear to be in the air."

From this point on, the Gulf Breeze affair spiraled into an abyss of charges and countercharges impenetrable to few outside the devoted cadres committed to particular rock-hard positions. Ed Walters immediately and vociferously denied Tommy Smith's charges, effectively challenging various details of his claims. The UFO model discovered in the attic of his former home proved a different sort of obstacle for Walters, who was forced to admit that the device had been constructed of drafting paper with his own writing on it. Walters insisted that debunkers had fished the drafting paper out of his garbage, fashioned a model resembling the craft in his widely publicized photos, and placed it in the the attic of his former home in order to diminish his credibility.

After examining the discovered artifact, Walters insisted that someone had taken and used a house-plan drawing he had created two years after his first UFO photos were made public. Smelling blood, Philip Klass — and many others — reached a different conclusion, namely that the preliminary house plan, made by Walters in late 1986, could indeed have been used by Walters to make the UFO model some months before he released his UFO photos. Many pro-UFO researchers were forced to agree with their archnemesis on this point.

As the debate grew more polarized (following the time-honored formula of well-publicized UFO sightings), Walt Andrus reluctantly gave in to pressure from within his organization to reopen its investigation of the case. When Florida MUFON investigators Rex and Carol Salisberry — longtime Andrus loyalists — subsequently announced their conclusion that "several, if not all of the photos are probable hoaxes," Andrus angrily announced that the Salisberrys "do not have grounds to arrive at that conclusion until it is submitted to us."

Convinced that the MUFON hierarchy was more committed to covering the tracks of its botched original investigation than to uncovering the truth of the Walters photos, the Salisberrys and several other top MUFON field investigators resigned from the organization. Ironically, twenty years earlier Andrus had led a walkout from the Aerial Phenomena Research Group, accusing its founders of authoritarian leadership. Now Andrus stood charged of the same offense by disappointed local members of his own group.

By mid-1991, most observers who didn't have a stake in the outcome came to see that the parallels between the Walters and Billy Meier cases were far more compelling than Budd Hopkins and many others supposed. Yet there was an important difference as well. Whereas Billy Meier wrote volumes about the vast religious meanings of his encounters, even at one point calling himself Christ's thirteenth disciple, in their book Ed and Frances Walters showed no indication of having reflected on the meanings — philosophical, spiritual, or other — of their alleged encounters.

"It means that either the aliens themselves had chosen an absolutely insensitive clod upon which to shower their favors," wrote ufological observer Robert Girard, ". . . or that this book's shocking shallowness could only be accounted for and written by someone whose over-riding motive was either greed, attention or the satisfaction of putting a big fat one over on a bunch of foolish human beings." Many others found the Walterses' resolute absence of wonder suspicious. But even if Ed did create all of the photographs fraudulently — perhaps to pocket more than half a million dollars in book advances and sales of television rights collected so far — still, there remained aspects of the case that seemed to defy the supposedly definitive nay-saying of Philip Klass and other religiously consistent debunkers.

A host of Gulf Breeze area witnesses told of seeing aerial objects similar in many respects to those depicted in the Walters photos. "I saw a bright orange object fly over without making a sound," insisted a Gulf Breeze city councilperson. A retired newspaper publisher reported, "We were walking along the bay when I saw a bright object with lights shining through what looked like portholes. It looked just like the photographs that we saw in the paper." A local physician said, "It hovered beyond our pier, shining a white beam on the water. We saw the exact same craft as shown" in Ed Walters's photographs.

These accounts were eagerly collected and put forward by Walters and his supporters as evidence that what he saw and photographed was real. No less significant — and perhaps more so, in the long run — are particular kinds of details that advocates of Walters's position knew about but chose not to make public in relation to the Gulf Breeze sightings.

Donald Ware is a leader in the pro-ET hierarchy of the Mutual UFO Network and one of the chief proponents of the view that Ed Walters is telling the truth about what he saw and photographed. While doing fieldwork in Gulf Breeze, investigative journalist Ed Conroy said he became aware through Ware of certain bizarre events in the Gulf Breeze area that Ware chose not to mention in his MUFON report of the Gulf Breeze UFO investigation. Conroy said Ware told him about reports of sightings of a nine-foot-tall, human-like, hairy creature two counties over from Gulf Breeze that date from December, 1987 (one month after Ed Walters reported his first UFO sighting) to March of 1990; and . . . a report of mutilated dog carcasses found on local beaches in 1988.

"There is no evident causal connection between the reports of the Gulf Breeze UFOs and those of 'Bigfoot,' " notes Conroy, "but students of the paranormal have often seen that UFO reports are known to have occurred during periods of other extremely unusual events that include poltergeist-like phenomena, reports of spontaneous human combustion, an upsurge in popular religious fervor and even — quite controversially — anomalous animal mutilations and disappearances."

According to Conroy, Donald Ware seemed to "believe it best to cover up certain kinds of stories in the public interest." Yet as the Gulf Breeze mythos continues to unfold, news that particular too-bizarre-to-be-believed details were thus "missed" can only raise new questions about what other equally fantastic "peripheral" data may likewise be regularly omitted from the files of the UFO orthodoxy.

Philip Klass and his school of debunkers are perhaps mistaken in their insistence that ufologists consistently shape their research to transform mundane events into fantastic episodes. Maybe just the opposite is true no less often. It seems important to wonder whether, unknowingly, mainstream UFO researchers habitually "smooth" details that don't corroborate the hidden assumptions of their quasi-religious "extraterrestrials coming to make contact with us" interpretation.

If Proteus, Hermes, Trickster, and Dionysus have shown us anything, it is that the so-called "secondary" data associated with UFOs — including paranormal experiences, apparitions of hairy monsters, visits from demonic Men in Black, telepathic channelings of apparent gibberish about bananas, babies, and flying dogs — may well be *primary*, precisely because they don't "fit."

It also remains distinctly possible that the UFO phenomenon is finally more bizarre than we dare — or even *can* — imagine.

SIXTEEN

$\times$

SETTING aside the question of who and what they are and where they may be from, there is no avoiding the fact that for over forty years it has come to seem natural to imagine aliens in human terms — to draw them close through our metaphors. They come to "our world." The procedures they perform on abductees are "medical." They are interested in "our genetic material." They seek to "crossbreed with us." And so forth.*

During my many months of research and writing, I felt a steadily increasing desire to reverse this equation — to try to imagine human experience in the context of the larger domain to which alien behaviors and capacities appear to point. For it occurs to me that we humans may already share significantly in *their* realm without realizing it, that we already inhabit *with them* a ground of shared forms, and that, from an evolutionary perspective, humankind may be following a largely unconscious course toward dimensions of "contact" at once more remarkable and more intrinsic than we have begun to imagine.

---

*My choice of the word *alien* rather than *angel* to describe *them* in this section should not be taken to indicate a bias for the extraterrestrial visitation hypothesis over other theories (such as those of Jung or Vallee). I have chosen to use *alien* simply because this metaphor more than any other has taken root in the popular imagination concerning UFOs.

Are we and they headed someplace together? Someplace overlapping *there* and *here*? Is it possible we might someday meet embodied in a new way? Do we already coinhabit what Michael Murphy calls a "larger earth"?

In one sense, these questions seem outrageous. If the aliens indeed are real, theirs *must* be a realm apart and beyond. But is this necessarily so? I think not, and I intend to show why. These four questions speak to my reading of the equally "outrageous" — and consistently compelling — experiences described by people who report UFO close encounters. Intuition tells me that these extraordinary encounters may reveal unseen human possibilities, mysteries at work inside the facade of mundane affairs, pointing to crucial links between our nature and theirs.

I confess I don't know where my hunches will lead, but in the spirit of exploration that characterized the early days of ufology, when the mere phrasing of provocative questions was considered more useful than the mouthing of rote answers, I will follow my speculations wherever they may travel. I invite you to join me along the way with your own conjectures.

More than forty years of UFO reports reveal nothing so clearly as that the aliens are exceptional and supernormal beings. No matter what may ultimately be discovered about their origins and substance, about the nature and level(s) of their being, an impressively consistent body of eyewitness testimony points to remarkable attributes: their capacity to change shape and form at will, to move at extraordinary speeds across great distances, to perform feats of great agility, to embody varying degrees of luminosity.

If the events described in these reports overlap with our world (as they appear to, although to what extent has yet to be determined), it is difficult to avoid the impression that they have mastered secrets of time, space, matter, and form, mysteries of "bodily transformation," that we humans have not.

Or have we — some of us, at least? Across many different fields of study and realms of practice, a view of strange, uncharted human capacities begins to come into view:

In the process of being treated for sleepwalking, an army officer exhibits deep indentations resembling rope marks on his arms. These appear as he painfully relives an earlier episode during which he is roped to his bed to inhibit his somnambulism.

Diagnosed as schizophrenic, a man who expresses a great desire to give birth begins feeling something moving in his stomach — "like a baby," he says. During the next three weeks his abdomen becomes more and more distended and he gains sixteen pounds without altering his diet. Repeated medical tests find no pathology to account for the growth.

A group of experimental subjects, told what to expect from a certain drug, is able to produce not only that exact effect when given a dummy pill, but also the side effects of the drugs they think they are taking.

A woman, skilled at modifying physiological functions once considered inaccessible to conscious will, demonstrates a capacity to vary the firing patterns of single, designated nerve cells and the muscle to which they are attached.

A man diagnosed with multiple personality disorder is found to be allergic to citrus juices in all but one of his personalities. He remains free of rashes and other symptoms so long as that one personality retains executive control.

Each of these instances has been described in prestigious medical journals or in books by respected scientific researchers. Connections between these cases, at face value, aren't immediately obvious. Yet looking more closely, patterns begin to emerge.

Mind-generated bodily marks, including hysterical stigmata, sometimes appear spontaneously in response to trauma and catharsis. They suggest the body's plasticity and its precise responsiveness to mental imagery. During a cathartic recall of a beating by her father, for example, a female patient of the British psychiatrist Robert Moody developed a bruise on her hand closely resembling the imprint of an elaborately carved stick.

False pregnancy (pseudocyesis) likewise reveals the body's extraordinary responsiveness to images and passionate desire. This syndrome occurs in more females than males, not surprisingly.

The facile appearance and disappearance of allergies in individuals diagnosed as having multiple personality offers additional evidence of the body's malleability — and of the intricate linkage of personality and physiology.

The placebo effect offers still another window on the close relationship between mental and physical change. In a study to discover whether occlusion of the mammary artery would relieve the pain caused by angina pectoris, 100 percent of the subjects who received mock incisions while under general anesthesia showed improvement compared to 76 percent of the subjects whose arteries were actually tied.

The woman who was able to vary the firing patterns of single, designated nerve cells and attached muscles is not alone in her talent. Among biofeedback researchers there is now a strong consensus that any physical process that can be brought to awareness through biofeedback can be voluntarily modified.

From these and other related examples of exceptional human functioning, an intriguing hypothesis might be drawn, namely that latent within the human personality there exist powers and potentialities that, when ignored or denied, either stagnate within us or take expression in the form of spontaneous extraordinary psychophysical phenomena. Conversely, could it be that latent mind-body capacities — some seemingly ordinary, others apparently extraordinary — might be susceptible to conscious direction through various specific actions, practices, and disciplines?

There is good reason to answer in the affirmative, as we will shortly see. Moreover, such phenomena may offer important clues to the nature of certain kinds of UFO encounters. With this possibility in sight, and remembering the decree that extraordinary claims require extraordinary evidence, we can continue examining data from a variety of experiential domains.

Medical research has shown that the achievement of physical fitness produces a great number of beneficial changes in cardiorespiratory capacity, muscle tone, bone elasticity and mass, hormonal balance, skin composition, immune response, vitality, mood, and appearance. There is little doubt about the basic plasticity of the human form through regular exercise.

There are numerous instances of sudden and complete cures triggered by religious figures, faith healers, or shrines. None is more striking than the case of Delizia Ciroli, a Sicilian girl whose metastatic bone cancer of the knee was so far advanced that her parents made plans for her funeral. The plans were canceled when, after she drank water from Lourdes, the cancer went into remission and she was declared permanently and completely cured.

In the increasingly impressive field of mental imagery research, numerous clinical and experimental studies have shown that imagery-based therapies can facilitate relief from depression, insomnia, obesity, chronic pain, phobias, anxieties, cancer, and other afflictions.

The area of religious practice offers many compelling instances of unusual mind-body interactions. For instance, without any noticeable physical manipulation, the Indian yogi Swami Rama produced a thirteen-degree Fahrenheit difference in temperature between two sides of his hands. Tibetan lamas have demonstrated the ability to raise the temperature of their feet by as much as fifteen degrees, a practice known as *tumo*.

In another Tibetan religious tradition, the ecstatic transcendence of gravity is evident in the long-distance walking of Tibetan ascetics trained in *long-gom*, a form of yogic walking during which enormous distances are traversed in a waking trance.

There have been more than 100 well-documented Catholic religious figures who developed visible marks on their hands and feet — stigmata — symbolizing the wounds of Christ's crucifixion. Such physical signs typically emerge in states of great mental and spiritual focus, as in the case of a stigmatic named Marie-Julie Jahenny, a French peasant girl who correctly predicted the day she would receive a new stigmatization on her breast consisting of a cross, a flower, and the words *O Crux ave*. In clinical studies, certain hypnotized subjects have exhibited "skin writing," sometimes at the precise moment specified by their hypnotist.

Saint Theresa of Avila, the celebrated Spanish mystic and founder of the Discalced Carmelites, was said to have levitated during her intense contemplative raptures. During her canonization proceedings, ten observers reported under oath that they had seen her rise from the ground while in ecstasy. Saint Joseph of Cupertino, a seventeenth-century Franciscan monk, was said to have been observed on more than 100 occasions while elevated from the ground in mystical rapture.

Such reports do not by any means confirm the reality of levitation. Still, it is important to bear in mind that it is a mortal sin to lie under oath during such proceedings and that those who testify in such proceedings typically are devoutly religious people. Father Herbert Thurston, author of *The Physical Phenomena of Mysticism*, writes: "There can be little doubt that [Pope] Benedict XIV, a critically minded man who knew the value of evidence and who studied the original depositions as probably no one else had studied them, believed that the witnesses of Saint Joseph's levitations had really seen what they professed to have seen."

Paranormal or quasi-mystical experiences frequently reported by both professional and amateur sportspeople indicate that athletic and religious practice share common features. These experiences include startling images of organs and cells, altered sense of time, supernormal energy, exceptional awareness of the playing field or general environment, telepathy, clairvoyance, out-of-body sensations, apparent weightlessness (and even the impression of momentary transcendence of gravity, or levitation), and instances of profound, all-encompassing peace.

To use Gregory Bateson's phrase, is there a "pattern which connects" this wide range of human activity? Michael Murphy, a longtime investigator of such patterns, believes the answer is yes, that such phenomena "may constitute a vast experiment of nature, by which, conceivably, the human race is learning how to effect its transition to new levels of functioning, even to a new kind of evolution."

Bold words from a bold thinker and a creative philosopher of the mysteries. While in his mid-twenties, Murphy first journeyed to India to practice meditation and study Eastern thought — a common enough rite of passage today, yet all but unheard of in the mid-1950s. While in India, Murphy stayed at the teaching center of Sri Aurobindo, one of the greatest minds in Indian religious and philosophic thought. Aurobindo's central premise was that "all nature is secret supernature," and that deep within the structures of ordinary life there pulses an intrinsic, never-sleeping transformational impulse.

Far from being an accomplished fact, said Aurobindo, evolution is still unfolding, still engaged in a struggle to transcend itself by giving birth to hidden dimensions of body, emotions, mind, will, and spirit. Deeply religious in the tradition of the great Eastern mystics, Aurobindo was an unusual Indian insofar as he held to a fundamentally evolutionary vision that embraced yet far transcended Western ideas about natural selection and adaptation. Evolution, in Aurobindo's view, is nothing less than the adventure of the Divine in the material world, realizing itself in time and space, returning to itself in a vast dance of form and consciousness.

To a young Michael Murphy, Aurobindo's idea of the whole of human experience as a laboratory for ongoing, long-term evolutionary unfoldment was both exciting and convergent with Murphy's lifelong intuition that "our truest world waits like a phantom limb" (in the words of a character in Murphy's novel *Jacob Atabet*). Likewise, Aurobindo's view that we either grow or stagnate seemed self-evident to Murphy. Thus as a scholar Murphy turned his eye toward patterns of "exceptional and supernormal human functioning" in fields including physiology; medicine; experimental psychology; meditation research; the lore of yoga and contemplative practice; studies of hypnosis, imagery, and biofeedback; shamanism; research with hallucinogenic drugs; and spiritual or mind-assisted healing, among others.

In his groundbreaking book *The Future of the Body*, Murphy finds evidence in the literatures of all these fields for his thesis that extraordinary mind-body phenomena attest to uncharted powers that tend to "either stagnate within us or erupt painfully and perversely, or get expressed in curious ways like the religious stigmata." He adds:

> My entire study is predicated on the idea that as some individuals get a glimpse of these possibilities, which can appear both beautiful and terrifying, they begin to undergo disciplines that facilitate a process of physical and spiritual transformation. One has to mount a significant effort to realize the promise of these strange and beautiful powers. One must cultivate them with wisdom and courage to make them health-giving, life-enhancing, and not mere curiosities or pathologies.

The challenge we face, Murphy adds, is to design practices and disciplines designed to

> give fruition to the whole being: body, emotions, mind, will, and spirit. Rather than being considered obstacles to the life of the soul, or hindrances to spiritual awakening or liberation, as supposed by the world's great religious paths, unusual mind-body phenomena may also be seen as emergent features of human development, as capacities native to the body we might one day inhabit. Clairvoyance, rapture, and luminosity in religious practice, along with painful stigmata, might point toward a multi-leveled transformation of our mind-body complex. They might be seen as the budding limbs and organs of our future nature.

Are there implications in Murphy's highly speculative ideas for our understanding of UFO close encounters? I have come to believe so. My own ideas, too, are quite speculative, and are offered with the aim of inspiring new and open-ended perspectives, especially as regards common ground between aliens (whoever or whatever they finally are) and human beings (whoever or whatever we finally are). In light of recurring patterns in close encounter reports, both of us become — in a very real sense — species with indeterminate boundaries.

Time after time in the preceding pages we have seen examples of alien-human interactions that lead to no small uncertainty about where to place the dividing line — or the buffer zone — between mind and matter. Carl Jung, we recall, stated that the deepest "layers" of psyche become increasingly collective as they descend into physical matter, becoming simply "world." Daemons — angels and demons — have been depicted throughout history as holding *terra intermedia*, middle ground, a status also ascribed to the beings encountered in fairy land and shamanic upper and lower realms, and to luminous presences keeping watch at the threshold of death.

In a similar vein, philosopher Michael Grosso has commented on "the tantalizing mixture [which UFOs] present of objective materiality and subjective elusiveness." He notes that the UFO phenomenon seems able to "affect radar, cause burns, leave traces in the ground and at the same time pass through walls, appear and disappear like ghosts, defy gravity, assume variable and symbolic shapes, and strike deep chords of psychic, mystic, or prophetic sentiment."

The question that interests me at this point is: are they indeed *coming to us*, as they appear to be, or are we in fact unknowingly *meeting them* on middle ground, owing to our own "tantalizing mixture . . . of objective materiality and subjective elusiveness"? My hypothesis is *both*. For this assertion to make sense, however, we must be willing to reenter the ancient imagination of "body" as multiple, diverse, and intrinsically dynamic.

The Taittirya upanishad, one of the great sacred texts of ancient India, speaks of human nature as comprising five interdependent *sariras*, or soul-sheaths whose ruling principles were *anna* (matter), *prana* (life-force), *manas* (mind), *vijana* (supramental consciousness), and *ananda* (delight in the fact of being, or self-existent delight). The first four entities, or "bodies," were grounded in different levels of the manifest world, the fifth in *Brahman*, the Absolute, although each responded to all the others in a coherent, self-organizing way.

Eminent Greek philosophers of antiquity described various *ochemata* or soul-sheaths or "vehicles" connected to the visible body. The Neo-Platonic philosopher Damascius wrote: "The soul possesses a certain shining (*augoeides*) vehicle (*ochema*) which is also called 'star-like' (*asteroides*) and is eternal." The Islamic Shiite philosopher Sheikh Ahmad Ahsa'i proposed a fourfold partition of the soul, distinguishing two *jasad*(s), "living organisms," and two *jism*(s), "body masses" or "body volumes." The first *jasad* is the ephemeral material body; the second *jasad* consists of subtle archetypal forms. The first *jism* is a thing of the intermediary world, a kind of astral body; the second *jism* is the essential subtle body, thought to be the imperishable, eternal, transcendental individuality and the "light body."

Ancient Egyptians believed in a system of interlocking subtle bodies, among them the *ka* and the *ba*, in which life was embedded. All of these formulations had roots in far older shamanistic traditions where soul-travel between three worlds — upper, middle, and lower — and interaction with nonordinary entities in each realm was taken for granted.

The idea was widespread that particular powers and states were associated with these separable yet interconnected vehicles. Although differing on particulars, these traditions "generally held that our physical form is only part of a fuller personhood available to introspection and inspired sight," writes Michael Murphy. It is fair to say that these images of multiple bodies prefigure the modern idea that we exist on many levels at once, knowingly or not; each level or realm having its own structures and processes.

Drawing on these images of human identity as intrinsically multiple, extending along a continuum of subtle mental and physical states, Murphy draws from his study of numerous disciplines to suggest that the human organism is radically plastic, capable of moving "*as a body* into strange inner realms, during 'near-death experience,' deep meditation, sensory deprivation, or other activities. *Something* in our mind-body complex, it seems, can carry the observing self to other worlds with extensions in space and chains of events that give a sense of passing time."

Through training of awareness and concentration, as in sport and religious practice, and sometimes apparently spontaneously, we may find ourselves apprehending forms, colors, sounds, touches that suggest that *other* worlds are embedded in *this* world. Mountain climbers and sailors noted for their ego strength have reported phantoms who helped them through crises or simply accompanied them on their adventures. Yogis, shamans, religious adepts, and ordinary people have offered vivid accounts of interactions with benign and malevolent figures, angelic figures, departed relatives, and entities that seemed to know what was happening in this world.

"In all this experience, from the subtlest alterations of awareness to three-dimensional visions, the subject typically feels as if he were apprehending something beyond this world, something with its own objective reality," Murphy writes.

Are those "somethings" aspects of a greater existence, distorted perhaps by the subject's perceptual filters? Are they first glimpses of a "larger earth"? To a frog with its simple eye, the world is a dim array of greys and blacks. Are we like frogs in our limited sensorium, apprehending just part of the universe we inhabit? Are we as a species now awakening to the reality of multidimensional worlds in which matter undergoes subtle reorganizations in some sort of hyperspace? Is visionary experience analogous to the first breathings of early amphibians? Are we ourselves coming ashore to a "larger earth"?

The English essayist Thomas Browne, in a much-quoted passage from his *Religio Medici*, characterized the human being as "that great and true Amphibian whose nature is to live, not only like other creatures in diverse elements, but in divided and distinguished worlds." If there is a "teaching" of the saucers, perhaps it is to remind us of the multiple worlds we inhabit, a reality with which most of humanity has lived for centuries.

In their very diversity, UFOs call forth an idea whose roots extend to antiquity: the universe as a Great Chain of Being, characterized by a plenitude of forms ordered by continuous gradation. Along this chain, according to the ancients, are to be found spiritual beings participating in Perfection to varying degrees, according to their capacity to know the Good. There were no gaps — how could the Divine fail to actualize a possibility? And there was continuous gradation between realms, or levels, each shading into another, with *many* intermediate dimensions.

Imagining the UFO phenomenon in these terms diminishes the apparent contradiction that some UFO beings appear to be more evolved than others, that is, beneficent in both action and intent, while others — especially those who kidnap humans and hold them against their will — behave more like terrorists than gracious "spirit guides." A few UFO researchers have proposed that there are actually several species of aliens currently interacting with humans, which is why no single "alien personality profile" emerges.

Classical theologians who adhered to the Great Chain/hierarchy of angels model of the universe, and modern-day ufologists who catalog various types of aliens, can be viewed as detectives following the same scent. The Chain of Being presents an image of the psyche and the cosmos alike, the personal and world souls alike, as populated by personified beings — friendly and not so — whose autonomy necessarily challenges the surety of the imperial human ego. The image of an interconnected chain gives continuity to a phenomenon seen as extending from outer to inner with a vast middle domain.

From this perspective, the truest anomaly is not that angels and aliens should exist, but rather, modern Western culture's project — unparalleled in history — of placing entire dimensions of reality off limits, thereby forcing these dimensions to "return with a vengeance" in various forms, including as UFOs. In this sense, taking seriously the "signals" of the phenomenon, even if we do not know how to "decode" them, is evidence of waking up after a long sleep of denial — of what is and always has been "right under our nose."

In this sense, the UFO myth carries historical necessity.

I am struck by Murphy's analogy between the limited vision of the frog and the human being. The visual apparatus of a frog, consisting of a mere handful of nerve cells, is rudimentary indeed when compared, say, with the structure of the human eye. The frog sees little more than indistinct shapes and forms, limited (as Murphy notes) to a gray-black hue. This is not to say the intrepid frog sees "incorrectly," but rather, *the frog sees what it can see according to its structure*, which is adequate for snaring insects with its tongue and — much of the time — eluding predators. We humans know there is "more" to see, but the frog does not — at least so far as we can tell.

Similar analogies present themselves in our realm. The psychologist Jean Piaget notes that the human infant does not realize that its mother still exists when she is out of baby's visual range. It takes a while for cognitive *object constancy* to develop, that is, for the child to realize that mother is "there" (still exists) even when she is "not there" (out of sight). This is not to say the infant perceives incorrectly, but rather, like the frog, perceives according to its structure. (One difference is that while the frog's structure does not change, the child's structure does. The child's cognitive apparatus develops over time, unlike the frog's.)

What do these examples have to do with humans and the UFO phenomenon? It is conceivable that we perceive UFOs and other "anomalous" phenomena according to our predominant yet still-evolving psychospiritual "structure." Just as the frog is "embedded" within a world of forms that it does not apprehend fully, and just as a human infant "operates upon reality" only partially according to its "primitive" cognitive structure, what we humans term "reality" may in fact be a limited spectrum of a much larger realm of possibilities, where what we call "mind" and "matter" have not yet distilled into the few dimensions that we can "capture."

Ours may well be a "world within worlds." In Michael Murphy's phrase, this earth may be embedded in a "larger earth." In certain altered states of consciousness we apprehend more of this greater domain. Entry into such "hyperdimensionality" may be spontaneous and "accidental," as in the UFO abductions phenomenon and other kinds of unexpected extraordinary raptures: the burning bush of Moses, the spinning wheel of Ezekiel. Or through an inexplicably compelling moment of contact during lovemaking, or when beholding a wildflower on a spring day, or hearing the voice of the gods in the ecstatic agony of a hungry baby.

Entry may also be gained intentionally, as through the strenuous practices of yogis and other religious adepts, through the intense psychic focus of artists and champion athletes, through vigorous psychotherapies involving hyperventilation, or through the ingestion of mind-altering substances, to name but a few possibilities.

An ancient Chinese aphorism holds that "the fish is the last one to know that it lives in water." The fish takes for granted that the medium it knows is the True Element — indeed, the *only* element. Why should it imagine otherwise? But then, one day, a particular fish swims into a remote part of the lake and sees a strange object above. The fish has no name for what it sees from below, but we who are above would call the object a "bobber." Amazed, the fish returns to its school and tells what it has seen. The story is impressive, but the other fish are not so interested. After all, there is always fresh kelp to find, not to mention larger, hungry fish to avoid. News of such strange objects can only be a dangerous distraction to the overall affairs of the school.

Over time, however, others see the bobber, and a robust set of legends grows. Then, on a particular day, a fish happens to swim too close to the object and gets "hooked." Suddenly this fish finds itself pulled *up* and *out*, into a vast and altogether amazing realm of forms *above* and *beyond*. Those who have snagged the fish and reeled it in, after analyzing the creature according to particular criteria, decide the fish is not a "keeper" and toss it back into the ocean. Bewildered, the fish makes its way back with an even more incredible tale to tell about another world — a very different kind of world — populated by the most marvelous of beings.

Depending on how this news is revealed and received, the fish is deified, eaten, or simply isolated from the rest of the school, where it is left to muse aloud, "Water! We live and swim in *water*! I have just now seen that which is *not* water: I have glimpsed 'dry land,' and 'open sky.' Does anyone hear me? Does anyone *care*?"

We are right, it seems to me, to identify with the prophetic fish. Each culture, each tribe needs its visionaries for the renewal of its collective life. Similarly isolated from the collective, the shaman has no doubts about the importance of intelligent congress with the Other of many faces and forms. Over time, many prophetic fish return with a consistent message: "The evidence is strong, there's more *being* to Being, there are so many other levels, we must be *explorers*! The bobber offers important clues to understanding our 'ordinary water' — if only we will dare discover their connections to the larger realms of which we are part. Don't you understand?"

Yet it seems natural to also identify with the resistance of the rest of the fish, the school as whole. Here is the other side of the issue: "And why *should* we welcome glimpses of marvelous beings inhabiting an element so different from our own? Isn't there enough on *this* side of that silly bobber to keep you interested? Don't you know that if we entertain fantasies about meeting those beings, we may be drawn to become amphibious, or to realize we *already are* amphibious at some level? Are we really *ready* for such a big change? Why, we've barely gotten used to being *fish*!"

And so it goes, and continues to go. I will not attempt here to resolve the tension between these perspectives on "UFO as evolutionary prod." I'm rather more interested in amplifying this tension by way of

ing its role in fostering the UFO myth, especially vis-à-vis
ctions.

ne alien abductions phenomenon is nothing if not complex. If we
honor the reports of those who have been "taken and returned," then
it is by no means clear that those responsible mean us well, any more
than most of the numinous personages of traditional spiritual cosmolo-
gies have ever been thought to be friends of human welfare. In pene-
trating our dreams and working us over in unknown backyards of the
universe, tampering with our genetics and rewiring our psyches, these
bona fide Agents of the Fantastic mirror the human shadow in uncanny
ways, magnifying our cruelty toward fellow humans and our studied
indifference toward various nonhuman species.

It is difficult, for instance, to mistake the look of abject terror in
the eyes of a steer held captive while its flesh is seared with a hot brand-
ing iron to take the imprint of a human hieroglyph signifying private
property. Simply stated, the abduction scenario contains much darkness,
much that seems ominous.

But aliens also *crossbreed* with us, one of the oldest myths of all:
gods and goddesses coupling with mortals, resulting in the birth of a
hero (Jesus, Confucius, and Achilles, among many others). And there
appear to be classes of beneficent abductions, according to those who
track this corner of the myth. ("Now, the 'Blondes' are real pros, very
much an evolved species of alien," I have been told by a researcher
who uses hypnosis to track alien-human contacts. "It's those damned
Grays, the lizard-faced thugs who pull people out of bed — they're
the ones giving aliens as a whole a bad name.")

Thus the abduction motif entangles and intercrosses ominous and
numinous, demonic and angelic, dark and light, placing portions of
each within the province of the human shadow. This is because our
divinity escapes our notice no less often than our barbarity — both
are easily projected outward.

There is much more worth exploring along these lines, but no less
important is Joseph Campbell's warning that the mythic traveler's
journey is complete only when he returns and realizes his extrahuman
vision in terms befitting the human condition. Hence, the questions
that interest me are these: What hero, what prodigious progeny issues
forth — and on how many levels at once — from the UFO-human
coupling? What rough beast is this, that "slouches towards Bethlehem"?

How shall we agree to define *human* in the context of these ideas — especially considering the multiple respects in which an apparently autonomous Other shows no regard for human autonomy?

Having learned from Proteus to be suspicious of "definitive" answers, I would rather ask more questions, by way of keeping our deliberations open. Are we and the UFO somehow aspects of one another's unlived lives, two sides of a larger coin of a larger realm? Are we as much a part of their dreams and myths as they are of ours? Does the UFO phenomenon as a whole represent a kind of "docking with our angel," as the character Darwin Fall suggests in Michael Murphy's novel *Jacob Atabet*? If so, how might we intend to meet this angel? What manner of extension is required from the human side of the equation? In light of Murphy's research suggesting a radical interface between form and consciousness, might human adventurers in far future times — Magellans yet to be born — learn to enter and explore hypersomatic realms, meeting the UFO halfway on turf *as much ours as theirs*? Should we even attempt such an enterprise?

Is the UFO a "cosmic shaman" (Kenneth Ring's phrase) guiding the individual and collective soul at times of initiation and transition? What can we learn about the UFO encounter experience from studying the physical and mental phenomena of trance, multiple personality, the near-death experience, stigmata, out-of-body travel, and legends about human bilocation and dematerialization? What did Thomas Aquinas mean when he said, "Angels need an assumed body, not for themselves, but on our account"?

These sorts of questions interest me much more than the popular questions of the television tabloid programs: "Where are they from?" and "Why are they here?" My queries reflect my enduring intuition that the UFO is a key of sorts to the human future — if not necessarily a near, inevitable, or altogether desirable one. But I am also interested in the sense in which the UFO closes off human options, functioning as a luminous fly in the ointment of fundamentalism, monotheism, and literalism; as a persistent nemesis to all manifestations of "single vision and Newton's sleep."

I have come to imagine the UFO a "cosmic Palestinian" seeking a homeland, demanding the return of lands captured by the Imperial Ego. Like Yasir Arafat, the UFO is not on the official guest list. So be it. We may have long ago cast aside our angelic hierarchies, but the demonic has not forgotten where we live, and means to enter through the least secure door — that is, if the abductions provide any clue.

Although the image of UFO as savior holds an honored place in UFO mythology, I admit I cheer each time the UFO refuses the caricature of *deus ex machina*, a mechanical god descending to redeem a weak human plot. I'm convinced this angel is simply too improvisational — not to mention too savvy — to be typecast in this dead-end role just as its career hits full stride. So if not salvation, perhaps initiation? If so, toward what ends?

There is a phrase used by the ancient alchemists — *opus contra naturam* — that refers to the spirit that works against, and ultimately transforms, nature itself. In this image the UFO becomes a presence that sets the natural order to work on itself, releasing gold from lead when the "inner temperature" is right, reminiscent of Michelangelo's prolonged chiseling in the service of "freeing the form inside the stone." Even if all UFOs could suddenly be explained in conventional terms, I suspect that few who lived during the UFO era will easily forget the recurring images of *presence* emerging from the shadows with enormous intensity, making vivid, contradiction-filled statements, retreating time and again; as if entering and leaving through massive wounds in the flesh of the World Soul.

These metaphors barely approach the tension of the matter, hinting at the strain within matter itself: Lucretius's "tear inside a stone," Wallace Stevens's "poem at the heart of things." Such images remind us that Jacob *wrestled* with his angel, in contrast to the Hallmark card notion of angelic presence: "females in nighties tripping through the sky." The philosopher Robert Avens offers an image closer to experiences reported throughout the UFO literature:

> Angels . . . are in reality demons of might and terror prompting man to conform to their image. As the Sufi mystics repeatedly emphasize: "We are wrestling not *against* but *for* the Angel" — i.e., for our "true" self, the archetypal image by which we are made. To know oneself is to know one's angel.

I like the idea that as we summon forth the resolve to wrestle with the angel UFO — beginning with the recognition that we find ourselves in an unknown alignment with an unknown phenomenon, the effects of whose presence are multiple, long-term, and irreversible — we find ourselves at last wrestling *for* the angel: for that alluring, imposing, and often terrifying dimension of nature with which sages, saints, poets, artists, and the rapturously mad have reckoned throughout the ages.

"*Demons of might and terror prompting man to conform to their image*" is the part the human ego would rather forgo, not least for the confirmation it gives that nothing is fixed — or, to the contrary, that what seems to be fixed ("laws of nature") may express something beyond our capacity to conceive, let alone our capacity to change.

Earlier I warned that my ideas in this chapter would be speculative. My goal has been to extend conventional thinking about UFOs, aliens, angels, and our relationship with all of them. Yet I am prepared to consider that, in the final analysis, we may share no true common ground with these forces. Possibly mainstream UFO researchers are correct in insisting that the abductors are from a cosmos entirely apart, inexorably alien to our universe, to our nature, to us.

Certainly this is their *formal* status in the UFO mythos: they cannot be other than *alien*. As such, they hold the cards; we can only respond to their agenda. We are their project. So the legend has developed.

Even so, the theme plays ambiguously. As usual. The current thinking of today's ufological orthodoxy curiously undercuts the hypothesis of UFOs as radically *other.* I'm speaking of the fact that, against the most incredible odds imaginable, our spacefaring visitors happen to be interfertile with us — at least the ones reported by the Budd Hopkins school of ufology. They are genetic engineers and baby stealers *par excellence*, a theme that provides mythic and religious underpinnings for today's adherents to the nuts-and-bolts, ET-oriented UFO perspective.

As with most of the UFO mythos, the image of the superalien biologist offers a better readout on our soul than theirs — in this instance revealing how incredibly little faith the proponents of the gene-tampering legend finally have in the ensouled, embodied experience of being human. Much of ufology is simply absurd, but this dark, self-fulfilling corner of its thinking fills me with great sorrow.

For it is only on the soil of our "original and unassailable integrity" that the term *alien* has any meaning whatever, writes Richard Grossinger. "The original ground on which we stand is this world, the familiarity of our body/minds, language, and civilization, however much in crisis that might seem and no matter that we judge ourselves to have made a mess of it." In a moving essay entitled "Giving Them a Name,"

Grossinger wonders why it should be "even remotely reassuring that we might be someone else's genetic experiment," in light of the fact that

> ... we exist only as the legitimate outcome of the forces that we express. We cannot be anything else, and I would argue that this is true even if we are someone else's experiment — and I will get right to the point on that one: even if we are the genetic experiment of a scientifically advanced race, the experiment can only be a manipulation of existing lifeforms; it does not include the invention of our whole existence. Our genes can be synthesized, or rearranged; the biological frame of life can be altered, but biology itself cannot be invented out of nothing by something that is itself an evolutionary product of the universe.

We are biological beings, as they logically must be if they have any use for our DNA. Thus "the experience to which biology refers remains intact," Grossinger insists. If alien scientists have learned to manipulate genetic material, this is an art they share with human scientists. Neither of us — alien or human — is intrinsically wiser as a result, for neither they nor we can take credit for *inventing*, as Grossinger puts it, "that creationary force ... the original phenomenology, the impulse for something to become in a universe where nothing might as easily have been."

So there is common ground after all: human and humanoid, *children of the same Creator.*

Michael Murphy's view that this shared footing may be far greater in practical terms than we imagine continues to fascinate me. I wonder whether his ideas might in fact be tested in action, given that a growing number of abductees claim to be "picked up" regularly.

What would happen if more abductees took up various martial arts, developing their *ki* and *chi*, their subtle energy bodies? Would they find themselves more able to navigate the "unearthly" elements in which they suddenly find themselves? Suppose first-time abductees later began practicing meditation and rudimentary sensory awareness exercises, training their attention to return to the present moment each time it fades or gets carried off by trains of thought. Suppose they practiced the shamanic art of remaining lucid in dream states. By the next abduction attempt, might they find it easier to stabilize their attention more fully at subtle bodily levels, to keep better track of external stimuli and internal responses, and to hone their imaging and concentration skills?

Would these subjects have an advantage over others — for instance, in remaining conscious during the transition between the mundane world in which they are picked up, and the fantastic realm into which they are floated or carried? ("Doorway amnesia" is the term given by UFO researchers to the characteristic absence of recall at this crucial threshold. In Greek mythology doorways, thresholds, and passages belong to the province of a particular god. Not surprisingly, his name is Hermes.)

Here is my point: If we are indeed "amphibians," then perhaps our emergent limbs require first our intention to use them. What would the abduction experience look like, feel like, sound like, to individuals who proposed to meet the aliens *as if* they share intrinsic middle ground with us as "hyperdimensional" beings?

I mean these proposals quite seriously — and with enormous respect for abductees themselves, who deserve nothing so much as to be empowered in a typically impossible situation. I'm not suggesting the equivalent of an Olympic program, either, but rather a modicum of training toward greater life mastery: body, mind, emotions, imagination, spirit. Essentially I'm suggesting an experiment. It's time to get bolder.

It is no doubt clear to the reader that I don't share what seems to me zealous paranoic theorizing on the part of many of today's abduction researchers. But I know many of them are providing genuine assistance to people who report personal experiences involving overwhelming anguish, and I salute them for this. I simply hope abduction counselors will adopt strategies that are more *proactive*, with less melodramatic shaking of fists toward the dark sky, especially if indeed most abductions are repeat experiences. UFO abductees need life skills, not invitations to join the personality cults of competing researchers.

In short, we could do some good science here by introducing a new variable into an existing experiment where certain parameters are already familiar (strange light in sky, stalled engine, missing time, strange dreams, horrifying memories, and so on). And we would no doubt gain a whole new body of travelers' tales: accounts from a new generation of abductees reporting their efforts to engage their experience in ways they hadn't thought possible.

Perhaps most abductees, during the actual experience, would still find themselves paralyzed by an overwhelming force — that is a distinct possibility. At the same time, if the aliens are indeed intelligent beings who respond to us responding to them, a change on our part might evoke something new on their end.

The possibilities are limitless. We're talking about *UFOs*, after all. Nothing could be stranger than what we've seen since Kenneth Arnold's fateful day in 1947.

Bite your tongue, a voice tells me. On second thought, the truly fantastic events may still be down the road. Or across the sky. Or stirring in unseen depths of the mythic imagination.

Probably all three.

EPILOGUE

$\mathbf{S}$ O IT has gone all these years; so it continues to go.

As the UFO phenomenon enters the fifth decade of its appearance on the modern world stage, no question is asked more often than this one: Are unidentified flying objects real, or merely symbolic? For hard-core disciples and debunkers alike, it continues to be the only question that matters — a kind of litmus test for the prodigy named UFO.

Based on what we have seen, however, the assumption that UFO events could be real *or* symbolic ("merely" symbolic, at that) is both arbitrary and gratuitous. *Symbolism*, derived from the Greek *symballein* ("to throw together"), denotes the drawing together of two worlds. An event, word, or image is "symbolic" not by standing for something *else*, but rather by indicating *more than* its obvious and immediate meaning, resisting precise definition or explanation while evoking unconscious realms.

When taken literally — as so much is taken by both ends of the UFO debate — the *real versus symbolic* dichotomy can only obscure the rich sense in which the UFO phenomenon becomes not less real, but more so, for its mythic, metaphoric, allegorical dimensions. Surely it is significant that the UFO's familiar images (flyovers, landings, close encounters, close calls, secret rumors and rumors of secrets, strained official denials, recurring fresh starts, and of course the alien abductions) continue to point to seemingly fathomless depths, frustrating pro- and anti-UFO researchers alike in their efforts to back the phenomenon into various ideological corners.

Perhaps we will someday know with certainty that UFOs are extraterrestrial spacecraft piloted by humanoid aliens; or that they emerge from parallel dimensions at will, whim, or in response to unwitting signals from the human psyche. Even then, what would matter is what is evoked from us: how any such revelation captures the mythic imagination. *Words in the news* become momentous when they become *worlds in our lives*. And who can doubt that humankind would interpret clear confirmation of either scenario as anything short of momentous?

Yet — as we have seen throughout this book — categorical proof of either breakthrough (or of any other final, all-encompassing outcome, including a definitive debunking) is exactly what continues to successfully elude all appropriately deputized ufological posses, and this despite several decades of constantly updated all-points-bulletins:

> Suspect last seen spinning at the edge of town, near the horizon of possibility. Rumored to be extremely complex, life-changing, and to possess hidden religious affiliations. Approach compulsively, with combination of awe, fear, arrogance, and irreverence — proportions unknown.

Thus as determined ET seekers await the Big News ("any day now, the lid on the government cover-up conspiracy's gonna blow sky-high"), UFOs consolidate their status as a cosmic chameleon darting back and forth between mind and matter, improvising brazenly with the core elements of each realm, making known their top-secret truths to high-level official bureaucrats (says the cover-up legend) but not to the rest of us.

As one school of researchers presses its claim that aliens are implanting physical probes in the skulls of human abductees, powerful mythic images take root in the culture's subconscious.

As investigators get local television news shows to feature videotapes of last week's strangely moving celestial lights, armies of alluring possibilities expand their subliminal occupation of imagination-at-large, leading to renewed calls for televised congressional hearings fueling new rounds of "take no prisoners" shelling between ufology's two camps: *those who know* and *those who don't*.

In short, not apart from the debate about whether or not it is real, but precisely within the fertile milieu this debate provides, the UFO phenomenon goes along doing what seems to be its job: nourishing within the collective psyche a free-floating expectation of unspecified yet inevitable "contact" between humankind and an elusive yet widely posited *otherkind*. And because the nature of the "contact" and "otherkind" remains largely unspecified, and therefore amenable to unbounded conjecture, the symbolic dimensions of the phenomenon develop increasingly greater allure.

So it has gone all these years; so it continues to go.

In UFO case after case, something remarkable is seen. Witnesses offer testimony. "Experts" dismiss this testimony. Witnesses and public at large reach for explanations; these, too, are dismissed. Pro-UFO researchers identify new patterns, reach definitive conclusions. Debunkers dismiss each new pattern, reach opposing definitive conclusions. UFO events take on increasingly bizarre forms; old patterns crumble. The overall debate becomes increasingly convoluted with each new round.

Meanwhile, compelling sighting reports continue to be made, often by highly credible witnesses. As experts — governmental, military, academic, and scientific — consistently refuse to consider the growing body of first-person accounts, witnesses and the public at large reach their own conclusions about the true nature of UFO events.

Eager for stories, news media return to "retired" witnesses — Betty Hill, Lonnie Zamora, Charlie Hickson, and Calvin Parker — for reflections on their life-changing experiences, thereby keeping realms of past images alive to the collective imagination. Pressed for answers, astronomers, psychologists, theologians, air force officials, and civilian investigators offer vastly differing opinions, effectively enhancing the overall significance of the initials UFO.

All along, debunkers recite their familiar mantra — *hoax, hallucination, mistaken identity* — while pro-UFO researchers keep insisting *UFOs are not only real, they are the most important story in human history*. Thus players can enter the game knowing which side to root for: ours. Players get to agree on rules: (1) try to be convincing, (2) try harder. And on procedure: each side's referees shall call the plays. And on the goal: to prevail. ("Any day now ... this time *finally*.")

All of this in the context of an unwritten, unspoken dictate: No one shall prevail.

Ever.

Above all else, the game must go on.

The jury never delivers a final verdict because there is no jury — or else everyone who has an opinion is part of a jury that remains perennially too divided to agree, too caught up to quit.

Time and again the saucer hovers only so close, seldom so near as to deny any legend its place in an ever-expanding UFO mythos, yet close enough that the finish line can remain within view.

Over forty years ago, air force UFO investigators Edward Ruppelt and J. Allen Hynek foresaw a swift resolution of the phenomenon they had been charged to study. Their prediction was repeated by many others during the following decades, especially during sighting lulls, until it became orthodox ufological liturgy.

Today, with fewer of what ufologists call "high-quality sightings" than in many years, longtime investigator (and ET-hypothesis champion) Jerome Clark predicts an imminent solution to the entire controversy.

Not just the tabloids but major news media, Clark recently announced, will soon confirm ufologists' findings with their own major investigations.

"Our long quest is almost over," Clark states. "We soon, I think, will know what UFOs are."

Alien abduction specialist Budd Hopkins is of a similar mind: "After decades of painstaking and persistent investigation, including many false leads and dead ends, the UFO phenomenon is at last revealing its core secrets."

Adds UFO historian and abduction researcher David M. Jacobs: "We may be on the threshold of momentous discoveries."

Maybe the end is indeed near.

Yes.

This time. At last.

Then again, maybe not. We have yet to meet one last figure from the shadowy nether world of myth, a man whose name has become synonymous with that which continues and does not end.

SISYPHUS has been sentenced by the gods to ceaselessly roll a rock to a mountain summit, whereupon the stone will fall to the bottom by its own weight. With good reason, writes Albert Camus, the gods assume there could be "no more dreadful punishment than futile and hopeless labor," especially when performed by one who "knows the whole extent of his wretched condition," as Sisyphus indeed does.

Camus found himself interested in the moment following each descent of the rock to the bottom of the hill — the few seconds before Sisyphus descends again to the lower world according to the terms of his lifelong sentence. "At each of those moments when he leaves the heights and gradually sinks toward the lairs of the gods, he is superior to his fate," Camus insists. "He is stronger than his rock."

We are to grasp this essential truth: There is no way out for Sisyphus, no reprieve, no commutation. He is a tragic hero because he is *conscious* of his futile task. "The lucidity that was to constitute his torture at the same time crowns his victory," writes Camus. This is the twist in the story, and the gods are of course surprised. Sisyphus, powerless and rebellious, *defies* them, becomes the master of his fate, by saying one simple word — *yes* — even though he knows this is equivalent to affirming an eternity of unceasing effort intended as torment.

By finding *meaning* in his assigned endeavor, Sisyphus succeeds in driving "from the world a god who had come into it with dissatisfaction and a preference for futile sufferings." To this day, Camus insists, Sisyphus is "still on the go," like "a blind man eager to see who knows that the night has no end.... His rock is his thing [and] the rock is still rolling."

Through the ages, various human commonwealths have developed guiding myths, and myths about these myths, for capturing the essence of *otherkind*. Sisyphus has been present each time any human tribe has felt itself on the verge of explaining — or explaining away — this history-haunting ghost whose face and form changes from age to age, yet whose beckoning remains so remarkably constant.

Each time a new theory of the UFO's origins is put forward, each time the UFO is *captured*, triumphant Sisyphus finds himself resting once again "at the top of the hill." And as each theory falls short of comprehensiveness and certainty, the boulder belonging to Sisyphus plummets to the ground below. Thus the ascent and descent are performed again and again, both sides of the debate agreed on the importance of "uncovering" the UFO's true unambiguous origins.

Just as significantly, both sides maintain that such origins can (and must) be found. In UFO case after case, definitive origins prove elusive.

Yet ufologists — pro and con — continue to try, expecting to succeed. This is the central difference between Sisyphus and modern ufologists. The man sentenced by the gods to an eternity of compulsive futility "knows the whole extent of his wretched condition; it is what he thinks of during his descent." Ufologists, by contrast, think of the impending culmination of their efforts, when their "rock" will lie still and the UFO will be finally and fully explained.

This wrestling with the angel UFO at the boundary where human and suprahuman face off represents a kind of eternal return, an unfolding cycle, an endlessly recurring ritual, a vivid instance of Ouroboris swallowing its tail. In Sisyphus's unending labor we find a constancy of the sort expressed by the UFO — always leaving, always returning; and by the human psyche's endless pursuit, born of seemingly limitless metaphysical restlessness.

What makes the UFO so compelling is its very persistence as an unfolding historical being who yet conjures primordial truths; its capacity to call forth successively, over long stretches of time, the mythical moment, punctuating mundane history with cosmic rhythms that — how could it be otherwise? — knock us right off our feet.

Thus it seems appropriate that we leave Sisyphus *steadying himself*, as Camus has it, at the foot of the mountain, "to raise the huge stone" one more time. Always the human spirit agrees to make the climb again, not knowing exactly why, somehow trusting that in the intercrossing and entangling of human and divine fates, to be human is not, finally, to be at a loss.

"What interests me is to know how to become a saint."
"But you do not believe in God."
"Exactly. How to be a saint without God: that is the only concrete problem I understand today."
"What interests me is how to be a man."
"We are looking for the same thing, but I am less ambitious."
— Albert Camus, *The Plague*

I AM struck by certain similarities between Homer's *Odyssey* and the UFO phenomenon. Both are epic in scope; both deal with the actions of a "hero" who wanders seemingly without end, enduring trials and tribulations. Both are "elevated" narrative forms, the *Odyssey* as inspired poetry, the UFO phenomenon as the appearance of fantastic events. Both are also allegorical — they concern much more than their surfaces suggest.

But there are important differences as well. Ulysses' wanderings only *seem* endless; eventually they culminate in what Henry Fielding calls the "one great end," the hero's return home. As we take leave of our subject, no such ending is apparent. Because the modern UFO's homestead remains a mystery, its wanderings continue. "I fancy Sisyphus returning toward his rock," Camus writes. "The rock is still rolling."

These thoughts touch on what the literary scholar Angus Fletcher sees as the single great weakness of allegory, namely a tendency toward "diffusion of inner coherence, since the typical allegory threatens never to end." When an allegory goes on and on, we "can be anesthetized by the ritual order of enigma and romance." The most sublime and picturesque qualities of an allegory — the very qualities that capture our imagination in the first place — can cast a spell. The riddles that startle at the outset eventually begin to lull.

It seems that something along these lines has taken place within the UFO universe in recent years. To be sure, UFOs still evoke the exceptional, the mythic, but no longer on a widespread basis. Once perceived as such a radical new possibility, the idea of UFOs no longer startles or amazes.*

For now, the main significance of UFOs for society may well rest not so much in their extraterrestrial origins, or lack thereof, as in the fact that a sizable segment of society believes and behaves as if they are real, regardless of the available evidence. Public opinion surveys show an increasing willingness of Americans to believe we are not alone

---

*Even so, new mysteries continue to press for entry into the UFO mythos; witness the remarkable crop circle phenomenon reported with increasing frequency in Great Britain, Australia, Japan, the Soviet Union, Canada, and Midwestern fields in the United States. The patterns (or "agriglyphs," as they have been dubbed), which typically appear overnight in knee- or waist-high grain without cutting or damaging plants, are said to be accompanied by electrical disturbances, hovering lights, humming sounds, and other unusual phenomena. Well over 600 occurrences of these circular impressions, some ranging up to 100 feet in diameter, have been reported since 1976. "Whatever the cause, the circles are particularly intriguing because they are beautiful geometric formations that level crops in a precise pattern," wrote *Time* magazine on September 18, 1989. (One formation resembled a Celtic cross.) The circles have become a lively topic of discussion at UFO research meetings, where many believe they must be caused by alien spaceships. Thus the beat goes on.

in the universe. That this increase corresponds to more than forty years of UFO sightings is surely significant.

As we come to the end of our study, certain questions that captivated us at the outset seem to have resolved themselves. Are UFOs from outer space or from the ongoing mythology of humankind? The answer could be: both. Even if UFOs are actual extraterrestrial spacecraft, they have succeeded in slipping into traditional mythology, next to other gods and goddesses. In that sense — if only in that sense — UFOs have indeed *landed* and may be here to stay.

Some longtime observers have concluded that, other than as mythology, the UFO phenomenon is for the most part over — for good. They cite as evidence the unusual quietude that has settled in on the UFO horizon. Abductions continue to be reported but not on the front pages, and there is no certainty that new abductions aren't simply symbolic echoes of the old ones, or for that matter, that the original ones weren't symbolic echoes of . . . who knows what? Likewise, no UFO sightings currently stir major controversy, so unlike the 1960s and 1970s when UFO fieldworkers eagerly awaited their next on-site assignment, their pronouncements conveyed to the nation on network television.

These and other signs are interpreted to mean the UFO phenomenon will simply fade away as strangely as its sudden arrival, that it will take its place in folklore with vampires, leprechauns, and werewolves as a folkloric motif specific to a particular historical epoch.

Don't bet on it, respond other ufologists. The UFO phenomenon is only stabilizing itself at its current plateau. We need to absorb what's already obvious before *otherkind* returns with a new revue, maintains this school of researchers. For now, the phenomenon is simply busy recycling itself, gathering together its images and effects, monitoring new drafts in the labyrinthine human psyche the way a thermostat monitors room temperature, ready to kick up the flame when the time is right.

Which view is correct? By now the futility of seeking yes-or-no, black-or-white answers to such questions seems obvious. We can say who is right about the future of the UFO phenomenon with as much certainty as we can say when Samuel Beckett's long-awaited Monsieur Godot will finally arrive.

But suppose the first group is correct. Suppose no new UFO reports are made and we are left with only memories, like negatives of photographs once so remarkably vivid. As a thought experiment, let's just say they stop coming around.

Maybe this development would be sufficient to deflect attention from the allegory's baroque surface-level debate about the origins and composition of UFOs, prompting us finally to take survey of how this debate has obscured an ongoing and roundabout discussion about what it means to be human. Perhaps it would then become clear that more than four decades since the term *flying saucer* was first spoken, the UFO phenomenon has revealed considerably more about our nature than about theirs.

UFOs may be the most important phenomenon since the dawn of human history. They may also turn out to be, in Angus Fletcher's phrase about one function of allegory, little more than "sheer ornamental display." Either way, there's a rock in front of us — as there always is. Will we still take our place behind it, even though it finally dawns on us that mythic realities always imply much more than can ever be precisely defined or fully explained?

Will we agree again to sweat our way back to the top even as we admit that whatever conclusions we reach about UFOs will lead inevitably to new questions about what it means to live a human life in a galaxy of uncertain hospitality?

If UFOs do disappear tomorrow, will we simply find another domain in which to continue what is inevitably a *religious* search to recover lost intimacy?

Of course we will, just as we always have. Because no less than for Sisyphus, pushing rocks is our thing. And the rock continues to roll: one more time up, again back down, then once more to the top.

SO IT has gone all these years; so it continues to go.

ACKNOWLEDGMENTS

IN THE creation of this book I enjoyed the assistance of a good many people representing a wonderful diversity of perspectives toward the prodigy called UFO.

For making themselves available for primary interviews and in some cases ongoing conversations, and/or for making available particular documentation, I am grateful to Walt Andrus, Jerome Clark, Ed Conroy, Richard Haines, Budd Hopkins, David Jacobs, Philip Klass, Gordon Melton, Leo Sprinkle, Dennis Stacy, Dennis Stillings, Whitley Strieber, John Timmerman, and Jacques Vallee.

Don Michael, David Pursglove, Ken Ring, Jane Rock, Charlie Sweet, and Mary Wickwire offered much encouragement, especially in their appreciation for that which thrives "at the edge." Michael Murphy supported the idea of this book from its inception, not least by sponsoring a small private gathering of UFO researchers to exchange ideas at Esalen Institute. Bocara Legendre's financial support of that meeting greatly contributed to its success.

Special thanks to my agent Fred Hill for many useful suggestions in the days when I was attempting to translate rough ideas into a concrete book project; and to Stuart Miller for his early interest and support.

I continue to be indebted to Laurance S. Rockefeller for his generous support of my work in recent years. I also acknowledge and thank Jean Lanier, George Lamb, and Elizabeth McCormack.

My editor, William Patrick, understood and supported the spirit of *Angels and Aliens* from the very beginning. His keen eye and novelist's ear made this book better, and his warmth and wit regularly eased my labors. Likewise I thank Beth Burleigh, Hartley Ferguson, Ted Laux, Richard Rossiter, Nancy Bell Scott, Sharon Stecher, and Joyce Weston for doing their work so well.

For many hours of deeply satisfying conversation about art, myth, symbols, and the soul of the world, and for their lasting friendship, I extend my hand to Phil Cousineau and Peter Rojcewicz: scholars, artists, rogues, fellow travelers.

Most of all, I thank you, Kathryn, for enduring the trials of my obsessions during the period that this book captured and swept me away. Knowing you were near, along with Tyler and Yoshi, made all the difference. I will never, ever forget.

Finally, this obvious but easily overlooked fact: Were it not for the unknown wanderer named UFO — its adventures and misadventures in a world that excludes it — there would be no book at all. "Such things commonly please us best which are most strange, and come farthest off." Indeed so.

NOTES

Prologue

P.xi In *Creation Myth*, R.J. Stewart . . . : Stewart, p. 11.
P.xii Joseph Campbell, in turn, writes that . . . : Campbell, 1986, p. 18.
P.xii "the supposed surety of fact . . .": Hillman, p. 55.
P.xii "We have here a golden opportunity . . .": Jung, 1978, p. 16.

Chapter One

P.1 PENDLETON, Ore., June 25 (AP) . . . : Strentz, p. 24.
P.2 "Skepticism changed to wonder and the journalists reported the incident . . .":
Jacobs, 1975, p. 37.
P.2 Army and CAA spokesmen expressed skepticism over a report . . . : Strentz, p. 24.
P.2 "I can't begin to estimate the number of people, letters, telegrams . . .": Lagrange,
p. 30.
P.2 PENDLETON, Ore., June 27 (UP) . . . : Strentz, p. 25.
PP.2-3 The *New York Times* editorialized . . . "atoms escaping from an overwrought
bomb" . . . : Jacobs, 1975, p. 41.
P.3 In a similar spirit, *Life* magazine quoted a Harvard . . . : *Life*, 21 July 1947,
pp. 14-16.
P.3 "If I saw a ten-story building flying through the air . . .": Jacobs, 1975, p. 38.
P.3 "practically a moron in the eyes of the majority . . .": Ibid.
P.4 "a modern myth of things seen in the skies" . . . : Jung, 1978.
P.4 A widely published Gallup poll of August 19, 1947 . . . : Gallup, p. 666.
P.5 A private pilot named Vernon Baird . . . : Jacobs, 1975, p. 39.
P.5 Flying saucers belong in the same category as the Loch Ness monster . . . : *New
York Times*, 27 December 1947, p. 28.
P.5 "the reported phenomenon is something real and not visionary . . .": Fawcett
and Greenwood, p. 213.
P.6 "The attitude toward this task varied from a state of near panic . . .": Ruppelt,
1956, pp. 13-14.
P.6 "an ice cream cone topped with red" . . . : Story, 1980, p. 220.
P.6 "it appears to be a metallic object . . .": Good, 1988, p. 146.

P.7 "powered by some jet or other type of power-shooting flame . . .": Clark, forthcoming, 1991.

P.7 "no astronomical explanation" was possible . . .: Ibid.

P.8 "Instead of seeking the origin of a possibly unique phenomenon . . .": Jacobs, 1975, p. 50.

P.8 a two-part *Saturday Evening Post* series . . .: *Saturday Evening Post*, 30 April 1949, 7 May 1949, pp. 20–21, 136–139; pp. 36, 184–186.

P.9 "For the past 175 years, the planet Earth has been under . . .": Keyhoe, 1967, p. 7.

P.9 "Charley, there's a rumor . . . it's a top level deal," said Charley: Keyhoe, 1950, p. 73.

Chapter Two

P.11 Mythic events . . . "form the ground or foundation of the world, since everything rests on them": Jung and Kerenyi, p. 7.

P.13 In an article in the British magazine *Magonia* . . .: Kottmeyer, 1990, pp. 3–10.

P.13 "a great deal of misunderstanding" . . .: Ibid., p. 4.

P.14 myth . . . "always sets up some precedent as an ideal . . .": Jung and Kerenyi, p. 6.

P.14 The myth . . . in its original living form . . .: Ibid., p. 5.

P.15 "It is the theory which decides what we can observe": Watzlawick, 1984, p. 101.

P.15 the German physicist Werner Heisenberg, namely that nature never reveals itself . . .: Ibid.

P.15 "If two observers habitually look for different kinds of pattern . . .": Keeney, p. 53.

P.16 Michel suggested, "then no matter what we do, it will forever remain . . .": Fitzgerald, p. 69.

P.17 Proteus's "ceaselessly changing image that could take on any shape . . .": Hillman, p. 203.

P.17 "This wily god never discloses even to the skillful questioner . . .": Campbell, 1949, p. 31.

P.18 Giambattista Vico, "since human knowledge is nothing else than the endeavor to make things correspond . . .": Watzlawick, 1984, p. 29.

P.19 First, we wish reality to exist independently of us . . .: Segal, p. 31.

P.19 "All this is banal enough but the implications are anything but . . .": Hayward, p. 8.

Chapter Three

P.21 "It appeared that the Air Force, after eighteen months of effort . . .": Jacobs, 1975, p. 62.

P.22 "Almost immediately . . . we perceived . . . six bright objects . . .": Clark, forthcoming, 1991; Sachs, pp. 218–19; Story, 1980, p. 243; Story, 1982, p. 138.

P.22 To the pilots it "looked very much as if an element of 'human' or 'intelligent' error . . . a ball ricocheting off a wall": Ibid.

P.23 "Our shift had been on duty about forty minutes . . . a very strange situation existed": Story, 1980, p. 388.

P.23 As had happened the previous week, numerous radar and visual correlations were made . . . : Jacobs, 1975, pp. 75–77; Sachs, p. 362; Story, 1980, pp. 361–62.

P.23 The air force insisted that "there has been no pattern that reveals . . .": Story, 1980, p. 389.

P.24 "There is no other conclusion I can reach but that . . . there were at least ten . . .": Strentz, p. 41.

P.25 WASHINGTON, July 28 (INS) . . .: Ibid., p. 42.

P.25 The Air Force is now ready to concede that many saucer and fireball sightings . . .: *Life*, 7 April 1952, p. 80.

P.25 Dr. Walther Reidel . . . "I am completely convinced . . .": *Life*, 7 April 1952, p. 86.

PP.25–26 Dr. Maurice A. Boit . . . "The least improbable explanation . . .": *Life*, 7 April 1952, p. 86.

P.26 The real depths of the saucer mystery . . .: Strentz, p. 89.

P.26 "The article is factual, but *Life*'s conclusions are their own": Jacobs, 1975, p. 71.

P.27 *Times* science writer Walter Kaempffert . . . weather balloons: *New York Times*, 12 April 1952, p. 10.

P.27 A *Times* editorial complained . . . "the idea was too fantastic to die": *New York Times*, 13 April 1952, Sec. IV, p. 9.

P.27 DAYTON, Ohio, July 19 (AP) . . .: Strentz, pp. 38–39.

P.28 "It was inevitable that someone, somewhere, sooner or later, would claim contact . . .": Stacy, p. 121.

P.29 "was in the presence of a man from outer space — A HUMAN BEING FROM ANOTHER WORLD!": Adamski, p. 66.

P.30 the contactees had no fear of ridicule and eagerly sought publicity: Jacobs, 1975, p. 109.

P.32 "luminous egg-shaped craft flying toward me at terrific speed": Story, 1980, p. 282.

P.33 "much more beautiful than that of any woman I have ever known before" . . .: Ibid.

P.33 "What they wanted of me [was] a good stallion to improve their own stock" . . .: Story, 1980, p. 383

Chapter Four

P.36 "allegory says one thing and means another . . .": Fletcher, p. 2

P.36 Henry Peacham . . . "may hardly be gathered": Peacham, p. 27.

P.36 "a fundamental process of encoding our speech": Fletcher, p. 3.

P.37 "But somehow this literal surface . . . if given interpretation": Ibid., p. 2.

P.38 "There were at least . . . aircraft could perform": Strentz, p. 41.

P.38 "Somebody must have been telling lies about Joseph K. . . .": Kafka, p. 1.

P.39 "By having a surrealistic surface texture . . . of thought": Fletcher, p. 107.

P.40 "If you strive to convey . . . in terms of ordinary meanings": Vallee, 1988, p. 107.

P.40 "manages to disturb . . . narrow-mindedness of the debunkers" . . .: Ibid., p. 178.

P.40 "leads to a rejection . . . of the symbols conveyed" . . .: Ibid., p. 179.

P.40 "the apprehension of these . . . two attitudes of mind": Fletcher, p. 18.

P.42　If it's a rumor ... don't know enough about it: Jung, 1978, p. vii.

P.42　"Something is seen ... but like weightless thoughts": Ibid., p. 6.

P.42　"this obviously complicated phenomenon ... as a possible physical basis": Ibid., p. 7.

P.42　"whether a primary perception ... with illusions and visions": Ibid., p. 6.

P.43　"an Elijah who calls down fire ... of the Messiah": Ibid., p. 21.

P.44　The deeper "layers" of ... the psyche is simply "world": Stevens, p. 71.

PP.45-46　Professor Peter M. Rojcewicz ...: Rojcewicz, 1987, pp. 148-160.

P.46　Veteran ufologist John Keel reported disturbing personal encounters ...: Keel, 1976, p. 255.

P.46　The real UFO story ... all of the many manifestations ...: Ibid., p. 39.

P.47　"the life-voyager wishing to be taught by Proteus ...": Campbell, 1949, p. 381.

Chapter Five

P.49　A thoroughly frustrated Keyhoe ... "machines under intelligent control": Clark, forthcoming, 1991.

P.49　"calculated to insinuate censorship, whether or not it actually existed": Ibid.

P.49　"Any indication that there ... were authorized to release": Ibid.

P.49　"enhanced rather than detracted ... sensational and unsupported claims": Jacobs, 1975, p. 56.

P.50　Ruppelt wrote: "I have visited ... are anything from outer space": Clark, forthcoming, 1991.

P.50　taking the old ostrich ... hell of a lot worse: Keyhoe, 1961, pp. 6-8.

P.50　"under pressure directly or indirectly ... to reverse his position": Keyhoe, 1959, pp. 5-6.

P.50　"Don't let them trick you ... put the record straight": Ibid.

P.51　"It seems odd," a dispirited ... able to find answers: Ruppelt, 1960, p. 6.

P.51　Looking to the sky ... "saw it descend toward us": Story, 1980, p. 150.

P.52　"as though adjusting or 'setting up' something" ...: Ibid.

P.52　"I stretched my arm ... motions back and forth" ...: Ibid.

P.53　"their great white leader ... what they were signing": Clark, 1978, p. 43.

P.53　"That 'great white leader' business ... not where I was": Ibid.

P.53　"I saw Venus, but ... [the large UFO] ... above Venus": Cruttwell, 1960.

P.53　"The slight irregularities on ... 'beings' inhabiting the saucer" ...: Menzel, p. 169.

P.54　"suggests his close friendship with Gill" ...: Klass, 1974, p. 279.

P.54　"When I arrived on ... been named after me?": Clark, 1978, p. 44.

P.54　"I simply could not believe my eyes" ...: Klass, 1974, p. 284.

P.54　"Actions speak louder than words" ...: Ibid., p. 288.

P.54　"Having had about four ... thing seemed really extraordinary": Clark, 1978, p. 44.

P.54　"any astronomical object would ... arc in that time" ...: Clark, forthcoming, 1991.

P.54　"how one can prop up ... history of human endeavor": Fitzgerald, p. 7.

P.55　Congressional hearings presented a serious ... from 1957 to 1964: Jacobs, 1975, p. 158.

PP.55-56 Captain George T. Gregory maintained . . . but only temporarily: Ibid., pp. 161-162.

P.56 On the one hand . . . *in a logical manner*: Ibid., p. 172.

PP.56-57 "it was pretty well . . . space that were unexplainable": Story, 1980, p. 410.

P.57 Despite being confronted with . . . this most important question: Ibid.

P.57 The public relations problem . . . was tantamount to surrender: Jacobs, 1975, p. 172.

P.58 "a step-like flight . . . leveling off, tilting upward" . . .: Story, 1980, p. 173.

P.58 "I don't believe it! . . . This is ridiculous!": Ibid.

P.60 The charisma of hypnosis . . . the ultimate nonpersonal truth: Story, 1982, p. 199.

P.61 California debunker Robert Schaeffer . . . fact the planet Jupiter: Ibid., p. 204.

P.61 The main problem with . . . as a genuine "unknown": Ibid.

P.61 "That is why . . . the famous Hill abduction has remained a subject of controversy": Ibid., pp. 204-205.

Chapter Six

P.62 "All the institutions of mythological . . . whose forms they are" . . .: Jung and Kerenyi, p. 9.

P.63 "if any aspect of the UFO phenomenon . . . may be true too": Hopkins, 1987, p. xiii.

PP.66-67 Barney Hill said or drew nothing . . . speak through its eyes: Kottmeyer, "Gauche Encounters . . .," pp. 8-9.

P.67 "The only [Star Trek . . . details of ufo experiences": Ibid., p. 4.

P.68 "Why don't you establish open contact?" asked Belans: Vallee, 1990, p. 179.

P.70 A publication prepared by the German scholar Hartmann Schaeden . . . toward the setting sun: Vallee, 1965, p. 9.

P.70 In Nuremberg (1561) and Basil (1566) . . .: Jung, 1978, pp. 95-96.

P.70 "I saw a pillar . . . them spoke unto me": Vallee, 1988, p. 213.

P.71 . . . a whirlwind came out . . . turned not when they went: Bullard, pp. 98-99.

Chapter Seven

P.74 looked up, and I saw . . . off immediately across country: Story, 1980, p. 342.

P.75 Astrophysicist and computer scientist Jacques . . . most imaginative hypothesis of all: Sachs, p. 299.

P.75 "Dulles had enough 'chutzpah' to order such a stunt": Ibid.

P.75 Klass began his attempted demolition . . . : Klass, 1974, pp. 124-134.

P.76 The property where the UFO . . . influx of tourist dollars: Ibid., p. 134.

P.76 "I wanted to keep it . . . I'll know what to do": *The El Paso Times*, 24 April 1965.

P.78 *June 29, 1964.* Businessman Beauford . . .: Hall, p. 248.

P.78 "something that moved at . . . or other characteristics": Ibid., pp. 252-253.

P.79 *August 19, 1965.* Harold Butcher . . . : Ibid., p. 254.

P.79 "Flying saucers are all but . . . that cannot be explained": *Christian Science Monitor*, 21 August 1965.

P.80 "It began to seem to us ... dawn of human consciousness" ...: Author interview with J. Allen Hynek, 16 April 1985.

P.81 "These objects could move at fantastic ...": Constable, p. 106.

P.82 "The situation was so charged ...": Ibid., pp. 107–108.

P.83 "I watched with horror ... rushed for the telephone" ...: Ibid., p. 109.

P.83 "the unenviable position ... occurence in the sky" ...: Jacobs, 1975, p. 206.

PP.83–84 "It wasn't until after ... fire for the air force": Hynek and Vallee, pp. 199–200.

P.84 Yes, I am. I am sorry ... would *you* think?: Strentz, p. 120.

P.84 "the most insulting thing ... in some time": Jacobs, 1975, p. 210.

P.84 "must look to beings from beyond ... boredom of everyday life": *Nation*, 26 September 1966, p. 269.

P.84 "the most significant development ...": Jacobs, 1975, p. 210.

P.85 "What a pleasure it was ... a Martian myself": Hynek, 1969, p. 39.

P.85 It is my inclination to ... conclusion for another year: Constable, p. 116.

PP.85–86 Our study would be conducted ... job off to our benefit: Flammonde, p. 213.

P.87 The *New York Times* praised Condon ...: *New York Times*, 8 January 1969, pp. 1–2.

P.87 "full-scale campaign to ... out in the open": Jacobs, 1975, p. 244.

P.87 "Mozart producing an uninspired ...": Hynek, 1969, p. 41.

P.87 Jacques Vallee later commented ...: Hynek and Vallee, p. 222.

PP.87–88 Both the public and the project ... further scientific attention?: Hynek, 1969, p. 42.

Chapter Eight

P.89 "peculiar doubleness of intention": Fletcher, p. 7.

PP.91–92 "If you want, I'll swear ... somebody listening to a lie": Boer, pp. 37–38.

P.92 "Hermes knows better than to collide ... effective as heroic confrontation": Paris, p. 74.

P.92 both involve acts of displacement: Ibid., p. 70.

P.92 "somewhere between the explicit ... in the right context": Ibid., p. 63.

P.93 "communication under the sign ... of Hermes are multiple": Ibid.

P.93 "wants to win over ... means twisting the truth" ...: Ibid., p. 82.

P.93 "seems fascinated with a specific ... untying, attaching and detaching": Ibid., p. 105.

P.93 "When we are in Hermes' field ... is correctly called quicksilver": Bly, p. 143.

P.94 "If we are to have success ... *what is strangely uncanny*": Kerenyi, 1974, p. 5.

P.94 "Laughter, humour and irony permeate everything Trickster does" ...: Radin, p. xxiv.

P.94 "a forerunner of the saviour ... characteristic is his unconsciousness": Ibid., p. 203.

PP.94–95 "is in many respects ... sheer unconsciousness and unrelatedness" ...: Ibid.

P.95 "playing tricks in the ghostly ... spirits and poltergeists reign": Ibid., p. 190.

P.95 Obviously there is some kind ... to be so easily teased: Keel, 1978, p. 133.

P.96 Ginette Paris makes the point . . .: Paris, p. 104.
P.96 "trust in our own performance": Ibid.
P.96 "puts all of himself . . . he pretends to be": Ibid.
P.96 *"Dionysus is not the God behind the mask. He is the mask"*: Ibid.
P.96 Karl Kerenyi, who studied cultures . . .: Kerenyi, 1960.
P.96 "This negative definition of the mask . . . or divinity it embodied": Paris, pp. 52–53.
P.97 The philosopher Gaston Bachelard . . . "all thoughts of positive and negative": Bachelard, p. 211.
P.98 "The latest incarnation of Oedipus . . . traffic light to change": Campbell, 1949, p. 4.

Chapter Nine

P.100 that one should not try . . . nonhuman emotions and perceptions: Vallee, 1965, p. v.
P.100 "modern science rules over . . . on an infinite theme": Vallee, 1969, p. 157.
P.100 "ufology has become such . . . left for general culture": Ibid., p. 25.
PP.101–102 Vallee put forth five self-evident "principle facts" . . . "model of religious miracles": Ibid., pp. 160–161.
P.102 "it is quite conceivable . . . mask the pattern to be solved": Ibid., p. 154.
P.103 that the universe might contain . . . beyond the human perceptual range: Ibid., p. 155.
P.103 "we are presented with . . . and of continued manifestation": Ibid.
P.104 told Yanacsek to "keep an eye on it": Story, 1982, p. 182.
P.104 "It wasn't cruising . . . twelve seconds — just *stopped*" . . .: Story, 1980, p. 93.
P.104 Five witnesses on the ground . . . "the road, the car — everything turned green": Ibid., pp. 94–95.
P.105 Philip Klass determined . . . really a large fireball of the Orinoid . . .: Klass, 1974, pp. 395–411.
P.105 UFO researcher Jenny Zeidman ruled out . . .: Story, 1980, p. 95.
P.105 Over the years, Klass attempted to diminish Coyne's credibility . . .: Klass, 1983, pp. 158–160.
P.105 "Coyne has become an international celebrity in the world of UFOlogy": Ibid., page 158.
P.106 Said Oberg: Something that behaved like an alien . . . one of the best on record: Story, 1982, p. 184.
P.106 "little buzzin' sound — *nnnnnnnn, nnnnnnnn* — just like that . . .": Blum, p. 31.
PP.106–107 PASCAGOULA, Mississippi. — Two shipyard workers . . .: San Francisco *Chronicle*, 13 October 1973.
P.107 "First thing they wanted to do was take a lie detector test": Blum, p. 14.
P.108 CALVIN: I got to get home and get to bed . . . I'm gettin' sick. I gotta get out of here: Ibid., pp. 35–36.
P.109 "If they were lying . . . they should be in Hollywood": Ibid., p. 10.
P.109 "There was definitely something here that was not terrestrial, of the earth": United Press International news dispatch, 14 October 1974.
P.109 "Terrifying experience of some sort, yes . . . premature to say anything like that": Ibid.

P.109 Why, Klass demanded to know . . .: Klass, 1974, pp. 342–344, 347–369.
P.111 "You know at night, I lie in bed . . . All I have to do is close my eyes": Blum, p. 139.
P.112 "induced the pre-Incan peoples . . . the landing strips" . . .: Fitzgerald, p. 23.
P.112 "nothing better to do than spend years . . . mere bunglers in comparison": Ibid.
P.112 "seizes upon every megalith . . . evolution of human intelligence": Ibid., p. 22.
P.112 Carl Sagan snorted: "The space vehicle sets . . . that they need airfields": Bradbury, p. 307.
P.113 Von Daniken had "touched a sensitive nerve in our collective unconscious": Hynek and Vallee, p. 231.
P.113 "There's a big credibility gap . . . the existence of the gap": Ibid.
P.113 the air force had acted . . . unrestrained interest in the phenomenon: Jacobs, 1975, pp. 280–281.
P.115 Many people would like . . . more about the UFOs: Ibid., p. 293.

Chapter Ten

P.117 "We have here a golden . . .": Jung, 1978, p. 16.
P.118 "allegories are based on . . . presented in the fable": Fletcher, p. 113.
P.118 "Allegorical stories exist, as it were . . .": Ibid., p. 79.
P.118 "nothing but a resurgence . . .": Vallee, 1969, pp. 36, 131, 149.
P.119 "the only object we know . . . is the space capsule": Ibid., p. 2.
P.120 October 27, 1180: Ibid., p. 4.
P.120 September 12, 1271: Ibid., p. 5.
P.120 March 8, 1468: Ibid., p. 6.
P.120 One day, among other instances . . . seen there was impossible: Ibid., p. 12.
P.121 "A crowd of boys . . . direction of the old fort": Ibid., p. 26.
P.121 They are not a working-class . . . through the earth: Ibid., p. 27.
P.121 "documented stories of babies . . . hunt and take away": Vallee, 1988, p. 52.
PP.121–122 folklorist Thomas Bullard pursued . . .: Bullard, p. 390.
P.123 "to begin to raise questions . . .": Vallee, 1988, p. vi.
P.123 The stewpot thinker "habitually tosses . . .": Hopkins, 1991, pp. 8–9, 12.
P.124 "Abductions are a decidedly recent . . .": Author interview with Budd Hopkins, 6 July 1990.
P.124 "Let us recall that while under hypnosis . . .": Author interview with Jacques Vallee, 8 August 1990.
P.124 As part of his exhaustive dissertation . . .: Bullard, p. 423.
P.125 The philosopher Ernst von Glasersfeld . . .: Watzlawick, 1984, pp. 17–40.
P.126 Allegory . . . "seems to aim . . . will aid this function?": Fletcher, p. 73.

Chapter Eleven

P.127 ALAMOSA, Colo. (AP) — Snippy . . .: Strentz, p. 276.
P.128 "a curious boy wondering what his knife would do to a dead horse": Ibid., p. 279.
P.129 Indeed, millions are still awaiting . . .: Denver Post, 11 November 1967, p. 69.

P.129 "I've yet to see a coyote . . .": Howe, p. 11.

PP.129-130 Each day, just before dusk, ranchers . . .: Ibid., p. 9.

P.130 had access to any experts in veterinary . . .: Clark, 1984.

P.131 The "clean, bloodless, sometimes incredibly . . . (or refusing to confront) a mutilated carcass": Adams, p. 46.

P.131 "Is it possible that we are being confronted with UFOs . . . them to operate surreptitiously": Ibid., p. 55.

P.132 at least one non-human intelligence . . . sustenance and genetic experimentation: Howe, p. xviii.

P.132 The story told by Linda Howe . . . fleeting images we see?: Ibid., p. xiii.

PP.132-133 *Tarragona, Spain* . . . We heard a very loud noise . . . but upside down: Buckle, pp. 2-3.

PP.133-134 *Milford Haven, Wales*. On a midsummer . . . Nor was anything ever reported: Holiday, p. 10.

P.134 *Matles-Barbosa, Brazil*. Brazilian newspapers . . . "Karen" after the experience: Creighton, p. 26.

P.136 Although little known in the United States . . . evidence be dismissed easily: Kinder, p. 220.

PP.136-137 "When I touched the oxide . . . something that was unusual": Ibid., p. 225.

P.137 "The pictures look good . . . anything that was fake about them": Ibid., p. 232.

P.137 As for the audio . . . produce those particular sounds: Ibid., p. 239.

P.137 Steve Ambrose, sound engineer . . . "money in special effects": Ibid., p. 241.

P.138 I am certain [Meier] . . . make people understand his experiences: Ibid., pp. 263-264.

P.138 "could very steadily move the object . . . lot of work for one guy": Ibid., p. 281.

PP.138-139 "He may simply be . . . contacts will never be known": Ibid., p. 306.

Chapter Twelve

P.140 *The pattern which connects*: Bateson, p. 8.

P.140 *What pattern connects the crab . . . back-ward schizophrenic in another?*: Ibid.

PP.140-141 I want you to produce arguments . . . arrive at that conclusion?: Ibid., p. 7.

P.141 *How are you related . . . pattern connects you to it?*: Ibid., p. 9.

P.141 "Very good. You mean . . . like a painting?": Ibid.

P.141 "Yes, one claw is bigger . . . made of the same parts": Ibid.

P.141 "the idea that size could be . . . deeper symmetry in formal relations" . . .: Ibid.

P.142 "We could recognize in every . . . pieces in the claw" . . .: Ibid.

P.142 "Humerus in the upper arm . . . fingers correspond to toes": Ibid., p. 10.

P.142 "My central thesis can now . . . indeed, *it is patterns which connect*": Ibid., p. 11.

P.143 "any A is relevant . . . components of the same 'story',": Ibid., p. 13.

P.144 In 1972, J. Allen Hynek introduced the following . . . and UFO occupants fall into this category: Hynek, 1972, pp. 115-206.

P.147 The piercing instruments used . . . potentially unpleasant moral inquisition: Bullard, p. 431.

P.148 Lactantius, a Christian apologist . . .: Schneweis, p. 47.

P.149   "a dynamic and constantly evolving panorama . . . Righteousness and Malevolence": Godwin, p. 11.

P.150   "But if the archangel . . . beat us to death": Rilke, 1982, ed. and trans. Mitchell, p. 157.

P.150   Plutarch, in his essay "On the Cessation of Oracles," . . . "one of the society of both": Fletcher, p. 40.

P.150   In Plato's *Symposium*, Diotima . . . "powers are many and diverse": Ibid., pp. 43–44.

P.150   "Very early in history the term demon . . . direct communication with intermediaries" . . .: Ibid., p. 43.

P.151   Abduction researcher Budd Hopkins's well-elaborated position . . .: Hopkins, 1983, 1987.

P.151   All the evidence points . . . "friendship of the thighs . . .": Godwin, p. 81.

P.152   . . . the daemonic, a character ascribed . . . which we call "shuddering": Fletcher, p. 41.

P.153   "a buzzing or humming . . . at the Lady's departure" . . .: Vallee, 1988, p. 97.

P.154   the final "miracle" had come . . . amnesia, the conversions, and the healings: Ibid., p. 200.

PP.154–155   "In the sense that the shaman . . . access to a defined cosmos" . . .: Drury, p. 3.

P.155   I have seen things as if . . . I could not hold up my hand: Nicholson, p. 62.

P.155   After his initiation is complete . . . unusual and sometimes disturbing presence: Ring, 1989, pp. 15–16.

P.157   "as though in a million . . . happened to you in your life" . . .: Ring, 1986, p. 76.

P.157   "You grasp the essential meaning . . . your children, need you": Ibid.

P.157   "You wish you could . . . adequate to describe it?": Ibid., p. 77.

P.157   "All you know is . . . will never again be the same": Ibid.

Chapter Thirteen

P.160   "buried under a section of superhighway along with Jimmy Hoffa": Early, p. 85.

P.160   In the late 1940s and maybe even later . . . will release the information: Clark, 1990, p. 57.

P.162   "was in a talkative mood," which . . . not like writing we would do: Berlitz and Moore, pp. 82–83.

P.162   small beams about 3/8ths . . . except that it wasn't tinfoil: Clark, 1990, p. 60.

PP.162–163   "The many rumors regarding . . . sheriff's office of Chaves County": Berlitz and Moore, p. 26

P.163   "The cover story about the balloon . . . someone else took it to Wright": Clark, 1990, p. 61.

P.163   "Back in those days . . . something, it wasn't discussed" . . .: Ibid., p. 62.

PP.163–164   "Seems like every time after a good . . . much area [as] a briefcase": Ibid.

P.164   "Naturally I said I would . . . I never found any more" . . .: Ibid.

P.164   One military witness, O.W. Henderson . . . from the Roswell base: Randle and Schmitt, p. 82.

P.166   This night O'Barski was complaining . . . leaving him "goddamn scared": Bloecher, p. 3.

P.166   "There's probably nothing to it . . . left my girlfriend's house": Hopkins, 1981 [a], p. 40.

P.167   A hypnosis session was arranged . . . recall the intervening events: Ibid., pp. 40–78.

P.167   "I don't want to remember. I'm not supposed to remember": Ibid., p. 56

P.167   "one basic and striking . . . undistinguished lights ahead of him": Author interview with Budd Hopkins, 5 August 1990.

P.168   Memory blocks may . . . be almost entirely invisible: Hopkins, 1981, p. 223.

P.169   "unjustifiably homogenizes the diversity" . . . fostering a new popular mythology: Author interview with Dennis Stillings, 12 November 1990.

P.169   "spiritual traditions throughout the world . . . mischievous tricks on human naiveté": Author interview with Michael Grosso, 29 June 1991.

P.170   "vague feeling that something . . . particular stretch of road": Klass, 1989, p. 82.

P.170   "an unknown mind control technology . . . with missing time in between": Author interview with Budd Hopkins, 5 August 1990.

P.170   "it would be surprising . . . about the claimed experiences" . . .: Klass, 1989, p. 81.

PP.170–171   Dr. Clamar stated: "The events recounted . . . nearly identical experiences": Hopkins, 1981 [a], p. 237.

P.171   "I cannot say whether . . . the UFO experience actually 'happened' ": Ibid., p. 238.

P.172   "If one wants to be truly jarred, . . . as there are UFO reports": Ibid., p. 57.

P.172   "Abductions practically *beg* to be read symbolically" . . .: Author interview with Jacques Vallee, 30 July 1990.

P.173   TOP/SECRET/MAJIC/EYES ONLY . . . : Maccabee.

P.176   Why, for instance, had the undeveloped film . . . : Klass, Winter 1987–88, Spring 1988; pp. 137–146, 279–289.

P.176   "Whoever typed the Hillenkoetter briefing document . . . since 1982, when our correspondence began": Ibid.

P.177   "My files of correspondence from Moore . . . the Hillenkoetter briefing document": Ibid.

P.177   "But thanks to the invention of the Xerox . . . prior to late 1984": Ibid.

P.177   "in contrast to the more elegant . . . at about the same time": Ibid.

P.177   "the logical choice for an assignment . . . with a crashed UFO": Moore, 1982, p. 101.

P.177   "if I was going to pick a panel . . . selected for such a committee": Klass, Winter 1987–88, Spring 1988; pp. 137–146, 279–289.

P.177   "Lady Luck smiled, allowing . . . on the 35 mm film": Ibid.

P.178   More significantly, Robert Cutler . . . housed in the Eisenhower library: Ibid.

P.179   "were confident that within . . . 'What are UFOs?' ": Ruppelt, 1956, p. 46.

P.179   Jacques Vallee's heretical suggestion . . . overall UFO mythos: Author interview with Jacques Vallee, 30 July 1990.

P.180   "major goal . . . county or parish in the U.S.A.": Andrus, p. 24.

P.180   "I would be desperately happy . . . for good tomorrow morning" . . .: Author interview with Philip Klass, 3 January 1991.

Chapter Fourteen

P.182 "rites which accompany every . . . state, social position, and age": Turner, p. 4.

P.183 Van Gennup showed . . . or consummation (return): Ibid., p. 5.

P.183 "A hero ventures forth . . . region of supernatural wonder": Campbell, 1949, p. 30.

PP.183–184 that destiny has summoned the hero . . . every corner of the world: Ibid., p. 58.

P.185 "One is harassed, both . . . there is no exit": Ibid., p. 60.

P.185 "Whitley" ceased to exist . . . humanity survived the transition: Strieber, p. 26.

P.185 "I don't believe it! . . . This is ridiculous!": Story, 1980, p. 173.

PP.185–186 "is *not* whether [UFOs] exist," . . . times on individual lives: Raschke, pp. 24–26.

P.186 "There is no place . . . must change your life": Rilke, 1982, Trans. Bly.

P.186 "that we very well . . . be an immense challenge": Strieber, p. 67.

P.187 "Betwixt and Between: The Liminal Period in Rites of Passage" . . . : Turner, p. 6.

P.187 For most of us it began . . . mind doing this to me?: Hopkins, 1981 [a], p. 197.

P.188 And then there was the problem . . . Because you believe you were abducted: Ibid., pp. 197–198.

P.188 "his special knowledge and sometimes disturbing presence": Ring, 1989, pp. 15–16.

P.190 "landing with both feet firmly planted in midair": Author interview with Donald Michael, 3 September 1986.

P.190 "changes in the constellation . . . transformations of the collective psyche": Jung, 1978, p. 12.

P.190 "life is in the transitions . . . in the terms connected": James, p. 1180.

PP.190–191 "As you look in the mirror . . . simultaneously perceived by the same witness": Rojcewicz, 1989, p. 12.

P.191 "the bringing together of two . . . poetic reality it will have": Schumer, p. 21.

P.192 The disciple has been blessed . . . vision: the Cosmic Man: Campbell, 1949, p. 234.

P.193 "It is possible that we are being . . . I have given up trying!": Author interview with Leo Sprinkle, 30 June 1990.

PP.193–194 "What we see emerging . . . no one can say for certain": Author interview with Jacques Vallee, 30 July 1990; Vallee, 1988, pp. 271–276.

P.194 "The very expectation of a 'culmination'" . . . role in the feedback loop: Author interview with Jacques Vallee, 30 July 1990.

P.194 "What kind of alien doctors . . . of the entire phenomenon": Vallee, 1988, pp. 268–269.

PP.194–195 "then it has no choice . . . man is hungry for knowledge . . . contribute to the reinforcement itself": Ibid., p. 275.

P.195 "when one of the messages . . . depending upon the circumstances": Watzlawick, 1983, p. 3.

Chapter Fifteen

P.196 "It seems that whenever a supposedly excellent . . .": Moseley, 5 February 1985, p. 1.

P.197 "usually reliable source in Washington" . . .: Moseley, April 1985, p. 1.

P.198 "Are there motives we have not yet the technology to imagine?": Hopkins, 1985, p. 75.

P.198 Stanton T. Friedman begins his talk . . .: Friedman, pp. 98, 11.

P.199 "arouse the public from its state of oblivion . . .": Christensen, p. 18.

P.200 Hynek "picked his way carefully through this minefield . . .": Jacobs, May–June 1986, p. 6.

P.200 When Dr. J. Allen Hynek, over twenty . . . never be the same: Steinberg, p. 6.

P.201 "The three of us got out of the car . . . privacy and emotion of others": Zeidman, p. 20.

P.201 "A cohesive force has gone . . . in the relatively near future": Tate, p. 1.

P.201 "the sheer magnitude of . . . and its inherent importance": Jacobs, September–October 1986, p. 21.

P.201 "a lackluster bunch of 'experts,' . . . various other assorted monkeys": Hackney, p. 5.

P.202 "playground for the botched and the bungled": Stillings, p. 3.

P.203 "The confused swirl resolved . . . terror and utter disbelief": Strieber, p. 35.

P.203 "*You may be going mad . . . have a brain tumor*": Ibid., p. 36.

P.203 "a peculiar whooshing, swirling . . . the living room downstairs" . . .: Ibid., p. 21.

PP.203–204 "If something is strange . . . some sort of instinct": Ibid.

P.204 "working busily at something . . . side of my head": Ibid., p. 25.

P.204 "so powerful that it . . . my personality completely evaporate": Ibid.

P.204 "an extremely shiny, hair-thin . . . mounted on a black surface": Ibid., p. 28.

P.204 "You'll ruin a beautiful . . . wires on the end": Ibid.

PP.204–205 "Abruptly, my memories end . . . sometime during the night": Ibid., pp. 30–31.

P.205 "as if it contained a coiled snake": Ibid., p. 40.

P.205 "But how could I call . . . Flying saucers. How idiotic": Ibid.

P.205 "Hopkins was a large . . . wanting to understand it" . . .: Ibid.

PP.205–206 "Of the more than two . . . undertaken for investigative purposes": Author interview with Budd Hopkins, 3 April 1991.

P.206 "describing what he believed . . . in their mystical complexity": Ibid.

P.206 "I think I've seen you . . . was on a shelf": Ibid.

P.207 "Of course I didn't . . . *and so does Budd*": Author interview with Whitley Strieber, 10 April 1991.

PP.207–208 When Hopkins received word . . . *I simply cannot trust*" . . .: Author interview with Budd Hopkins, 3 April 1991.

P.208 I don't know anyone outside . . . out of touch with reality: Hopkins, early 1987, pp. 3–4.

P.208 "was not able to accept . . . *Intruders* was by and large a failure": Author interview with Whitley Strieber, 10 April 1991.

P.208 It may be that the human . . . this effort, in my opinion: Conroy, 1989, pp. 354–360.

P.209   A reviewer for *Nation* . . . sold it as fact: Ibid., pp. 126–130.

P.209   Martin Kottmeyer, in an essay . . . "subsequent withdrawal into himself": Kottmeyer, unpublished, no date.

PP.209–210   *When I had journeyed half . . . tell of other things I saw*: Mandelbaum, p. 1.

P.210   As Walters began screaming . . . the UFO was gone, too: Walters and Walters, p. 29.

P.211   "They won't hurt you . . . tests. That's all": Ibid., p. 45.

P.211   heard voices speaking in Spanish . . . fed bananas by "abductors": Ibid., p. 56

P.211   "stared at me with eyes . . . seemed somehow curious": Ibid., p. 64.

P.211   "You are in danger . . . Come forward": Ibid., p. 123.

P.212   "The whole thing was almost . . .what seemed to be happening": Ibid., p. 19.

P.213   Zan Overall — regarded as . . . to perform such feats: Overall, 1990, pp. 1–44.

P.214   "ranks as one of . . . in the past forty years": Walters and Walters, p. 345.

P.214   If one were to briefly . . . scientific community as factual: Ibid., pp. 346–347.

P.214   STUDENT EXPLAINS DOUBLE . . . "appear to be in the air": Conroy, 1990, p. 4.

P.215   "several, if not all . . . are probably hoaxes" . . .: Klass, November 1990, p. 1.

P.215   "do not have grounds . . . it is submitted to us": Ibid.

P.216   "It means that either the aliens . . . bunch of foolish human beings": Klass, May 1990, p. 3.

P.216   "I saw a bright" . . . Gulf Breeze city councilperson: Walters and Walters, from book jacket.

P.216   "We were walking along . . . that we saw in the paper": Ibid.

P.216   "It hovered beyond our pier" . . . in Ed Walters' photographs: Ibid.

P.217   reports on sightings of a nine-foot-tall . . . local beaches in 1988: Conroy, 1990, p. 10.

P.217   "There is no evident causal . . . anomalous animal mutilations and disappearances": Ibid.

P.217   "believe it best to . . . in the public interest": Ibid.

Chapter Sixteen

P.219   In the process of being treated . . . to inhibit his somnambulism: Moody, 1946, p. 721.

P.220   Diagnosed as schizophrenic . . . account for the growth: Evans and Seely, p. 38.

P.220   A group of experimental . . . think they are taking: Murphy, forthcoming, 1992.

P.220   A woman, skilled at modifying . . . which they are attached: Simard and Basmajian, pp. 12–19.

P.220   A man diagnosed with multiple . . . personality retains executive control: Institute of Noetic Sciences, pp. 3–6.

P.220   British psychiatrist Robert Moody . . . an elaborately carved stick: Moody, 1948, p. 964.

PP.220–221   In a study to discover . . . arteries were actually tied: Dimon, Kittle, and Crockett, pp. 483–486.

P.221   Delizia Ciroli, a Sicilian . . . permanently and completely cured: Dowling, p. 636.

P.222 Indian yogi Swami Rama ... sides of his hands: Green and Green, pp. 197–199.

P.222 Tibetan lamas have demonstrated ... practice known as *tumo*: Benson, pp. 46–61.

P.222 Marie-Julie Jahenny, a French ... words *O Crux ave*: Thurston, pp. 63–64.

P.222 "There can be little doubt ... professed to have seen": Ibid., pp. 17–18.

P.223 "may constitute a vast ... new kind of evolution": Author interview with Michael Murphy, 5 December 1989.

P.224 In his groundbreaking book ... mere curiosities or pathologies: Ibid.

P.225 "the tantalizing mixture [which UFOs] ... psychic, mystic, or prophetic sentiment": Grosso, p. 10.

PP.225–226 "The soul possesses a certain ... (*asteroides*) and is eternal": von Franz, p. 136.

P.226 The Islamic Shiite philosopher ... and the "light body": Ibid., p. 138.

P.226 "generally held that our ... introspection and inspired sight" ...: Murphy, forthcoming, 1992.

P.226 "*as a body* into strange ... sense of passing time": Ibid.

P.227 "In all this experience" ... ashore to a "larger earth"?: Ibid.

P.233 Angels ... are in reality ... to know one's angel: Avens, p. 5.

P.234 "The original ground on which we stand ...": Grossinger, p. 48.

Epilogue

P.241 "Our long quest is almost ... know what UFOs are": Klass, 1991, p. 8.

P.241 "After decades of painstaking ... revealing its core secrets": Author interview with Budd Hopkins, 3 April 1991.

P.241 "We may be on the threshold ...": Author interview with David Jacobs, 6 May 1991.

P.242 "no more dreadful punishment than futile and hopeless labor" ...: Camus, 1991, pp. 119–123.

P.243 "What interests me is to know ... but I am less ambitious": Camus, 1990, p. 136.

P.244 "diffusion of inner coherence ... order of enigma and romance": Fletcher, p. 367.

P.246 "sheer ornamental display": Fletcher, p. 368.

BIBLIOGRAPHY

Adams, Thomas R. "Animal Mutilations: A Decade of Mystery." *MUFON Symposium Proceedings* (1984): 44–63.

Adamski, George. *Inside the Space Ships*. New York: Abelard-Schuman, 1955.

Andrus, Walt. "Director's Message." *MUFON UFO Journal* 269 (September 1990): 1–24.

Avens, Robert. *The New Gnosis*. Dallas: Spring Publications, 1984.

Bachelard, Gaston. *The Poetics of Space*. Translated by Maria Jalas. Boston: Beacon Press, 1969.

Bateson, Gregory. *Mind and Nature: A Necessary Unity*. New York: E.P. Dutton, 1979.

Benson, Herbert. *Beyond the Relaxation Response*. New York: Times Books, 1984.

Berlitz, Charles and William L. Moore. *The Roswell Incident*. New York: Grosset and Dunlap, 1980.

Bloecher, Ted. "The 'Stonehenge' Incidents of January 1975." *Flying Saucer Review* 22, no. 3 (October 1976): 3–7.

Blum, Ralph and Judy Blum. *Beyond Earth*. New York: Bantam Books, 1974.

Blumrich, Joseph. *The Spaceships of Ezekiel*. New York: Bantam Books, 1974.

Bly, Robert. *Iron John: A Book About Men*. Reading, Mass.: Addison-Wesley Publishing Co., 1990.

Boer, Charles, trans. *The Homeric Hymns*. 2nd Ed. Dallas: Spring Publications, 1970.

Bradbury, Will, ed. *Into the Unknown*. Pleasantville, N.Y.: Reader's Digest Assoc., 1981.

Buckle, Eileen. "Spanish UFO Fiesta." *Flying Saucer Review* 20, no. 3 (December 1974): 2–7.

Bullard, Thomas Eddie. "Mysteries in the Eye of the Beholder: UFOs and Their Correlates as a Folkloric Theme Past and Present." Ph.D. dissertation, Indiana University, 1982.

Campbell, Joseph. *The Hero with a Thousand Faces*. Princeton: Princeton University Press, 1949.

———. *The Inner Reaches of Outer Space*. New York: Alfred van der Marck, 1986.

Camus, Albert. *The Myth of Sisyphus and Other Essays*. Translated by Justin O'Brien. New York: Vintage International Books, 1991.

———. *The Plague*. New York: Vintage International Books, 1990.

Christensen, Marge. "Shifting the Burden of Proof." *MUFON Symposium Proceedings* (1985): 14–20.

Clark, Jerome. *The Emergence of a Phenomenon: UFOs from the Beginning Through 1959.* Volume II of *The UFO Encyclopedia.* Detroit: Apogee Books, forthcoming 1991.

———. "Close Encounters: History's Best Case." *Fate* 31, no. 2 (February 1978): 38–46.

———. "Reality Mutilation." *Fate* 37, no. 415 (October 1984): 99–103.

———. *UFOs in the 1980s.* Detroit: Apogee Books, 1990.

Condon, Edward U. *Scientific Study of Unidentified Flying Objects.* New York: Bantam Books, 1969.

Conroy, Ed. *Report on Communion.* New York: William Morrow and Co., 1989.

———. "Who is the Joker in the Gulf Breeze UFO 'Hoax'?" *The Communion Letter* 2, no. 2 (Summer 1990): 1–16.

Constable, George, ed. *The UFO Phenomenon.* Richmond: Time-Life Books, 1987.

Creighton, Gordon. "Uproar in Brazil." *Flying Saucer Review* (December 1971): 24–28.

Cruttwell, N.E.G. "What Happened in Papua in 1959?" *Flying Saucer Review* 6, no. 6 (November/December 1960): 3–7.

Dimon, E.G., C.F. Kittle, and J.E. Crockett. "Comparison of Internal Mammary Artery Ligation and Sham Operation for Angina Pectoris." *American Journal of Cardiology* 5 (1960): 483–486.

Dowling, St. John. "Lourdes Cures and Their Medical Assessment." *Journal of the Royal Society of Medicine* 77 (1984): 636.

Drury, Nevil. *The Shaman and the Magician.* London: Arcana, 1982.

Early, George W. "Crashed Saucers and Pickled Aliens." Part 2. *Fate* 34, no. 4 (April 1981): 84–89.

Eliade, Mircea. *Myth and Reality.* New York: Harper Torchbooks, 1963.

Evans, D. and T. Seeley. "Pseudocyesis in the Male." *The Journal of Nervous and Mental Disease* 172 (1984): 38.

Fawcett, Lawrence and Barry J. Greenwood. *The UFO Coverup.* Prentice-Hall, 1984.

Fitzgerald, Randall. *The Complete Book of Extraterrestrial Encounters.* New York: Macmillan, 1979.

Flammonde, Paris. *The Age of Flying Saucers.* New York: Hawthorne Books, 1971.

Fletcher, Angus. *Allegory: The Theory of a Symbolic Mode.* Ithaca, N.Y.: Cornell University Press, 1964.

Franz, Marie-Louise von. *On Dreams and Death.* Boston: Shambhala Publications, 1986.

Friedman, Stanton T. "Flying Saucers, Noisy Negativists and Truth." *MUFON Symposium Proceedings* (1985): 98–112.

Gallup, George H. *The Gallup Poll: Public Opinion 1935–1948.* New York: Random House, 1972.

Godwin, Malcolm. *Angels: An Endangered Species.* New York: Simon and Schuster, 1990.

Good, Timothy. *Above Top Secret: The Worldwide UFO Coverup.* New York: William Morrow and Co., 1988.

Green, E. and A. Green. *Beyond Biofeedback.* New York: Delta, 1979.

Grossinger, Richard. "Giving Them a Name." *ReVISION* 11, no. 4 (Spring 1989): 43–48.

Grosso, Michael. "Transcending the 'ET Hypothesis.'" *California UFO* 3, no. 3 (1988): 9–11.

Hackney, Tom. *Saucer Smear* 34, no. 8 (15 November 1987): 1–8.

Haines, Richard F. *Advanced Aerial Devices Reported During the Korean War.* Los Altos, Calif.: LDA Press, 1990.

Hall, Richard. *Uninvited Guests.* Santa Fe: Aurora Press, 1988.

Hayward, Jeremy W. *Shifting Worlds, Changing Minds*. Boston: Shambhala Publications, 1987.

Hillman, James. *Healing Fiction*. Barrytown, N.Y.: Station Hill, 1983.

Holiday, F. W. "Some Recent Welsh Cases." *Flying Saucer Review* (October 1974): 9–12.

Hopkins, Budd. *Intruders*. New York: Random House, 1987.

_____. Letter to Whitley Strieber, early 1987.

_____. *Missing Time*. New York: Berkley Books, 1983.

_____. "Stewpot Thinking — An Obstacle to Science." *MUFON UFO Journal* 251 (March 1991): 8–9, 12.

_____. "The Evidence Supporting UFO Abduction Reports." *MUFON Symposium Proceedings* (1985): 66–77.

_____. "UFO Abductions: The Invisible Epidemic." *MUFON Symposium Proceedings* (1981 [a]): 44–59.

Howe, Linda Moulton. *An Alien Harvest*. Littleton, Colo.: Linda Moulton Howe Productions, 1989.

Hynek, J. Allen. *The UFO Experience*. London: Corgi Books, 1972.

_____. "The Condon Report and UFOs." *Bulletin of the Atomic Scientists* 25 (April 1969): 39–42.

Hynek, J. Allen and Jacques Vallee. *The Edge of Reality*. Chicago: Henry Regnery Co., 1975.

Institute of Noetic Sciences. "Multiple Personality: Mirrors of a New Model of Mind?" *Investigations* (Sausalito, Calif.) I (1985): 3–6.

Jacobs, David M. "J. Allen Hynek and the UFO Phenomenon." *International UFO Reporter* 11, no. 3 (May–June 1986): 4–8.

_____. "Does UFO Research Have a Future?" *International UFO Reporter* 11, no. 5 (September–October 1986): 14–16.

_____. *The UFO Controversy in America*. Bloomington: Indiana University Press, 1975.

James, William. "A World of Pure Experience." In *William James 1902–1910*, edited by Bruce Kuklick. New York: Library of America, 1987.

Jansma, Sidney J. *UFOs, Satan and Evolution*. Publisher not given, 1980.

Jung, Carl G. *Flying Saucers: A Modern Myth of Things Seen in the Sky*. Princeton: Princeton University Press, 1978.

Jung, Carl G. and Carl Kerenyi. *Essays on a Science of Mythology*. Princeton: Princeton University Press, 1973.

Kafka, Franz. *The Trial*. New York: Knopf, 1953.

Keel, John A. *The Cosmic Question*. New York, London: Granada Publishing, 1978.

_____. *UFOs?: Operation Trojan Horse*. New York: Manor Books, 1976; New York: E.P. Putnam's Sons, 1970.

Keeney, Bradford P. *Aesthetics of Change*. New York: Guilford Press, 1983.

Kerenyi, Carl. "Man and Mask." In *Spiritual Disciplines*, Papers from the Eranos Yearbooks. Vol. 4. New York: Pantheon Books, 1960.

_____. *Hermes: Guide of Souls*. Dallas: Spring Publications, 1974.

Keyhoe, Donald. "Captain Keyhoe Revising His UFO Book: Air Force Rumored to be Pressuring Former Project Chief." *The UFO Investigator* 1, no. 8 (June 1959): 5–6.

_____. "The Captain Ruppelt Letters." *The UFO Investigator* 11, no. 1 (October 1961): 6–8.

_____. *The Flying Saucers Are Real*. New York: Fawcett Publications, 1950.

_____. *The TRUE Report on Flying Saucers*. New York: Fawcett Publications, 1967.

Kinder, Gary. *Light Years*. New York: Pocket Books, 1987.

Klass, Philip J. "The MJ-12 Crashed Saucer Documents." Parts 1, 2. *Skeptical Inquirer* 12 (Winter 1987-88, Spring 1988): 137-146, 279-289.

_____. *Skeptics UFO Newsletter* 3 (May 1990).

_____. *Skeptics UFO Newsletter* 6 (November 1990).

_____. *Skeptics UFO Newsletter* 9 (May 1991).

_____. *UFO Abductions: A Dangerous Game*. Buffalo, N.Y.: Prometheus Books, 1989.

_____. *UFOs Explained*. New York: Vintage Books, 1974.

_____. *UFOs: The Public Deceived*. Buffalo, N.Y.: Prometheus Books, 1983.

Kottmeyer, Martin. "Dying Worlds, Dying Selves." Unpublished, no date.

_____. "Entirely Unpredisposed." *Magonia* 35 (January 1990): 3-10.

_____. "Gauche Encounters: Badfilms and the Ufo Mythos." Unpublished, no date.

Lagrange, Pierre. "It Seems Impossible But There It Is." In *Phenomenon: Forty Years of Flying Saucers*, edited by John Spencer and Hilary Evans, 26-45. New York: Avon Books, 1988.

Maccabee, Bruce, ed. *Documents and Supporting Information Related to Crashed Flying Saucers and Operation Majestic Twelve*. Mount Rainier, Md.: Fund for UFO Research, 1987.

Mandelbaum, Allen, trans. *The Divine Comedy by Dante Alighieri; Inferno*. New York: Bantam Books, 1980.

Menzel, Donald H. "UFO's — The Modern Myth." In *UFO's — A Scientific Debate*, edited by Carl Sagan and Thornton Page. New York: W. W. Norton and Co., 1972.

Moody, Raymond. *Life After Life*. Atlanta: Mockingbird Books, 1975.

Moody, Robert L. "Bodily Changes During Abreaction." *The Lancet* (1946): 721.

_____. "Bodily Changes During Abreaction." *The Lancet*, Letter of June 19, (1948): 964.

Moore, William L. "The Roswell Investigation: New Evidence in the Search for a Crashed UFO." *MUFON Symposium Proceedings* (1982): 84-104.

Moore, William L., and Stanton T. Friedman. "MJ-12 and Phil Klass: What Are the Facts?" *MUFON Symposium Proceedings* (1988): 205-241.

Moseley, James W. *Saucer Smear* 32, no. 2 (5 February 1985): 1-8.

_____. *Saucer Smear* 32, no. 4 (20 April 1985): 1-8.

Murphy, Michael. *The Future of the Body*. Los Angeles: Jeremy P. Tarcher, forthcoming, 1992.

Nicholson, Mary, ed. *Shamanism*. Wheaton, Ill.: Theosophical Publishing House, 1987.

Overall, Zan. *Gulf Breeze Double Exposed*. Chicago: J. Allen Hynek Center for UFO Studies, 1990.

Paris, Ginette. *Pagan Grace*. Dallas: Spring Publications, 1990.

Peacham, Henry. *The Garden of Eloquence*. Gainesville, Fl.: Ed. in facsimile by W.G. Crane, 1954.

Radin, Paul. *The Trickster*. New York: Shocken Books, 1972.

Randle, Kevin D. and Donald R. Schmitt. *UFO Crash at Roswell*. New York: Avon Books, 1991.

Raschke, Carl. "UFOs: Ultraterrestrial Agents of Cultural Deconstruction." *Archaeus: Cyberbiological Studies of the Imaginal Component in the UFO Contact Experience* 5 (1989): 21-32.

Rilke, Rainer Maria. *Selected Poems of Rainer Maria Rilke*. Translated by Robert Bly. New York: Harper and Row, 1982.

_____. *The Selected Poetry of Rainer Maria Rilke*. Edited and translated by Stephen Mitchell. New York: Random House, 1982.

Ring, Kenneth. *Life at Death*. New York: Cowan, McMann & Geohegan, 1980.

_____. "Near Death and UFO Encounters as Shamanic Initiations: Some Conceptual and Evolutionary Implications." *ReVISION Journal* 11, no. 3 (Winter 1989): 14–22.

_____. "Near-Death Experiences: Implications for Human Evolution and Planetary Transformation." *ReVISION Journal* 8, no. 2 (Winter/Spring 1986): 75–86.

Rojcewicz, Peter M. "The Folklore of the 'Men in Black': A Challenge to the Prevailing Paradigm." *ReVISION Journal* 11, no. 14 (Spring 1989): 5–16.

_____. "The 'Men in Black' Experience and Tradition: Analogues with the Traditional Devil Hypothesis." *Journal of American Folklore* 100, no. 396 (April–June 1987): 149–160.

Ruppelt, Edward J. *The Report on Unidentified Flying Objects*. New York: Ace Books, 1956.

_____. "Ruppelt Reverses Stand on UFOs." *The UFO Investigator* 1, no. 9 (March 1960): 6.

Sachs, Margaret. *The UFO Encyclopedia*. New York: Perigree Books, 1980.

Schneweis, Emil. *Angels and Demons According to Lactantius*. Washington, D.C.: Catholic University Press, 1944.

Schumer, Arlen. *Visions from the Twilight Zone*. San Francisco: Chronicle Books, 1991.

Scully, Frank. *Behind the Flying Saucers*. New York: Henry Holt, 1950.

Segal, Lynn. *The Dream of Reality*. New York: W. W. Norton and Co., 1986.

Simard, T. and J. Basmajian. "Methods in Training the Conscious Control of Motor Units." *Archives of Physical Medicine* 48 (1967) 12–19.

Stacy, Dennis. "The Contactee Era." In *Phenomenon: Forty Years of Flying Saucers*, edited by John Spencer and Hilary Evans, 121–133. New York: Avon Books, 1988.

Steinberg, Eugene. *Saucer Smear* 33, no. 5 (15 November 1987): 1–8.

Stevens, Anthony. *Archetypes*. New York: William Morrow and Co., 1982.

Stewart, R.J. *Creation Myth*. Longmead, England: Element Books, 1989.

Stillings, Dennis. *Saucer Smear* 36, no. 2 (5 February 1989): 1–8.

Story, Ronald D. *The Encylopedia of UFOs*. New York: Doubleday, 1980.

_____. *Sightings*. New York: Quill, 1982.

Strieber, Whitley. *Communion*. New York: William Morrow and Co., 1987.

Strentz, Herbert. "An Analysis of Press Coverage of Unidentified Flying Objects, 1947–1966." Ph.D. dissertation, Northwestern University, 1970.

Tate, Pete. *Saucer Smear* 33, no. 5 (25 June 1986): 1–8.

Thurston, Herbert. *The Physical Phenomena of Mysticism*. London: Burns Oates, 1952.

Turner, Victor. "Betwixt and Between: The Liminal Period in Rites of Passage." In *Betwixt and Between: Patterns of Masculine and Feminine Initiation*, edited by Louise Carus Mahdi, Steven Foster, and Meredith Little, 3–19. La Salle, Ill.: Open Court Press, 1987.

Von Daniken, Erich. *Chariots of the Gods?* New York: G.P. Putnam's Son's, 1970.

Vallee, Jacques. *Anatomy of a Phenomenon: UFOs in Space*. New York: Ballantine, 1965.

_____. *Confrontation: A Scientist's Search for Alien Contact*. New York: Ballantine Books, 1990

_____. *Dimensions: A Casebook of Alien Contact*. Chicago: Contemporary Books, 1988.

_____. *Passport to Magonia*. Chicago: Henry Regnery Co., 1969.

Vycinas, Vincent. *Earth and Gods*. The Hague: Martinus Nijhoff, 1961.

Walters, Ed and Frances Walters. *The Gulf Breeze Sightings*. New York, William Morrow and Co., 1990.

Watzlawick, Paul. *How Real is Real?* London: Souvenir Press, 1983.

_____. "Self-Fulfilling Prophecies." In *The Invented Reality*, edited by Paul Watzlawick, pp. 95–116. New York: W. W. Norton, 1984.

Watzlawick, Paul, John H. Weakland, and Richard Fisch. *Change*. New York: W. W. Norton, 1974.

Zeidman, Jennie. *International UFO Reporter*. 11, no. 3 (May–June 1986): 20.

INDEX

Ananias (sighting witness), 52
Anatomy of a Phenomenon (Vallee), 99
Andrews Air Force Base, UFOs on
radar at, 23
Andrus, Walt
on Gulf Breeze sightings, 214–215
Mutual UFO Network started by, 114
Angels, 148–152, 232–233
at Fatima, 152–154
wrestling with, 185, 233–234, 243
Angels: An Endangered Species
(Godwin), 149
Angelucci, Orfeo, contact by, 30–31
Animal Farm (Orwell), 118
Animals, mutilation of, 127–132
Antarctica, sighting in, 78–79
Apollo, and Hermes, 91–93
APRO (Aerial Phenomena Research
Organization)
and Condon committee, 86
and contactees, 34
defection of members from, 114
founding of, 21
APRO Bulletin, appeal to Ruppelt in, 50
Aquinas, Thomas, on angels, 148, 151,
232
Archetypes
as first principles, 11
manifestation of, 46, 190
patterns of, 44–46
Aristotle, on drama, 36
"Armstrong Circle Theater," 48–50, 56
Arnold, Doris, 2
Arnold, Kenneth
on "Armstrong Circle Theater,"
48–49
and Eternal Beginning, 11–13, 116
sighting by, 1–4, 17
Atwater, Gordon A., debunking by, 4
Audio recordings, 135–137
Aurobindo, Sri, 223–224
Avens, Robert, on angels, 233
Aztec, NM, crashed UFO at, 160

Bachelard, Gaston, *The Poetics of
Space*, 97
Baird, Vernon, hoax by, 5
Barnes, Harry, radar sighting by, 23–24

Barrera, Mario Jahn, sighting by, 78–79
Basil, Germany, sighting at, 70
Bateson, Gregory, on patterns, 140–143,
154, 223
Battos, Hermes observed by, 91
Beamships, 135–138
Beckett, Samuel, *Waiting for Godot*,
102n–103n
Behind the Flying Saucers (Skully), 9,
160
Belans, Mr., contact by, 67–68
Belgium, contact in, 67–68
"Bellero Shield" ("Outer Limits"
episode), 66–67
Benedict XIV (Pope), and levitation, 222
Bequette, Bill, report of Arnold sighting
by, 2, 14
Bergson, Henri, on laughable situations,
102n
Berlitz, Charles, *The Roswell Incident*,
161
Bethurum, Truman, contact by, 30
"Betwixt and Between: The Liminal
Period in Rites of Passage" (Turner),
187
Bible, angels described in, 148–150
Biofeedback, 221
Biological archetypes, 44
Bloecher, Ted, sightings investigated by,
166, 170
Blum, Ralph, abduction investigated by,
107–109, 111
Blumrich, Joseph, *The Spaceships of
Ezekiel*, 71
Bly, Robert, on Hermes, 93
Bodily transformations, 219–222
Boer, Charles, *The Homeric Hymns*, 91
Boit, Maurice A., on UFOs, 25–26
Brabant, Belgium, contact near, 67–68
Brahman, 225
Brazel, Bessie, on crashed UFO, 163
Brazel, Bill, crashed UFO pieces
collected by, 163–164
Brazel, W. W. "Mac," crashed UFO
discovered by, 162–163
Brazil
contact in, 32–34
sighting in, 134

ANGELS AND ALIENS · 271

Constantine (emperor), sighting by, 70
Contacts
  vs. abductions, 148
  by Adamski, 28–31
  by Meier, 135–139
  repeat, 147
  and savior stories, 144–145
  by Villas-Boas, 32–34
Cook, Duane, and Gulf Breeze
  sightings, 211
Cooper, Austin, on Condon committee,
  84
Cosmic Man, 192
Cosmic shamans, 157, 232
Cosmopolitan, on UFOs, 9
Cove de Ira, Portugal, miracle at,
  152–154
Coverups, allegations of, 7, 15, 26–28,
  34, 56–57, 175
Coyne, Lawrence J., sighting by,
  103–106
Crashed UFOs
  documentation of, 173–180
  rumors of, 159–165
Creation Myth (Stewart), xi–xii
Crop circles, 244n
Crystals from contact, 136–137
CUFOS (Center for UFO Studies),
  107, 114
Culture
  and observation, 125–126
  reactions to UFOs by, 100
  rejection of other worlds by, 228
  UFOs as destructors of, 186
Cutler, Robert, crashed UFO memo by,
  175, 177–178

Damascius, on souls, 225–226
Dante Alighieri, 209–210
Dark Night of the Soul, The (Saint
  John of the Cross), 147
Davenport, W.I., sighting by, 4
Davidson, Leon, on Socorro sighting
  insignia, 75
Davis, Kathy, and Strieber, 206–207
Deathbed visions, 156
Debunkers, refusal of Call to Adventure
  by, 185n

Deception by air force, 7, 15, 26–28,
  34, 56–57, 175
Demons, 146–147
  angels as, 149–152
  on old calendars, 124
Denver Post, on investigating UFOs, 79
Depth literalists, 39
Desert Center, CA, contact at, 28–30
Deserts, contacts in, 145
Dexter, MI, sightings at, 81–84
Diamond (Sheriff), and Mississippi
  abduction, 107–109
Dionysus, 95–97
Dirigibles, sightings of, 3, 69–70, 122
Doorway amnesia, 236
Double language of UFOs, 40
Drake, W.R., "Spacemen in the
  Middle Ages," 70
Dramatic arts, 95–97
Dream of Reality, The (Segal), 18–19
Drury, Nevil, *The Shaman and the
  Magician*, 155
Dulles, Allen, 75
Dwarfs and UFOs, 122–123
"Dying Worlds, Dying Selves"
  (Kottmeyer), 209n

Early, George W., on crashed UFO, 160
Eduardo (shaman), 155
Education, UFOs as, 193–195, 227
Egyptians and souls, 226
Einstein, Albert, on theories and
  observations, 15, 125
Eisenhower, Dwight D., briefed about
  crashed UFO, 173–174, 176
Elementals, 120
Eros, description of, 150
"Estimate of the Situation" (Project
  Sign), 7, 16, 48, 56
Eternal Beginnings, 11
Evidence, 33
  of crashed UFOs, 173–180
  of Gulf Breeze sightings, 211–215
  of Meier sighting, 135–139
  and theories, 54
  ufologist covering up of, 217
Evolution, 223
Exercise, 221

Goralski, Miroslaw, sighting by, 133
Government. *See* Air force
Grammar of UFOs, 195
Great Chain of Being, 227–228
Greece
   angels in, 148
   gods of, 14, 90–98
Gregory, George T., on Blue Book
   Project evidence, 55
Grossinger, Richard, on aliens, 234–235
Grosso, Michael
   on materiality of UFOs, 225
   on spirits, 169
Guides, spiritual
   myths of, 186–187
   in near-death experiences, 157
Gulf Breeze, FL, sightings at, 210–217
Gulf Breeze Sightings, The (Walters),
   212–214

Hackney, Tom, on Hynek, 201
Hades, 146
Harder, James, on Mississippi abduc-
   tion, 109
Harris, D.J., sighting by, 133–134
Haut, Walter, dispatch on crashed
   UFO prepared by, 162–163
Healey, John, sighting by, 103–106
Healings
   faith, 221
   at Fatima, 153–154
Heidegger, Martin, on new gods, 190
Heisenberg, Werner, 15
Henderson, O.W., alien bodies
   transported by, 164
Hermes, 90–94
   and angels, 149
   garbled messages from, 195
Hero with a Thousand Faces, The
   (Campbell), 183
Heroes
   aggregation of, 191–195, 231
   marginality of, 187–191
   separation of, 183–187
Hickson, Charlie, abduction of, 106–111
Hill, Betty and Barney, abduction of,
   58–61
   film parallels with, 65–67

later abductions influenced by, 171
   as primordial precedent, 62–64, 117,
   124
Hillenkoetter, Roscoe H., crashed UFO
   briefing by, 173–174, 176–177
Hillman, James
   on archetypes, 44
   on fact and fiction, xii
   on Proteus, 17
Hillsdale, MI, sighting at, 81–83
Hinwil, Switzerland, contact at,
   135–139
Historical parallel to UFOs, 101–103,
   117–126, 172, 184
"Hodomur, Man of Infinity" (Tilms), 68
Homer, *Odyssey*, 17, 244
Homeric Hymns, The (Boer), 91
Homologies, 142–143
Hopkins, April, 207
Hopkins, Budd
   on Gulf Breeze sightings, 212
   on Hills abduction, 63
   on historical UFO parallels, 121n,
   123–125, 169, 195
   on marginality of abductees, 187–188
   Missing Time by, 159, 165–172
   at Mutual UFO Network conferences,
   172, 198
   on repeat abductions, 147
   on sexual contacts, 151
   sighting by, 165
   solution to UFOs expected by, 241
   and Strieber, 205–209
   and Vallee, 169, 195
House Armed Services Committee
   hearings, 83
Howe, Linda Moulton, on animal
   mutilations, 131–132
Humanity, threat to concept of, 185–186
Hynek, J. Allen
   on Alabama sighting, 7
   close encounters defined by, 144, 201
   on Condon committee, 85, 87–88
   conversion of, 80, 83–84, 117
   death of, 199–202
   and Gregory, 55
   Mississippi abduction investigated
   by, 107–110

on New Guinea sighting, 54
Socorro sighting investigated by, 73
and swamp gas debacle, 81–83
at U.N. discussion, 105
on von Däniken, 113
Hypnosis
of Hickson and Parker, 109
of Hills, 59
of Kilburn, 166–167

Idea of the Holy, The (Otto), 152, 154
Incident at Pascagoula, 106–111
Incubus, 151
Initiation and UFOs, 181–182,
193–194, 233
Insignia on UFO, 75
Intruders (Hopkins), 63, 187, 206–208
Invaders from Mars (film), 65–66
Invisibility of abductees, 187–188
Iron John (Bly), 93

Jacob, wrestling with angel by, 185, 233
Jacob Atabet (Murphy), 223, 232
Jacobs, David M., *The UFO Controversy
in America*, 2
on air force efforts, 21, 57
on Condon committee, 83
on contactees, 30
on end of air force investigations, 113
on Hynek, 200–201
on Keyhoe and conspiracy, 56
on Project Grudge, 8
solution to UFOs expected by, 241
Jahenny, Marie-Julie, stigmata on, 222
James, William, on transitions, 190
Jansma, Sidney J., *UFOs, Satan and
Evolution*, 186n
Japan
ancient statues in, 119–120
sightings in, 3, 69, 120
Jezzi, Arrigo, sighting by, 103–106
John of the Cross, Saint, *The Dark
Night of the Soul*, 147
John Paul II (Pope), on devil, 149
Joseph of Cupertino, Saint, levitation
by, 222
Jung, Carl Gustav
on archetypal patterns, 44–46, 190

on changes from UFOs, 43
*Flying Saucers: A Modern Myth of
Things Seen in the Sky* by, 41
on myths, xii, 4, 43, 116–118
on symbols of UFOs, 42
on Trickster, 94–95
and UFOs as materialized psychisms,
44, 225
Juxtaposition, 191

K., Joseph (*Trial* character), 38–39
Kaempffert, Walter, on *Life* article, 27
Kafka, Franz, *The Trial*, 38–40
Kalendrier des Bergiers, demons depicted
on, 124
Kansas City, MO, sighting at, 4
Karagasy shaman, 155
Karen (alien), 134
Karth, Joseph E., on UFOs, 57
Kasuga, Mount, in Japan, sightings at,
120
Kazantsev, Alexander, on ancient astronauts, 119
Keel, John
on animal mutilations, 129
and Men in Black, 46
on origin of UFOs, 95
Kegan, Daniel, on animal mutilations,
130
Kentucky, sighting in, 6
Kerenyi, Karl
on Hermes, 94
on masks, 96
on myths, 11, 14, 62–63
on origins, 62–63
on Trickster, 95
Keyhoe, Donald E.
on "Armstrong Circle Theater," 48–50
on Condon committee, 84–85, 87
Condon committee memo leaked to,
86
Congressional hearings urged by, 55–56
and contactees, 31–32
coverup speculations by, 8–9, 16,
27–28
The Flying Saucers Are Real by, 9
plan to meet aliens by, 114
on Ruppelt, 50–51

National security
  censorship for, 49, 84
  UFOs as threat to, 6
Nazca, Peru, landing strips at, 112
NDE (near-death experiences)
  description of, 155–157
  marginality after, 188
Neptune (alien), 30
New Guinea, sighting at, 51–54
New Hampshire, abduction in, 58–61
New Mexico
  capturing of UFO in, 4–5, 159–165,
    173–180
  contact in, 30
  sighting in, 73–77
New York
  abduction in, 202–206
  sightings in, 79, 166
New York Times
  on Arnold sighting, 2–3
  on Condon committee report, 87
  on *Life* article, 27
  on silliness of UFOs, 16
Newport News, VA, sighting at, 22,
  24, 37
News Journal on Gulf Breeze photos, 214
Newsweek on animal mutilations,
  129–130
NICAP (National Investigations Com-
    mittee on Aerial Phenomena), 32
  and Condon committee, 86
  and contactees, 34
  stature of, 114
Nichiren (priest) and 1271 sighting, 120
Nietzsche, Friedrich, on Dionysus, 96
Night Church, The (Strieber), 209n
Nuclear weapons and contacts, 30
Nugent, Ed, radar sighting by, 23
Nuremberg, Germany, sighting at, 70

O'Barski, George, sighting by, 166
Oberg, James
  criticism of, 199
  on Mansfield sighting, 105–106
Object constancy, 228–229
Observations based on theories, 15–17
Odyssey (Homer), 17, 244
Ohio, sighting in, 103–106

Okeanos (father of Proteus), 17
"On the Cessation of Oracles"
  (Plutarch), 150
Oracles and Hermes, 90
Origin in myths, 12, 14, 62
Orwell, George, *Animal Farm*, 118
Otto, Rudolph, on demons, 152, 154
Our Lady, appearance of, at Fatima,
  152–154
"Outer Limits" and Hills abduction,
  66–67
Overall, Zan, on Gulf Breeze photos, 213

Pagan Grace (Paris), 92–93
Parallels
  in allegories, 89–90, 118
  historical, to UFOs, 101–103, 117–126,
    172, 184
Paraphysical domain and UFOs, 45,
  134–135
Parham, Beauford E., sighting by, 78
Paris, Ginette
  on Dionysus, 96
  on Hermes, 92–93
Parker, Calvin, abduction of, 106–111
Pascagoula, MS, abduction at, 106–111
Passport to Magonia (Vallee), 101, 103
Patterns
  archetypal, 44–46
  connecting, 140–143, 152, 154, 158,
    223–224
  searching for, 15–17
Peacham, Harry, on allegory, 36
Pelletier, Joseph, *The Sun Danced at
  Fatima*, 153
Pensacola News Journal on Gulf Breeze
  photos, 214
Perception
  limited nature of, 227–229
  and marginality, 189
Perceptual readiness, 19–20
Peru, landing strips in, 112
Phillips (Mr. and Mrs.) and Socorro
  sighting, 75
Photographs
  of Gulf Breeze sightings, 211–215
  of Meier sightings, 135–139
Physical evidence. *See* Evidence

Physical examinations of abductees, 59
Physical Phenomena of Mysticism, The
(Thurston), 222
Piaget, Jean, on object constancy,
228–229
Pioneers of Space (Adamski), 28
Placebo effects, 220
Plasma, and Hills abduction, 61
Plato, on spirits as mediators, 150
Pleiadeans, contact with, 136, 139
Plutarch
on angels, 150
contact report by, 120
Pod marks at Socorro sighting, 74–75
Poetics of Space, The (Bachelard), 97
Poland, sighting in, 133
Poltergeists, 95
Portugal, miracle in, 152–154
Post, Bob, on Meier photographs, 137
*Presentation of Self in Everyday Life,
The* (Goffman), 96
Primordial Beginnings
Arnold sighting as, 12
Hills abduction as, 62–64
Principal facts on UFOs and parallel
experiences, 101–102
Proctor, Floyd, on crashed UFO, 162
Professional archetypes, 44
Project Blue Book, 25, 31, 50–51, 73, 113
Project Grudge, 8, 21–22, 25, 27
Project Sign, 6–8, 17
Prophetic powers
of Hermes, 92
of UFOs, 17
Proteus, 17–20, 47, 69, 71–72
Psychic component of UFOs, 42–44, 225
Psychological archetypes, 44
Publicity for contactees, 30–31
Pyramid of Inscriptions, 119

Questions, answers based on, 16–17
Quicksilver, Hermes as, 93–94
Quintanella, Hector, and swamp gas
debacle, 82

Radar, UFOs sighted on, 23–25
Radiation and radioactivity
at animal mutilation sites, 128

from contacts, 33
from UFOs, 78
Radin, Paul, *The Trickster,* 94
Rainier, Mount, sighting at, 1–3
Rama, Swami, 222
Ramey, Roger M., crashed UFO covered
up by, 163
Raschke, Carl, on purpose of UFOs,
185–186
Reality
boundary between multiple, 191
human wishes for, 18–19
mental and material, 45
myths forming, 14
and theories, 126
UFO effect on defining, 182–183
Recursive unsolvability, 193
Reidel, Walther, on UFOs, 25
Reis, Herminio and Bianca, sighting
by, 134
Religio Medici (Browne), 227
Religion
encounters as experiences in, 147
and mind-body interaction, 222
Religious visions, 42–43
Repeat encounters
instances of, 147
preparation for, 235–237
*Report on Unidentified Flying Objects,
The* (Ruppelt), 6, 48, 50–51
Reverdy, Pierre, on juxtaposition, 191
Rhanes, Aura (alien), 30
Rilke, Rainer Maria
angels described by, 150
on meeting the Other, 186
Ring, Kenneth
and cosmic shamans, 157, 232
on near-death experiences, 156–157
on shamans, 155, 157, 188
Rites of passage, 182
aggregation in, 191–195
marginality in, 187–191
separation in, 183–187
Rojcewicz, Peter M.
on blurred reality, 190–191
on Men in Black, 45–46
Roswell, NM, capturing of UFO at,
4–5, 159–165, 173–180